Educational Policies and Youth in the 21st Century

Educational Policies and Youth in the 21st Century

Problems, Potential, and Progress

edited by

Sharon L. Nichols
University of Texas at San Antonio

INFORMATION AGE PUBLISHING, INC.
Charlotte, NC • www.infoagepub.com

Library of Congress Cataloging-in-Publication Data

A CIP record for this book is available from the Library of Congress
http://www.loc.gov

ISBN: 978-1-68123-529-5 (Paperback)
      978-1-68123-530-1 (Hardcover)
      978-1-68123-531-8 (ebook)

Printed in the United States of America

To all marginalized youth who strive to be heard, seen, valued, and respected. You are not forgotten.

CONTENTS

PART I

CHARACTERISTICS AND EXPERIENCES OF 21ST CENTURY YOUTH

PART II

PROMINENT EDUCATIONAL POLICIES AFFECTING YOUTH

PART III

IMPLICATIONS FOR BETTER POLICY DEVELOPMENT
FOR 21ST CENTURY YOUTH

PREFACE

For decades, American citizens have been besieged by negative rhetoric about their public education system. Schools, many argue, are not adequately preparing students for 21st century knowledge and skills needed for 21st century jobs. As evidence of this problem, critics point to international and national standardized test data that show on average, American students performing in the middle of the international pack. Critics argue that students' putative "mediocre" academic performance warrants an externally imposed system of change. Over time, ongoing criticism leveled at public schools and their teachers has led to increasingly demanding and rigid policies that culminated in the No Child Left Behind (NCLB) Act of 2002. Although its 2009 successor, Race to the Top (RTTT) alleviated some of the pressures, schools are still susceptible to the mandates of high-stakes testing accountability—the most invasive provision of NCLB.

High-stakes testing (HST) is the use of standardized tests to distribute consequences to teachers, administrators, and their students. The underlying theory of HST is that the promise of incentives for good test scores coupled with the threat of punishments for bad test scores will compel teachers into more efficient and effective teaching. Schools improve, it is assumed, when test scores rise. Tests, in this approach, are deemed the effectors and detectors of change. However, after more than a decade of implementation, we know that HST has had mostly bad consequences for education. For example, we know that high-stakes testing has had little or no effect on students' academic performance (Nichols, Glass, & Berliner, 2006, 2012; Timar & Maxwell-Jolly, 2012). And, it has altered how teachers teach and

Educational Policies and Youth in the 21st Century, pages ix–xiv
Copyright © 2016 by Information Age Publishing
All rights of reproduction in any form reserved.

how students experience learning in mostly negative ways (Nichols & Berliner, 2007; Ravitch, 2011).

One important flaw of high-stakes testing as the primary mechanism of reform is its assumption that learners are all the same and that they are equally interested in the same topics, and able to learn them (and demonstrate that learning) at the same rate and in the exact same ways. This assumption denies the reality that our student population varies widely across a limitless number of variables all of which intersect with learning experiences in known and unknown ways. For example, some students are monolingual English-only speakers. For them, English-based, high-stakes tests are much easier than they are for students for whom English is a second language (ESL). For ESL students, high-stakes tests are more challenging when they must first translate questions before answering them. But even this analysis is a blunt representation of students' linguistic (and other types of) diversities. Although policies cannot reasonably address all types of variation, the lack of meaningful tolerance for any type of student diversity in NCLB and RTTT (and other policies) is the impetus for this book.

Our student population is changing in ways that cannot be ignored. One significant change is the proportion of students of color is growing quickly. Soon, White students will be the minority in schools and Black and Hispanic students (of varying origins, ethnicities and languages) collectively will be the majority. According to the U.S. Department of Education, the percentage of White students enrolled in school fell from 60.3% in 2001 to 51.7% in 2011. Over the same time period, the percentage of Hispanics students grew from 17.1% to 23.7% and the percentage of Black students stayed relatively the same at 17.2% in 2001 to 15.8% in 2011. Importantly, by 2023 it is estimated that White students will drop further down to 45% of all public school students, whereas Hispanics will represent approximately 30%. The composition of the Hispanic population alone is diverse including English-only and bilingual students from many different types of backgrounds (Puerto Rico, Guatemala, Dominican Republic, Colombia, Mexico, and Spain to name a few). Many Hispanic students are undocumented, or live with family members who are, posing unique school challenges for them. Some Hispanic students are bilingual, and some are English-only speakers presenting identity challenges as they are forced to navigate home-school spaces.

This book is a response to this growing diversity and is guided by two primary goals. The first goal is to sensitize readers to the vast diversity of American youth who attend our schools and their wide-ranging interests, experiences, cultures, and values. It is a critical wake-up call to politicians, educators, and the concerned citizens who support them of the need to be more thoughtfully proactive about the impact of educational policies that are intended to serve our youth. America's students and the world in which they live are changing at a rapid pace. This book sheds light on these changes to help readers become better consumers of and advocates for (or against) policies that impact youth. A second goal of this book is to fore-ground a few of the more prominent and ongoing education policies and practices and to examine how they serve these youth.

OVERVIEW OF CHAPTERS

In Part I, authors deconstruct the identities and experiences of various youth groups. In Chapter 1, Morales, Trujillo, and Kissell explore the identities of Latin@ youth by examining the social, historical, and contextual factors that impact their lives. As one of the fastest growing segments of the population, this chapter sets the stage to think through how various sociopolitical and economic factors influence educational opportunities, access, and outcomes for this diverse subgroup of youth. Next in Chapter 2, Penn, Kinloch, and Burkhard help us understand the "languaging" practices of African American youth and the ways in which they are used to help them navigate educational and geographical spaces. In this era of racial hostility toward Black youth, especially Black males, it seems important to pay attention to how these youth navigate their emergent racial identities. In Chapter 3, Alvarez Gutiérrez and Quijada Cerecer present narratives from a group of undocumented youth to explore the challenges of living in spaces where their residency status is in question or temporary. Undocumented youth live in highly precarious situations and are forced to navigate questionable statuses and the constant threat of deportation of them or loved ones. In Chapter 4, Patterson, Blanchfield, and Riskind discuss what we know about the everyday lived experiences of LGBT youth. It wasn't so long ago, LGBT youth remained largely hidden; however, now younger and younger youth are coming out to themselves to their families, friends, and teachers. And yet, there are still extremely visible cases of suicide by these teens who undergo excessive bullying. Although as a country we have made great strides in the past decade becoming more tolerant and accepting, we have far to go. Finally, the widening wealth gap, and the 20+ million school-aged kids who live in poverty demand that we examine how poverty interacts with schooling (Biddle, 2014). Alarmingly, a much greater percentage of public school students are poor (eligible for free or reduced-price lunches) rising from 38.3% in 2000–2001 to 49.6% in 2011–2012. It is important to better understand what are the unique challenges and opportunities of being a poor student in today's schools. In Chapter 5, Biddle provides compelling data to show the powerful effects of poverty on students' educational experiences and outcomes.

In Part II, authors examine more closely our national policy climate by targeting some of the more prominent ones affecting these diverse youth. For example, in Chapter 6, López explores the role of language policies in America's schools. Although our students speak at least 39 different languages in schools across America, the focus of this chapter is on bilingual education and its features as it relates to Hispanic populations. The role and value of bilingual education varies widely across the states, and therefore this chapter helps to uncover what are some of the more prominent issues involved in how these varying programs are implemented and their effects. Similarly, the recent tragedy of the thousands of Latin American kids migrating to the United States and the resulting debates and controversies makes the topic of immigrated students and the policies that govern their educational experiences timely. In Chapter 7, Alvear and Turley focus on our national immigration political climate to suggest how students navigate the transitions between home and school amidst the constant threat of deportation. The last chapter in this section of the book focuses on the broader impact of high-stakes testing policies as it relates to marginalized students' general well-being. Vasquez Heilig, Marachi, and Cruz deconstruct the notion of "grit" that has recently been appropriated by many to justify harmful test-based policies especially as it relates to our poorer students and students of color.

In Part III, authors take a step back and provide some overarching conclusions regarding the range of topics presented throughout the book. Authors of Chapters 9 and 10 offer new ways to think about 21st century skills and policies. In Chapter 9, Reynolds argues that to move forward, it is necessary that we embrace educational goals of creativity and joy in learning. The current (global) emphasis on tests and data restrict students' learning experiences in alarming ways. Reynolds argues that 21st century skills necessarily require a shift from data-driven learning experiences to humanistic ones that embrace creativity, enjoyment, interest, and passion. In Chapter 10, Nichols and Svenkerud-Hale argue that newer policies must reframe educational problems. Past and current reform efforts are subject to narrowly defined problem definitions that have the effect of blinding us from seeing alternative solutions to complex educational problems. Nichols and Svenkerud-Hale offer alternative frames for thinking about how to construct policies that will better serve our youth. Finally, in Chapter 11, McCaslin offers her analysis of some of the most pressing takeaways and cross-cutting themes from the book. Framed by the concept of problem representation, McCaslin argues for the importance of carefully considering the needs and motivational dispositions and struggles of youth as policies are constructed and enacted.

CONCLUDING COMMENT

This edited book, including leading authors from across the country, high-lights how educational policies impact youth's development and socialization in school contexts. In most cases, policies are constructed by adults, implemented by adults, but are rarely informed by the needs and opinions of youth: not only are youth not consulted, but policymakers often neglect what we know about the psychological, emotional, and educational health of youth. Therefore, both the short- and long-term impact of these policies have but limited effects on improving students' school performance or personal health issues such as depression or suicide.

This book spotlights the growing diversity and changing landscape of the 21st century youth culture. It is also about educational policy and the ways in which policy constructions—largely written by adults—impact youth who are left out of the discussion. Throughout my work (e.g., Nichols & Berliner, 2007; Nichols & Good, 2004; Nichols, 2013; Nichols & Valenzuela, 2013) I have noticed over and over how policy misrepresents, distorts, and negatively impacts youth they are designed to serve. For example, the pressures of high-stakes testing influences teachers in ways that undermine their capacity to develop meaningful relationships with their students (Perlstein, 2007). This is problematic since we know that students do better when they believe their teachers care about them (Noddings, 2005). The pressures of high-stakes testing accountability are counterproductive to learning.

I have also noticed over and over how adults who are asked to abide by these laws and policies often have little knowledge about the history, impact, or rationale for the policies they implement. Teachers are asked to abide by the daunting and controlling demands of the No Child Left Behind Act (and its successor Race to the Top), and yet they are relatively uneducated about the vastness of the law, its scope, or its consequences. Of course, working hard to keep up with day-to-day teaching demands quite unsurprisingly leaves little room to ponder such things. Teachers and principals have too much to worry about when it comes to their own students to wonder why NCLB asks so much of them or to worry how it impacts students in another school, community, or state. Therefore it is hoped this book will help to inspire an education work force that is better equipped to advocate for meaningful policies that impact their work and their students' lives.

—Sharon L. Nichols

REFERENCES

Biddle, B. J. (2014). *The unacknowledged disaster: Youth poverty and educational failure in America.* New York, NY: Sense.

Nichols, S. L. (Ed.). (2013, Summer). This issue. *Theory into practice special issue: Educational policy and the socialization of youth for the 21st century, 52*(3), 149–151.

Nichols, S. L., & Berliner. D. C. (2007). *Collateral damage: How high-stakes testing corrupts America's schools.* Cambridge, MA: Harvard Education Press.

Nichols, S. L., & Good, T. (2004). *America's teenagers—Myths and realities: Media images, schooling, and the social costs of careless indifference.* Mahwah, NJ: Erlbaum.

Nichols, S. L., Glass, G. V., & Berliner, D. C. (2006). High-stakes testing and student achievement: Does accountability pressure increase student learning? *Education Policy Analysis Archives, 14*(1). Retrieved July 20, 2009, from http://epaa.asu.edu/epaa/v14n1/.

Nichols, S. L., Glass, G. V., & Berliner, D. C. (2012) High-stakes testing and student achievement: Updated analyses with NAEP data. *Education Policy Analysis Archives, 20*(20). Retrieved September 16, 2012, from http://epaa.asu.edu/ojs/article/view/1048

Nichols, S. L., & Valenzuela, A. (2013, Summer). Educational policy and youth: Effects of policy on practice. *Theory Into Practice, Special Issue: Educational Policy and the Socialization of Youth for the 21st Century, 52*(3), 152–159.

No Child Left Behind (NCLB) Act of 2001, 20 U.S.C.A. § 6301 *et seq.* (West 2003)

Noddings, N. (2005). *The challenge to care in schools: An alternative approach to education* (2nd ed.). New York, NY: Teachers College Press.

Perlstein, L. (2007). *Tested: One American school struggles to make the grade.* New York, NY: Henry Holt.

Ravitch, D. (2011). *The death and life of the great American school system: How testing and choice are undermining education.* New York, NY: Basic Books.

Timar, T. B., & Maxwell-Jolly, J. (Eds.). (2012). *Narrowing the achievement gap: Perspectives and strategies for challenging times.* Cambridge, MA: Harvard Education Press.

ACKNOWLEDGMENTS

I would like to acknowledge my dear mentors, each of whom played a role in making this project happen. There is much I could say about each of these individuals, all of whom have made an indelible impact on me both professionally and personally. I turn to them often (perhaps too often, if you ask them) for support, advice, and guidance. I have never been turned down or led astray. I am fortunate to have such wonderful and esteemed academicians who have helped guide me over the years. Their support for this project has been no different.

My heartfelt thanks go to David Berliner, who initially gave me the idea of turning these ideas into a book; to Gene Glass, who unquestioningly supported and advocated for this project; to Tom Good, whose feedback helped me to clarify my vision for this project; and to Mary McCaslin, whose insight makes this book better and whose academic contributions on student motivation and development have been an inspiration.

Finally, a big thank you to George Johnson of Information Age Publishing, who believed in and supported this project from the start.

PART I

CHARACTERISTICS AND EXPERIENCES
OF 21ST CENTURY YOUTH

CHAPTER 1

EDUCATIONAL POLICY AND LATIN@[1] YOUTH

P. Zitlali Morales
University of Illinois, Chicago

Tina M. Trujillo
University of California, Berkeley

René Espinoza Kissell
University of California, Berkeley

WHY FOCUS ON LATIN@ YOUTH?

The research on the schooling of Latin@s in the United States is as diverse as the Latina population itself, spanning topics as varied as literacy and language (Gándara & Orfield, 2012; Gutiérrez & Orellana, 2006; Gutiérrez & Rogoff, 2003; Nieto, 2009; Valdés, Capitelli, & Alvarez, 2011), historical analyses (Donato, 1997; Gonzalez, 1999, 2013), the particular experiences of immigrant youth (Gándara & Contreras, 2009; Gonzales, 2010; Poza, Brooks, & Valdés, 2014; Valenzuela, 1999), continued segregation (Orfield & Ee, 2015; Valencia, 2011b), culturally responsive teaching and curricular politics (Darder, 2011, 2012; Nieto, 1999; Valenzuela, 1999), and higher education access and retention (Abrego & Gonzales, 2010; Contreras, 2011).

Educational Policies and Youth in the 21st Century, pages 3–22
Copyright © 2016 by Information Age Publishing
All rights of reproduction in any form reserved.

3

Most of this body of literature examines the inequitable schooling conditions for Latin@ students. The social, political, and historical foundations of these inequities include particular policies that have shaped and continue to shape the opportunities, experiences, and outcomes for Latin@ students.

Alongside these scholarly developments, immigration influxes from Latin America over the last half century have resulted in the "Latinization" of cities and schools (Dávila, 2004), where one in every three students is now Latin@ (United States Department of Education, 2013; Fry & Lopez, n.d.). Many of the public schools with the highest concentrations of Latin@s have the highest dropout rates and are chronically underfunded, overcrowded, and segregated (Noguera, 2003). Yet, historically, the Latin@ community has actively organized to advocate for or resist different educational reforms related to bilingual education, school closures, and school choice reforms, to name a few. The rapid growth of the Latin@ student population, coupled with the persistent inequalities they face in schools and society, makes learning from the research evidence on the policies that impact this community all the more critical (Reyes & Valencia, 1993).

Fortunately, a small, but growing number of scholars studying Latin@ education have already contributed much to our understanding about which policies shape educational opportunities for Latin@ youth and why (Gándara & Contreras, 2009; Gándara & Hopkins, 2010; Reyes & Valencia, 1993; Valencia, 2011a; Valenzuela, 2005). This chapter picks up where this scholarship leaves off in order to help explain the range of policy interventions that have uniquely influenced Latin@ students' educational experiences. It also considers the ways in which particular obstacles and opportunities facilitated by these policies are shared with other students from marginalized communities, such as other students of color, English learners, and students from low-income families.

To accomplish our goals, we first describe who these youth are, including the multiple ways that Latin@s are defined, and the complexities and limitations that accompany these definitions. We then outline a brief history of the schooling of Latin@s in the United States, highlighting the most relevant policies, legislation, and court cases, and their impact on certain subgroups of the Latin@ population. From there, we review the research on the educational, social, and economic policies that have had the greatest impact on the lives and educational outcomes of Latin@ youth. We conclude by considering the new directions that scholars and policymakers are poised to take, as well as pointing out what educators can learn from this literature.

DEFINING LATIN@S

When reviewing the educational policies that impact the schooling of Latin@[2] youth, it is important to clarify who is included in the broad label of Latin@ because its definition is continuously revised and often contested. The most common definition of Latin@ is "the segment of the U.S. population that traces its descent to the Spanish-speaking, Caribbean, and Latin American worlds" (Suárez-Orozco & Páez, 2002, p. 4). At the intersection of race, ethnicity, and culture, Latin@ is an identity with boundaries defined by historical and political processes. The encompassing pan ethnic label has been used to serve various institutional needs of the American government, the Spanish-speaking media, and community groups and political leaders alike (Mora, 2014). Alcoff (2000) suggests the term "ethnorace" to conceptualize *Latinidad*. She argues that "using only ethnicity belies the reality of most Latin@s' everyday experiences in that it obscures our own awareness about how ethnic identifications often do the work of race while seeming to be theoretically correct and politically advanced" (Alcoff, 2000, p. 246 as cited in García Bedolla, 2009, p. 5). Nonetheless, we find the term Latin@ to be a useful label, as it brings together populations with some shared political history—of colonization, immigration, and language use—as well as shared struggle.

Latin@s are the fastest growing demographic in the United States. They are predicted to reach nearly one third of the American population by 2060 (U.S. Census Bureau, 2012). Those of Mexican descent make up most of the Latin@ population at 65.5%, followed by Puerto Ricans (8.6%), and Cubans (3.7%). An influx of migration from Central American countries has brought the population to 8.2% of the Latin@ population and South Americans to 6%. Almost 40% of Latin@s are immigrants, and 34.3% are under the age of 18 compared to 25.2% of the total U.S. population (Current Population Survey 2006 as cited in García Bedolla, 2009). Research indicates that 58% of native-born Latin@ youth from foreign-born parents still speak primarily Spanish at home, compared to 43% of native-born Asians with immigrant parents. This suggests that Latin@ families are more likely to retain their native language than other groups, such as Asians (Kao, 1999). Income and socioeconomic status also varies: More than one third of Mexicans and Puerto Ricans make less than $25,000 per year, while one fourth of Cubans make more than $75,000 a year and have the highest educational attainment among the three ethnic groups (García Bedolla, 2009).

These statistics illustrate that Latin@s are not monolithic; however, it is essential to understand why diverse communities have coalesced under the identity of Latin@. In other words, what unites Latin@s if they are so heterogeneous? To put it simply yet broadly, Latin@s are a marginalized community of color in the United States, one that is characterized by a subordinate position in the racial order that devalues "foreign" culture, concentration in low-wage work, high poverty rates, and political exclusion (García Bedolla, 2009; Leal & Meier, 2010; San Miguel & Donato, 2010). This reality has contributed to the inequitable schooling conditions that lead to the high dropout rates and low levels of educational achievement for this population. Contreras calls this issue the *brown paradox*, or the "discrepancy between the dramatic increase of Latin@s as a proportion of the population and the significant gap they experience in educational achievement, access, and integration into the social and economic fabric of the United States represents an interesting contradiction" (Contreras, 2011, p. 2).

Latin@ identity and politics are not static. Thus, considering the role of their historical contexts becomes essential when studying educational policies that most impact this community. Many scholars have argued for a more nuanced understanding of the Latin@ student population, one that extends beyond first- and second-generation immigrants. Telles and Ortiz (2008), for example, conducted a longitudinal study of Mexican Americans primarily from Texas and California examining the generational progress of participants from a 1970 study and their children using socioeconomic status, language use, and neighborhood integration as some of the indicators to measure progress. They found that Latin@s' educational attainment stalled among third and fourth generations, and they attributed this limited progress, in part, to chronic underfunding and a lack of resources in school systems that serve high concentrations of Mexican Americans.

In these ways, a shared experience of discrimination in the United States, along with the desire to celebrate a collective culture, is a politicizing factor in community organizing for Latin@ education reform. Latin@s continue to be marginalized as they are racialized as the "nonwhite other," which has immediate academic implications and long-term social and economic ones (Suárez-Orozco & Páez, 2009). As this large and young population of 52 million expands, how Latin@s are represented and served in the educational policy arena becomes an increasingly vital question for scholars, policymakers, and practitioners.

SOCIO-HISTORICAL CONTEXT
OF LATIN@ SCHOOLING IN THE UNITED STATES

The history of schooling for Latin@s in the United States is closely linked to three areas: labor, the eugenics movement, and the issue of incorporation. American public schools both reproduce the social order and are sites of contestation that challenge the social order; the schooling of Latin@s is no exception. While communities now considered Latin@s have always been part of the United States, at the time that the United States annexed a large part of Mexico, they were called Californios, Tejanos, and Hispanos (Martinez, 2011). The Treaty of Guadalupe Hidalgo of 1848, which declared that anyone living on annexed land was immediately an American citizen, made this identity official. Significantly, the treaty also promised these communities the right to keep their culture and traditions, including their language(s).

Labor

González (1999) details how after the 1848 war between Mexico and the United States, the U.S. economy was in great need of an inexhaustible labor supply. As a result, "illegal" Mexican immigration to the United States was in fact "state sanctioned labor crossing of the border to satisfy corporate demand" (p. 53). Bracero programs employed individual men because the U.S. government did not want migrant workers to settle down with their families. In districts with a high proportion of migrant workers and youth, such as the cotton-growing regions of Texas, Colorado's sugar beet fields, and the various farming areas of California, one could find signs that read, "No Migrant Children Allowed" (Gonzalez, 1999). School officials and teachers feared that educating Latin@ youth would compromise their supply of manual labor. For them, expectations for lifelong manual labor were consistent with their deeply ingrained beliefs about Latin@s' lower intelligence and general aptitude. Labor was seen as the rational alternative to academic studies for this group deemed intellectually and socially inferior.

Eugenics

In schools, it was common for students of Mexican descent to be segregated from their White peers in the Southwest and in California. Officials justified the segregation by citing presumably scientific evidence about differences in language and overall lower abilities. "Mexican schools," as they were known, placed a strict emphasis on vocational training, usually using eugenics-based intelligence testing to justify stratification in the schools and workplace (González, 1999). With the exception of a few cases of upward mobility, vocational education largely served to train Latin@s to work low-skilled jobs and maintain minimal participation in American society (San Miguel & Donato, 2010). Several scholars have painstakingly documented how this tracking of Latin@s and other students of color into vocational training or other non honors/AP curriculum continues to this day (Gonzalez, 1999; Valenzuela, 2005; Valencia, Menchaca, & Donato, 2002). Today, high-stakes testing continues to be used to sort these students, a policy development whose roots can be traced back to the beliefs that some races are biologically superior and more deserving than others.

Incorporation

In contrast to the sporadic and localized boycotts prior to the 1920s, the 1930s marked a more systemic era of organizing against unequal schooling practices. In part spurred by the return of veterans of Mexican descent, Mexican American organizations filed lawsuits against segregation by lobbying state authorities to issue policy statements against the practice and further investigate the issue. Post-1960s education reform Latin@ activists and community members tackled school discrimination, segregation, unequal schools, and testing using a range of organizing tactics, including walkouts, boycotts, protests, and litigation. White resistance to integrated schools hampered these goals, and Latin@ activists turned to curricular issues, particularly around bilingual education.

Beyond contestation, activists and educators fought for inclusion in three major areas of public education: school governance, educational administration, and teaching (San Miguel & Donato, 2010). The community control movement of the late 1960s and early 1970s mobilized coalitions of Blacks and Puerto Ricans in New York to gain decision-making power of local schools and schools boards. These efforts led to temporary control of three local school districts in that city (I.S. 201, Two Bridges, and Ocean-Hill Brownsville), increased hiring of Latin@ administrators and teachers, and the establishment of bilingual education programs. These reforms, however, were "short-lived and by the mid-1970s, established school elites regained control of the schools" (Nieto, 2000; San Miguel & Donato, 2010, p. 41). Limited resources and positions in schools and districts as superintendents, principals, and teachers also heightened tensions between Latin@s and African Americans (Leal, Meier, & Rocha, 2010; San Miguel & Donato, 2010).

POLICIES AFFECTING LATIN@ YOUTH

The invisibility of Latin@s in the educational policy arena is what Orfield terms "policy by nonpolicy" (2002, p. 389). That is, policies that are crafted to mitigate racial and economic inequalities often fail to achieve their stated aims. For example, decreasing class sizes in theory should give low-performing students more specialized attention; however, when most Latin@ urban schools lack sufficient teachers and classroom resources to implement this type of reform, they are left with untrained, less experienced teachers. Or high-stakes, standards-based reforms driven by the No Child Left Behind Act and the Race to the Top program, which were intended to be equity focused by disaggregating data by race and holding schools to higher test-based standards, did not provide the necessary resources to schools, administrators, or teachers to be able to make improvements that would lead to higher test scores. What is more, educational policies explicitly focused on Latin@s have tended to have the most detrimental effects, such as restrictive language policies and ethnic studies bans. Implicit in these policies are not just beliefs about the conditions that lead to the best educational opportunities for Latin@ youth; they are fueled in large part by xenophobic and racist fears about how communities characterized as "non-American" might negatively influence the U.S. culture, economy, and society as a whole.

While a wide range of policy instruments have influenced Latin@s' schooling experiences, the primary policies that have perhaps had the greatest impact on Latin@ education include legislation related to segregation, language, testing and tracking, school choice, as well as broader social and economic policies. In what follows, we detail the ways in which these major policy instruments have shaped the educational experiences of Latin@ youth.

Segregation

The history of segregation in this country is often recounted as revolving almost entirely around White and African American students, yet Latin@ communities have an equally elaborate history of segregationist educational policies. As far back as 1899, American universities recruited students from Cuba and the island of Puerto Rico, but,

> the mixed-race population posed dilemmas for host U.S. institutions during an era of racial segregation. Afro-Cubans and dark-skinned Puerto Ricans were not allowed to enroll in White institutions, but were welcomed by historically Black colleges such as Hampton and Tuskegee. (San Miguel & Donato, 2010, p. 30)

In California, the case of Álvarez v. *Lemon Grove School District* (1931) was the first successful school desegregation case in U.S. history. After the district's school board forced Mexican students in the integrated town of Lemon Grove to attend a separate school, a group of Mexican parents fought back. They charged that the alternate school was substandard and likened it to a stable. The judge in that case ruled in favor of Álvarez. However, he did so because he reasoned that because Mexicans were considered Caucasian at that time under the law, they could not be legally segregated. It was not until the case of *Mendez v. Westminster* (1947) that segregation statewide was prohibited. Though not commonly a part of the discourse on school segregation, these cases served as important predecessors to the more prominent case of *Brown v. Board of Education of Topeka* (1954).

After the initial gains of the Civil Rights era, where the extent of segregation in schools decreased, particularly in the South, the trend has been steadily reversing. Today, segregation is still on the rise. The number of Black and Latin@ students attending schools with a high concentration of poverty saw a dramatic increase in the last 20 years. In California, on average, Black and Latin@ students attended schools with 52% and 58% poor children in 1993, respectively, and by 2012, Blacks attended schools that served 66% poor children and Latin@s in schools that were more than 70% poor (Orfield & Ee, 2015). Also in California, Latin@ students "on average attended schools that were 54% white in 1970, but now attend schools that are 84% nonwhite" (Orfield & Ee, 2015). Debates around segregation have reignited with the proliferation of charter schools over the past 20 years, which, as other chapters in this book detail, have often been marketed toward Latin@s or other communities of color.

Language Policy

Other educational policies that have significantly affected Latin@ youth come in the form of language policies, despite the fact that not all Latin@ youth speak a language other than English. Of the more than 2.5 million students classified as English learners in the United States, 75% are Spanish speakers, presumably of Latin@ descent (García & Kleifgen, 2010). Of children who speak a language other than English at home, 81% are U.S.-born or naturalized U.S. citizens (Lapkoff & Li, 2007).

The Bilingual Education Act of 1968 ushered in federal monies and a phase of increased educational access for students whose first language was not English. Yet increased access to "equal" educational opportunities was not tantamount to more "equitable" access. The case that served to best clarify this distinction was *Lau v. Nichols* (1974), where the court's ruling determined that, "There is no equality of treatment merely by providing students with the same facilities, textbooks, teachers, and curriculum; for students who do not understand English are effectively foreclosed from any meaningful education." In Lau, the courts recognized linguistic minorities' right to access the same education as their English-dominant peers by stating that school districts could facilitate this access by any means necessary, including the implementation of bilingual education programs (Gándara & Gomez, 2009).

A backlash against increasing numbers of immigrants and speakers of other languages, particularly in California and the Southwest, resulted in an English-only movement in the 1990s in several states: Proposition 227 in California, Question 2 in Massachusetts, and Proposition 203 in Arizona. Scholars posit that this legislation was successfully passed in part due to wide misunderstandings and stigmatization of bilingual education by both the general public and policymakers (Cline, Necochea, & Rios, 2004). Others argue that bilingual education has never come to full fruition because it was never fully funded. Yet, increasingly, dual-language programs, which represent one type of bilingual program, are growing in popularity. These programs have the advantage of serving students who are already English proficient and want to learn another language, in addition to English learners. They also hold the potential for integrating students from different socioeconomic, linguistic, and racial backgrounds (Morales & Razfar, in press). However, as Gándara and Contreras (2009) argue, focusing solely on within-school language programs detracts from larger disparities in educational resources and access that Latin@ communities have faced since the founding of the nation.

Testing and Tracking

The use of tests as gatekeepers for Latin@s has an elaborate political and ideological history. As early as 1904, psychometricians were using intelligence tests to sort immigrant students, language minorities, and other nondominant racial groups. Buttressed by deeply ingrained ideological beliefs about the intellectual inferiority of Latin@s, IQ tests were promoted as seemingly objective, scientific instruments for segregating these groups from mainstream educational and workplace opportunities. Despite a long line of scholarship that points to the cultural and linguistic biases and overall lack of validity that continue to characterize these assessments, testing continues to function as one of the most common tracking instruments in schools today.

Unlike the IQ tests of the early 20th century, however, today's tests carry with them even greater stakes for Latin@ youth. At the federal level, high-stakes testing and accountability policies like the No Child Left Behind Act and the Race to the Top program have tied strict consequences to Latin@ students' test scores. Schools serving large percentages of Latin@ students and English learners (among other nondominant populations) are under pressure to rapidly increase test scores or face sanctions that range from restructuring the school to replacing the staff, to converting the school to a charter status, to closing the school altogether (Trujillo & Renée, 2012, 2015). At the same time, challenges to correctly classifying limited English proficient[3] students compromise the validity of several of these policies' reporting requirements, which places undue pressure on schools with large numbers of Latin@ students, many of whom may be classified as limited English proficient (Abedi, 2004). Under these policies, schools that serve these populations are under heightened scrutiny; their students require more specialized resources to meet their students' unique academic, linguistic, and cultural needs, yet the policies themselves bring with them little to no such resources to build their capacity (Trujillo & Renée, 2012).

At the state level, high school graduation tests have served a similar gatekeeping function for Latin@ youth. Several states have now experimented with such test-based graduation requirements, yet rigorous research has confirmed that the students least likely to pass the tests, and therefore be denied a diploma, are students of color, English learners, and students from high-poverty communities. Furthermore, the National Academy of Sciences (National Research Council, 1999) concluded that such tests do not improve students' quality of education. Those students most likely to be penalized are those who have had inadequate access to high quality educational opportunities—Latin@s and other marginalized youth.

Such testing requirements have also caused various forms of collateral damage (Nichols & Berliner, 2007) for Latin@ youth. Valenzuela (2005), for example, has documented the multiple ways in which high-stakes testing in Texas—the state whose policies largely motivated national high-stakes accountability policies—effectively increased existing inequalities for Latin@ and English learner students. Curricula were narrowed to only those subjects that were tested. Simple, basic-skills instruction ensued. Instructional needs particular to English learners were not met. And, importantly, the presumed test-based improvements were later debunked. Such Texas-style accountability, according to Valenzuela, had the effect of relegating limited English proficient Latin@ youth to a second-class status. It also drastically diminished the role of democratic accountability in a public school system (Valenzuela, 2005).

School Choice

These trends in high-stakes testing exist alongside other educational policies that are deeply influenced by increasing globalization and market-oriented reforms (Suárez-Orozco & Páez, 2002). School choice policies, one prominent form of market-oriented educational reform that banks on competition and consumerist values, can be traced back to the support from community, state, and market actors in the emerging post-1970s, market-oriented policy era. The dwindling tax base of urban school districts post *Brown v. Board* has also made market-based school choice reforms, like charter schools and voucher programs, attractive to members of disenfranchised communities. Proponents of school choice policies reason that they benefit the least advantaged families by placing education in the hands of local educators, communities, and parents (Chubb & Moe, 1990). In fact, several members of Latin@ communities were early voucher advocates in the 1990s, and the last 10 years has witnessed a proliferation of charter schools in Latin@ communities. The strong link between school segregation and inequalities in school opportunities has drawn potent criticism of charter schools, which tend to be either predominantly African American or predominantly Latin@ (Lipman, 2011), but that do not consistently outperform (and usually perform worse than) traditional public schools.

Scholars have also documented a shift in Latin@-dominant charter schools from initially focusing on cultural empowerment to increasingly emphasizing a college-going culture by concentrating narrowly on test-based content and standardized testing (San Miguel & Donato, 2010). The scholarship on the relationship between Latin@s and school choice is quite limited, however. One exception includes a study in which researchers conducted a regression analysis of charter schools in Texas (Leal, Bohte, Polinard, Wenzel, & Winkle, 2010). The study examined the competitive effects between charter schools and traditional public schools, specifically the effects of charters on traditional public school enrollment and Latin@ student performance. The results were decidedly mixed.

For Latin@ families hoping to secure the best educational experience for their children by taking advantage of the increasingly common option to attend schools other than their local public school, the promise of school choice policies has usually gone unfulfilled. Their allure for many Latin@ families is strong, particularly for those whose neighborhood schools, often racially and economically segregated ones, are underresourced and, as a result, underperforming. Yet thus far the evidence suggests that choice policies, despite their prevalence in low-income, communities of color, do not result in Latin@ youth receiving a better education and, in many cases, are associated with lower academic outcomes for this population.

Social and Economic Policies

Scholars have argued that educational policies for Latin@s and non-Latin@ students alike are inextricably linked to broader social policies (Anyon, 1997, 2005). In other words, where Latin@s work and live—and the quality and equity of those experiences—shapes their children's educational opportunity. Social and economic policies that solidify patterns of poverty have weighty implications for teachers and students inside school districts (Anyon, 2005). Understanding the broader socioeconomic contexts surrounding Latin@ youth's educational crisis, therefore, is important for creating and choosing policy instruments intended to mitigate educational inequities (Gándara & Contreras, 2009).

Housing policy is one example of social policy that can create conditions that exacerbate cycles of poverty and disadvantage. One study of low-income housing in southern California found that by concentrating participants in poor, minority neighborhoods, the program effectively channeled families into racially segregated and underperforming schools (Pfeiffer, 2009). Thus, researching the relationship between government-sanctioned housing regulations, many of which have the unintended consequence of segregating nondominant racial groups into low-income communities, can help explain how schools that serve high concentrations of lower-income Latin@ families face disproportionately heavy burdens of educating students who bring with them particular cultural, linguistic, or academic needs. Such studies can also help explain why educational policies alone, usually those aimed at closing the test-based achievement gap between Latin@ students and their White counterparts, ultimately predict only a small fraction of variance in student outcomes (Rothstein, 2014; see also Biddle, Chapter 5).

Understanding how municipalities' gentrification efforts influence Latin@ youth's opportunities to attend high-functioning schools also illuminates the pervasive influence of social and economic policy on their academic performance. For example, Lipman's research on Chicago's government-facilitated economic development projects in the city's most financially impoverished, inner city, and working class neighborhoods demonstrates how African American and Latino families were effectively driven out of their communities and displaced by middle class, oftentimes White families (Lipman, 2011). In this case, city-assisted capital accumulation projects, intended to increase real estate tax and other revenues, had the effect of privatizing once affordable housing, dismantling public housing, and pushing longtime inner-city residents to the lowest-income, least resourced urban neighborhoods. The result is a phenomenon known as the "Latinization" of U.S. cities, or the displacement and ghettoization of Latin@ communities in the least resourced, usually highest crime neighborhoods (Dávila, 2004; Irizarry, 2011).

Alongside such market-driven gentrification efforts are usually school- and city-managed educational policies for closing neighborhood schools (usually in the most racially and economically isolated areas) and replacing them with privately run charter schools—schools whose performance is not better than, and oftentimes worse than, the traditional neighborhood public schools (Dávila, 2004; Lipman, 2011; Trujillo, in press; Trujillo & Renée, 2015). Attending to the role of these broader socioeconomic trends helps contextualize the roots and drivers of Latin@ students' persistent inequalities in schools.

Immigration policies also profoundly shape the educational experiences of Latin@ students. State-level legislation, such as Proposition 187 in California (passed in 1994) bars immigrants from accessing public services including education, dissuading many from remaining in the United States. Although this proposition was later ruled unconstitutional, entrance into higher education is still limited for undocumented students due in part to prohibitive costs. While higher education costs have increased for all students, undocumented students have significantly less access to financial resources because they cannot legally use federal student loans. Legislation proposed at the national level, such as the DREAM Act (Development, Relief, and Education for Alien Minors), would allow undocumented youth the opportunity to be treated as U.S. citizens with regard to paying for postsecondary education (see Chapter 3 for more on this topic).

Concurrently, there has been an exponential increase in the Latin@ incarceration rate over the past two decades, where one in four federal prison inmates is Latin@/a, even though fewer than one in eight U.S. residents is Latin@ (Morin, 2009). Known as disproportionate minority contact (DMC), DMC occurs when the proportion of youth of color who pass through the juvenile justice system exceeds the proportion of youth of color in the general population. Today, the rate of DMC increases as Latin@s and other youth of color move on through the criminal justice system (Short & Sharp, 2005).

LOOKING TO THE FUTURE: LEARNING FROM EVIDENCE IN LATIN@ EDUCATIONAL POLICYMAKING

The negative consequences of the educational, social, and economic policies reviewed in this chapter are, in many cases, a result of policymaking that focuses on compensating for Latin@ youth's perceived social and economic shortcomings. In most cases, these regulations, programs, and practices are intended to assimilate Latin@ youth and their families. In a minority of cases, however, a small number of policies or decisions have been made with a different aim in mind: to build on Latin@s' unique assets and to invest in the social, economic, and academic capacity of their schools and communities. In light of the Latin@ population's rapid growth, more policies that focus on the latter goals will be needed to effectively meet the needs of this historically underserved group.

For example, several Latin@ education scholars and Latino policy leaders have advocated for culturally responsive instruction and curriculum, including multilingual and multiliteracy opportunities to leverage what students know (Valenzuela, 1999; Yosso, 2005). Valenzuela's early work identified the phenomenon of culturally subtractive schooling, a process that she explains "encourages youth to de-identify from Mexican culture and the immigrants in their midst, [and that] results in the latter becoming unavailable as role models for, and co-creators of, achievement" (Valenzuela, 1999, p. 262). She maintains that the weak academic achievement of Latin@s is a consequence of these culturally subtractive schooling processes, and she advocates for an additive schooling model, one that promotes a pluralistic model of schooling by building on the students' bicultural experience and knowledge. Such work departs from more traditional policy scholarship that some scholars have argued frames Latin@s' experiences from a cultural deficit perspective (e.g., Fuller, Bein, Kim, & Rabe-Hesketh, 2015).

Latin@ policy scholars also contend that when researchers do not frame their inquiries from broader sociopolitical or sociocultural perspectives, the consequences can be detrimental in that they risk influencing the formation of more misinformed educational policies (Nieto, 2013; Valenzuela, 2015). This means recognizing that the problems of the Latin@ community, such as lower than average graduation rates or education levels of adults,

> are not an accumulated sum total of deficiencies that we collectively inherit or "possess," but rather a very deep history of educational neglect, underinvestment, and cultural chauvinism in an otherwise highly alienating, test-driven curriculum where the knowledge of the dominant group is what counts in our state curriculum. (Valenzuela, 2015)

Studies that contextualize Latin@ youth's performance within the larger social, economic, and historical conditions that have facilitated unequal access to high quality, equitable education opportunities, rather the concentrating solely on their within-school academic achievement or narrowly on what their families are not doing to support their academic achievement, represent one tool for expanding the discourse on Latin@ youth and policy.

As for policymakers, they can respond to the evidence on Latin@ youth's educational experiences by calling for more investments in the teaching force itself. For these scholars, more equitable educational opportunities for Latin@s can be facilitated, in part, by policies that diversify the teaching force. One persistent obstacle to Latin@ youth's educational success, some posit, is the shortage of Latin@ teachers, which has continued to increase in its disproportionality with the growing Latin@ student population. Orfield notes that "[s]trong outreach for Latin@ teachers has been replaced, in many states, by teacher exams that sharply reduce Latin@ certification" (2002, p. 393). Some institutions of higher education are partnering with community organizations to increase the number of teacher candidates coming out of their own communities, thereby increasing the number of teachers of color as well as teachers who understand the particular context of the neighborhoods in which they teach.

In response to today's high-stakes testing and accountability environment, a number of scholars are calling for more contextualized federal and state education policies—ones that take into account the unique economic and social conditions and historical legacies that have coalesced to create unequal learning opportunities for schools serving large numbers of Latin@s. Trujillo and Renée (2015), for example, recommend replacing more punitive federal accountability policies, such as those that mandate massive personnel layoffs or school closures (most of which take place in high-poverty communities with heavy concentrations of students of color) with ones that facilitate a more prominent role for the community in schools. Full-service community schools, for example, represent one type of reform that they suggest has the potential to meet the full needs of historically disenfranchised groups such as the Latin@ community, by providing not just academic resources for students, but physical health, mental health, occupational, and other resources for their families.

Despite a large volume of social science research that demonstrates how making mistakes is a healthy part of adolescence, recent policies and practices have criminalized the coming-of-age process for youth of color (Rios, 2009). This "adultification" of boys of color labels their actions as intentional and strips them of any element of childish naïveté (Ferguson, 2000). Unsurprisingly, this mistrust of authority has created a culture of resistance among Latin@ youth (Valenzuela, 1999). With the beginning of the War on Drugs, the 1980s and 1990s gave rise to the use of symbolic racism to portray young men of color as inherently criminal. Research demonstrates how implicit biases are embedded in the criminal justice system, which further enable the differential treatment of Latin@s.

Regardless of their particulars, all of these policy recommendations have one assumption in common. Each suggestion assumes that the public school system has the responsibility to create equitable educational opportunities for Latin@ youth. Whether it focuses on the classroom, school building, or federal level, each recommendation is built on the original principle espoused in *Lau v. Nichols:* that every school system in the country has the responsibility to design whatever educational policy or change that will effectively create equitable access for language minorities, many of whom are Latin@, to the same educational opportunities as their more privileged counterparts. The onus is on today's scholars, policymakers, and communities to design inquiries, make decisions, and promote policies that reflect this assumption.

NOTES

1. The term "Latin@" is used instead of "Hispanic" because the latter connotes a "sense of community through a connection *to* Spain," and the authors prefer the "sense of community through a history of colonization *from* Spain" that "Latino" encompasses (Mora, 2014). "Latin@" is used, rather than "Latina/o," to be gender inclusive.
2. See previous note.
3. Many scholars prefer the term English learner or English language learner over Limited English Proficient (LEP), due to its deficit-oriented phrasing, but LEP is still used by the federal government.

REFERENCES

Abedi, J. (2004). The No Child Left Behind Act and English language learners: Assessment and accountability issues. *Educational Researcher, 33*(1), 4–14.

Abrego, L. J., & Gonzales, R. G. (2010). Blocked paths, uncertain futures: The postsecondary education and labor market prospects of undocumented Latino youth. *Journal of Education for Students Placed at Risk (JESPAR), 15*(1/2), 144–157.

Alcoff, L. M. (2000). Is Latina/o identity a racial identity? In J. J. E. Gracia & P. De Greiff (Eds.), *Hispanics/Latinos in the United States: Ethnicity, race, and rights* (pp. 23–44). New York, NY: Routledge.

Anyon, J. (1997). *Ghetto schooling: A political economy of urban educational reform.* New York, NY: Teachers College Press.

Anyon, J. (2005). What "counts" as educational policy? Notes toward a new paradigm. *Harvard Educational Review, 75*(1), 65–88.

Chubb, J. E., & Moe, T. M. (1990). *Politics, markets, and America's schools.* Washington, DC: Brookings Institution Press.

Cline, Z., Necochea, J., & Rios, F. (2004). The tyranny of democracy: Deconstructing the passage of racist propositions. *Journal of Latinos and Education, 3*(2), 67–85.

Contreras, F. (2011). *Achieving equity for Latino students: Expanding the pathway to higher education through public policy.* New York, NY: Teachers College Press.

Darder, A. (2011). *A dissident voice: Essays on culture, pedagogy, and power.* New York, NY: Peter Lang.

Darder, A. (2012). *Culture and power in the classroom: Educational foundations for the schooling of bicultural students.* Boulder, CO: Paradigm.

Dávila, A. (2004). *Barrio dreams: Puerto Ricans, Latinos, and the neoliberal city.* Berkeley, CA: University of California Press.

Donato, R. (1997). *The other struggle for equal schools: Mexican Americans during the Civil Rights era.* Albany, NY: State University of New York Press.

Ferguson, A. A. (2000). *Bad boys: Public schools in the making of Black masculinity.* Ann Arbor, MI: University of Michigan Press.

Fry, R., & Lopez, M. H. (n.d.). *Hispanic student enrollments reach new highs in 2011.* Retrieved from http://www.pewhispanic.org/2012/08/20/hispanic-student-enrollments-reach-new-highs-in-2011/

Fuller, B., Bein, E., Kim, Y., & Rabe-Hesketh, S. (2015). Differing cognitive trajectories of Mexican American toddlers the role of class, nativity, and maternal practices. *Hispanic Journal of Behavioral Sciences, 37*(2), 139–169.

Gándara, P., & Gómez, M. C. (2009). Language policy in education. In B. Schneider, G. Sykes, & D. Plank (Eds.), *AERA handbook on educational policy research* (pp. 581–595). Washington, DC: American Educational Research Association.

Gándara, P., & Hopkins, M. (Eds.). (2010). *Forbidden language: English learners and restrictive language policies.* New York: Teachers College Press.

Gándara, P., & Orfield, G. (2012). Why Arizona matters: The historical, legal, and political contexts of Arizona's instructional policies and U.S. linguistic hegemony. *Language Policy, 11*(1), 7–19.

Gándara, P. C., & Contreras, F. (2009). *The Latino education crisis: The consequences of failed social policies.* Cambridge, MA: Harvard University Press.

García Bedolla, L. (2009). *Latino politics.* Cambridge, England: Polity.

García, O., & Kleifgen, J. A. (2010). *Educating emergent bilinguals.* New York, NY: Teachers College Press.

Gonzalez, G. G. (1999). Segregation and the education of Mexican children, 1900–1940. In J. F. Moreno (Ed.), *The elusive quest for equality: 150 years of Chicano/Chicana education* (pp. 53–76). Cambridge, MA: Harvard Educational Review.

Gonzalez, G. G. (2013). *Chicano education in the era of segregation.* Denton, TX: University of North Texas Press.

Gonzales, R. G. (2010). On the wrong side of the tracks: The consequences of school stratification systems for unauthorized Mexican students. *Peabody Journal of Education, 85*(4), 469.

Gutiérrez, K. D., & Orellana, M. F. (2006). The "problem" of English learners: Constructing genres of difference. *Research in the Teaching of English, 40*(4), 502–507.

Gutiérrez, K. D., & Rogoff, B. (2003). Cultural ways of learning: Individual traits or repertoires of practice. *Educational Researcher, 32*(5), 19–25.

Heubert, J. P., & Hauser, R. M. (Eds.). (1999). *High stakes: Testing for tracking, promotion, and graduation.* Washington, DC: National Academies Press.

Irizarry, J. (2011). Buscando la libertad: Latino youths in search of freedom in school. *Democracy and Education, 19*(1), 1–11.

Kao, G. (1999). Psychological well-being and educational achievement among immigrant youth. In D. J. Hernandez (Ed.), *Children of immigrants: Health, adjustment, and public assistance* (pp. 410–477). Washington, DC: National Academy Press.

Lapkoff, S., & Li, R. M., (2007). Five trends for schools. *Educational Leadership, 64*(6), 8–15.

Leal, D. L., Bohte, J., Polinard, J. L., Wenzel, J. P., & Winkle, R. D. (2010). Problem or solution? Charter schools, Latino students, and traditional Texas public schools. In D. L. Leal & K. J. Meier (Eds.), *The politics of Latino education.* New York, NY: Teachers College Press.

Leal, D. L., & Meier, K. J. (2010). Introduction. In D. L. Leal & K. J. Meier (Eds.), *The politics of Latino education.* New York, NY: Teachers College Press.

Leal, D. L., Meier, K. J., & Rocha, R. R. (Eds.). (2010). Black empowerment and representation of Latinos on local school boards. In D. L. Leal & K. J. Meier (Eds.), *The politics of Latino education.* New York, NY: Teachers College Press.

Lipman, P. (2011). *The new political economy of urban education: Neoliberalism, race and the right to the city.* New York, NY: Routledge.

Martinez, R. O. (2011). Introduction. In R. O. Martinez (Ed.), *Latinos in the Midwest* (pp. 1–15). East Lansing, MI: Michigan State University Press.

Mora, G. C. (2014). *Making Hispanics: How activists, bureaucrats, and media constructed a new American.* Chicago, IL: University of Chicago Press.

Morales, P. Z., & Razfar, A. (2016). Advancing integration through bilingualism for all. In E. Frankenberg, L. Garces, & M. B. Hopkins (Eds.), *School integration matters: Research-based strategies to advance equity* (pp. 135–144). New York: Teachers College Press.

Morin, J. L. (2009). Latinos and U.S. prisons: Trends and challenges. In S. Oboler (Ed.), *Behind bars: Latinos and prison in the United States.* New York, NY: Palgrave Macmillan.

National Research Council. (1999). *High Stakes: Testing for Tracking, Promotion, and Graduation.* Washington, DC: The National Academies Press. Retrieved from http://www.nap.edu/catalog/6336/high-stakes-testing-for-tracking-promotion-and-graduation

Nichols, S. L., & Berliner, D. C. (2007). *Collateral damage: How high-stakes testing corrupts America's schools.* Cambridge, MA: Harvard Education Press.

Nieto, S. (1999). *The light in their eyes: Creating multicultural learning communities.* New York, NY: Teachers College Press.

Nieto, S. (2000). *Puerto Rican students in U.S. schools.* Mahwah, NJ: Erlbaum.

Nieto, S. (2009). *Language, culture, and teaching: Critical perspectives.* New York NY: Routledge.

Nieto, S. (2013). *Finding joy in teaching students of diverse backgrounds: Culturally responsive and socially just practices in U.S. classrooms.* Portsmouth, NH: Heinemann.

Noguera, P. A. (2003). *City schools and the American dream: Reclaiming the promise of public education.* New York, NY: Teachers College Press.

Orfield, G. (2002). Commentary. In M. M. Suárez-Orozco & M. Páez (Eds.), *Latinos: Remaking America.* Berkeley, CA: University of California Press.

Orfield, G., & Ee, J. (2015). *Segregating California's future: Inequality and its alternative 60 years after Brown v. Board of Education.* Los Angeles, CA: UCLA Civil Rights Project.

Pfeiffer, D. (2009). *The opportunity illusion: Subsidized housing and failing schools in California.* Los Angeles, CA: UCLA Civil Rights Project.

Poza, L., Brooks, M. D., & Valdés, G. (2014). "Entre Familia": Immigrant parents' strategies for involvement in children's schooling. *School Community Journal, 24*(1), 119–148.

Reyes, P., & Valencia, R. R. (1993). Educational policy and the growing Latino student population: Problems and prospects. *Hispanic Journal of Behavioral Sciences, 15*(2), 258–283.

Rios, V. M. (2009). The racial politics of youth crime. In S. Oboler (Ed.), *Behind bars: Latinos and prison in the United States.* New York, NY: Palgrave Macmillan.

Rothstein, R. (2014). The racial achievement gap, segregated schools, and segregated neighborhoods: A constitutional insult. *Race and Social Problems, 7*(1), 21–30.

San Miguel, G. Jr., & Donato, R. (2010). Latino education in twentieth century America. In E. G. Murillo, *Handbook of Latinos and education: Theory, research, and practice* (pp. 27–62). New York, NY: Routledge.

Short, J., & Sharp, C. (2005). *Disproportionate minority contact in the juvenile justice system.* Washington, DC: Child Welfare League of America, National Center for Program Leadership.

Suárez-Orozco, M. M., & Páez, M. (2002). Introduction. In M. M. Suárez-Orozco, M. Páez, & David Rockefeller Center for Latin American Studies, *Latinos: Remaking America.* Berkeley, CA: University of California Press.

Telles, E. M., & Ortiz, V. (2008). *Generations of exclusion: Mexican-Americans, assimilation, and race.* New York, NY: Russell Sage Foundation.

Trujillo, T. (2016). Why the federal school improvement grant program triggers civil rights complaints. In E. Frankenberg, L. M. Garces, & M. Hopkins (Eds.), *School integration matters: Research-based strategies to advance equity* (pp. 89–104). New York: Teachers College Press.

Trujillo, T., & Renée, M. (2012). *Democratic school turnarounds: Pursuing equity and learning from evidence* (Legislative research brief). Boulder, CO: National Education Policy Center. Retrieved from http://nepc.colorado.edu/publication/democratic-school-turnarounds

Trujillo, T., & Renée, M. (2015). Irrational exuberance for market-based reform: How federal turnaround policies thwart democratic schooling. *Teachers College Record, 117*(6).

U.S. Census Bureau. (2012, December 12). *2012 national population projections.* Retrieved January 25, 2015, from https://www.census.gov/population/projections/data/national/2012.html

U.S. Department of Education, National Center for Education Statistics, Common Core of Data. (2013, Fall). *Public elementary/secondary school universe survey, 2013–14* (version 1a). Table *B.1.b.-1: Number and percentage distribution of public elementary and secondary students, by race/ethnicity and school urban-centric 12-category locale.* Retrieved from http://nces.ed.gov/programs/digest/d09/tables/dt09_151.asp

Valdés, G., Capitelli, S., & Alvarez, L. (2011). *Latino children learning English: Steps in the journey.* New York, NY: Teachers College Press.

Valencia, R. R. (1997). *The evolution of deficit thinking: Educational thought and practice, the Stanford series on education and public policy.* Bristol, PA: Falmer Press.

Valencia, R. R. (Ed.). (2011a). *Chicano school failure and success: Past, present, and future* (3rd ed.). New York: Routledge Falmer.

Valencia, R. R. (2011b). Segregation, desegregation, and integration of Chicano students. In R. R. Valencia (Ed.), *Chicano school failure and success: Past, present, and future* (3rd ed., pp. 42–75). New York: Routledge.

Valenzuela, A. (1999). *Subtractive schooling: issues of caring in education of U.S.-Mexican youth.* Albany, NY: State University of New York Press.

Valenzuela, A. (2005). *Leaving children behind: How "Texas-style" accountability fails Latino youth.* Albany, NY: SUNY Press.

Valenzuela, A. (2015, April 9). Mexican-American toddlers: (Mis)understanding the achievement gap. *Educational equity, politics & policy in Texas.* Retrieved from   http://texasedequity.blogspot.com/2015/04/mexican-american-tod-dlers-understanding.html

Yosso, T. J. (2005). Whose culture has capital? A critical race theory discussion of community cultural wealth. *Race Ethnicity and Education, 8*(1), 69–91.

CHAPTER 2

THE LANGUAGING PRACTICES AND COUNTERNARRATIVE PRODUCTION OF BLACK YOUTH

Carlotta Penn, Valerie Kinloch, and Tanja Burkhard
Ohio State University

> *You see me . . . I'm a Black male standing here. Not a statistic.*
> —Rendell, 2013

During the summer of 2013, four high school students (Chelsea, Christian, Rendell, and Scott), their teacher (Tori), a researcher (Valerie), and the former president of a teachers' union in the state of Ohio (Rhonda) participated in the Raise Your Hand day of learning held in Atlanta, Georgia, and sponsored by the National Education Association (NEA). This gathering, which precedes NEA's annual meeting, serves as an occasion for union, district, and school leaders to examine ways to improve teaching and learning conditions, contexts, and practices for students in U.S. public schools. Teachers, school support staff, superintendents, union representatives, and researchers shared examples of school and district collaborations, assessment and Common Core trends, and community-engaged practices. For the final presentation, Chelsea, Christian, Rendell, and Scott described

Educational Policies and Youth in the 21st Century, pages 23–38

23

their experiences working in a critical service-learning project, where they partnered with Tori and members of a church to design an urban garden, and to sponsor awareness campaigns at the school and in the community. Describing his desire to be a part of something that can impact the local, urban community, Rendell shared with his peers after the presentation:

> I was sitting there listening to the other presenter talk about statistics and I thought, "I attend an urban school and I'm out there doing this garden thing. You see me... I'm a Black male standing here. Not a statistic. And look at me."

Rendell's sentiments about being "a Black male" who is "not a statistic" open this chapter on the languaging practices and counternarrative production of Black youth. His sentiments are grounded in a desire to language his experiences—that is, to use communicative tools to counter deficit-oriented narratives—about his identity, competence, and ability. In an interview with Rendell, he referenced his presentation at the Raise Your Hand event as paramount to how he has come to publicly reject statistics that portray Black males in criminalizing ways. According to Rendell,

> I'm a Black male who went to urban schools. I grew up with a working single mother. People want you thinking Black kids aren't smart and capable of success. That's not true. We gotta work against that; tell our stories about who we are. That's what I did on the stage in Atlanta.

As he stood "on the stage," Rendell engaged in counternarrative production by languaging his experiences. In other words, he described his involvement in a project, explained that he is not a statistic, and concluded that he, in fact, is one of many Black youth who is "smart and capable of success." His narrative about who he is counters attempts to demean the identities of many Black youth.

In this chapter, we draw on Rendell's sentiments about not being a statistic to examine how some Black youth language their experiences related to racism, inequity, and marginalization in schools and the larger society. As referenced above, we conceptualize languaging as the multiple ways people employ communicative tools and practices to voice their experiences as they navigate a variety of sociocultural and sociopolitical contexts (e.g., schools, community spaces, church, work, popular culture, etc.). It is our belief that the practice of languaging can result in a disruption of deficit-oriented perspectives about the lives, literacies, languages, and identities of Black youth. More specifically, Black youth languaging their experiences can also lead to the production of counternarratives: the intentional use of narratives to resist normalized, or White middle class, practices, expectations, and ways of being that get imposed on them. Ultimately, counternarrative production supports the establishment of what McLaren and Hammer (2007)

refer to as "communities of resistance, counterpublic spheres, and oppositional pedagogies that can resist dominant forms of meaning by offering
new channels of communication" (p. 134).

To make the case for the importance of the languaging practices and
counternarrative production of Black youth, we ask: What are some of the
ways Black youth language their experiences with racism, inequity, and
marginalization; how can teachers, teacher educators, and educational
researchers create learning environments for Black students to produce
counternarratives through languaging their experiences? To address these
questions, we frame languaging as a strategy of counternarrative production through which Black youth can assert agency and critique hegemonic
power and structural racism. Then, we examine three contemporary examples of linguistic and racial injustices experienced by Black youth: Rachel Jeantel, a witness in the George Zimmerman murder trial; the Black
Student Forum of Boston College; and Rendell Buckhalter, a high school
graduate from the Midwest. Finally, we outline starting points for teachers,
teacher educators, and educational researchers to create learning environments that facilitate and support Black youth languaging and producing
counternarratives.

COUNTERNARRATIVES
AND COUNTERNARRATIVE PRODUCTION

According to critical race theory, counternarratives are stories told by
people who are marginalized by structural oppression in society. Matsuda
(1987) argues that "those who have experienced discrimination speak with
a special voice to which we should listen" (p. 324). It is imperative that we
listen to and take these voices seriously if we believe that all people deserve
freedom. In the United States, systematic racial discrimination has most
profoundly impacted the freedom of indigenous, Black, Latin@, and Asian
communities. It is important to note, however, that with the White, American, heterosexual male as the "normalized" identity in the United States,
gender, sexuality, language, and documentation status intersect with race
to marginalize people in different ways. Counternarratives help to uncover
the important histories, insights, and cultural identities of people who are
suffocated by dominating forces of oppression. Such accounts also offer alternative representations of their identities, experiences, and knowledges,
and therefore oppose the "majoritarian stories" that dominate mainstream
discourse. As Solórzano and Yosso (2002) contend, majoritarian stories
"purport to be neutral and objective yet implicitly make assumptions according to negative stereotypes about people of color" (p. 29).

Solórzano and Yosso's (2002) assertion points to the valuable role of recognizing, hearing, and circulating counternarratives, particularly from Black people. In other words, critical race theory promotes "the voice of color thesis [which] holds that because of their different histories and experiences with oppression, black...thinkers may be able to communicate to their white counterparts matters that the whites are unlikely to know" (Delgado & Stephancic, 2012, p. 10). Furthermore, counternarratives are important because of the correlation between how a person is perceived based on her racial identity and the opportunities afforded to her in society. If Black people do not reject the racist categorizations of them as morally bankrupt, violent, and uninterested in learning, then they might continue to disproportionately occupy the lowest positions in social, economic, political, and educational spheres. Therefore, it is necessary that we continue to work to "free the black body and personality from white control and domination" (Haymes, 1995, p. 28).

One way to move toward freedom for Black people is through the production of counternarratives—stories of resistance grounded in Black cultural practices and intellectual traditions—in which languaging plays a crucial role. The term languaging has been used differently across various disciplines. Some linguists, such as Knouzi, Swain, Lapkin, & Brooks, (2010), Swain (2006), and Swain, Lapkin, Knouzi, Suzuki, and Brooks, (2009), use the term to describe language production for self-scaffolding, solving problems, and making meaning. In this way, languaging refers to the process of using language to mediate cognition in second language acquisition. However, Lado (1979), who conceptualizes languaging from a psycholinguistic perspective, utilizes the term to distinguish "full linguistic performance in contrast to partial linguistic performance" (p. 3), which denotes a shift from the mechanics of language (e.g., pronunciation, grammar points) to wholistic linguistic performances. Additionally, Jørgensen (2008), who situates languaging in the realm of language use and production, uses the term to reference a speaker's employment of accessible linguistic features to reach a communicative goal. Finally, García (2010) frames languaging as a process through which ethnic identities and linguistic practices are mediated and negotiated. She argues that people employ "discursive and ethnic practices" to "signify what it is they want to be" (p. 519).

While the aforementioned definitions of languaging differ in terms of disciplinary usage (and from how we, ourselves, use the term), they mostly refer to a productive process. In this chapter, we conceptualize languaging as the multiple and nuanced ways Black people utilize language and other communicative tools to "talk back" (hooks, 1989) to deficit-oriented narratives that get (re)-produced in society. For us, the term denotes Black people's active resistance to such narratives through the use of languages and/or linguistic varieties that are oftentimes devalued in public spaces.

CONTEMPORARY EXAMPLES
OF BLACK YOUTH LANGUAGING

Solórzano and Yosso (2002) contend that "we must look to experiences with and responses to racism, sexism, classism, and heterosexism in and out of schools as valid, appropriate, and necessary forms of data" as we substantiate "critical discourse in education" (p. 37). In so doing, scholars, educators, and students can "turn the margins into places of transformative resistance" (Solórzano & Yosso, 2002, p. 37). In this section, we examine some of the ways Black youth engage in resistance and self-care within hostile, racist environments. Specifically, we focus on their languaging practices to demonstrate that one by-product of languaging is the counternarrative, or "a tool for exposing, analyzing, and challenging the majoritarian stories" (p. 32) that too readily privilege White life while demeaning Black life. We explore the languaging practices of Rachel Jeantel, who testified against George Zimmerman, the man who killed Black teenager Trayvon Martin; the Black Student Forum of Boston College, which penned an open letter to the college administration chastising them for their silence on assaults against Black life; and Rendell Buckhalter, a former high school student who rejected the statistical stereotyping of Black males. Their stories demonstrate how they language their experiences against racism, and the ways they remain resilient in "carrying on" despite abuses to their humanity. Additionally, their stories present learning opportunities for educators to better support Black students' intellectual, emotional, and social development.

Case 1: Rachel Jeantel

On March 19, 2012, Rachel Jeantel wrote a letter to Trayvon Martin's parents, describing her last conversation with him on the day George Zimmerman followed, attacked, and shot him dead. She concludes the letter by stating, "Then Trevon turned around and said, 'Why are you following me!!' Then I heard him fall. Then the phone hung up. I called back and got no response. In my mind I thought it was just a fight. Then I found out this tragic story. Thank you" (cited in Quigley, 2013). As a close friend to Martin and the last person to speak with him before he was killed, Jeantel was an important witness for the prosecution. She was 19-years-old during the time of her court testimony and had not yet graduated from high school. Even though Zimmerman was on trial for murder, Jeantel was cast by the defense and in the media as untruthful, uncooperative, uneducated, and as a criminal. For example, in a *Daily Mail* article published on June 27, 2013, Rachel Quigley (2013) writes that Jeantel "grew annoyed and confused several times throughout her second day of testimony," and "had to admit that she couldn't read cursive in court" In her Jeantel-bashing article, Quigley also includes tweets from Jeantel's Twitter account about drinking and smoking, and a picture Jeantel took of her newly polished fingernails. Quigley's article is one of many that dominated mainstream media in their collective effort to discredit Rachel Jeantel and Trayvon Martin, as well as other young Black people in the United States.

The focus on Jeantel's language, reading ability, and use of alcohol and marijuana reaffirms the majoritarian story that Black youth are likely to be uneducated people and engage in criminal drug behaviors. However, there are studies indicating that Black youth are not more likely to use or sell drugs than White youth (NAACP, 2015), and that they have positive experiences with education when provided similar opportunities afforded to their White peers. Furthermore, underage drinking, smoking marijuana, and having trouble reading do not invalidate a person's humanity or capacity to meaningfully contribute to society. Despite the public abuse directed at Jeantel, she defended her story and her friend. Jeantel languaged her experiences (e.g., her memories of Martin; her feelings of dismay over the murder of Martin; her identity as a Black youth in a racist country) by unapologetically telling her story using "her own particular, idiosyncratic black girl idiom, a mashup of her Haitian and Dominican working-class background, her U.S. Southern upbringing, and the three languages—Haitian Kreyol (or Creole), Spanish and English—that she speaks" (Cooper, 2013, p. 1).

In one instance deemed particularly offensive by Quigley, Jeantel responded to the defense attorney's suggestion that Martin attacked Zimmerman with, "That's retarded, sir" (cited in Quigley, 2013). This calling out of the older White male attorney in a court of law can be seen as a form of resistance. It was "retarded" that Martin would be cast as the aggressor when Zimmerman admits to following him even after dispatchers advised him not to. It was retarded because Martin was a teenager who expressed fear and Zimmerman was an adult with a history of racial profiling. It was retarded because Martin was unarmed and Zimmerman was wielding a gun. However, the word retarded has a negative connotation in mainstream discourse. It is viewed as insensitive because of its historical application to persons with mental and physical disabilities, or special rights. It is a brash and accusatory word, but for her own reasons, Jeantel decided it best captured the unfeasibility of Martin being a violent Black youth who was responsible for Zimmerman assaulting and, subsequently, murdering him. Taken together, Jeantel's letter, testimony, and use of Black English—a language that June Jordan (1989) claims "is not a linguistic buffalo" (p. 175)—counter the majoritarian story told about Trayvon Martin. They also counter the demeaning image the public painted of Jeantel. In fact, these things provide evidence into Jeantel's compassion and care for her friend and his family, her authority and reliability as a witness, and her self-determination to speak her own truth by using Black English as a language of power (Jordan, 1989; Kinloch; 2005; Smitherman, 1977).

Case 2: The Black Student Forum of Boston College

Created in 1970, the Black Student Forum at Boston College derived from the Black Talent Program, which was "an effort to recruit talented Black students from across the country" (https://www.facebook.com/BlackStudentForum). Beginning in 1971, the Black Talent Program assumed full leadership of the initiative and became responsible for "recruiting educationally and economically disadvantaged students of color," awarding them financial support, and advocating for a culturally diverse college environment. Their work led to the creation of the college's Black Student Forum, the Options Through Education experience, and the Black Family Weekend. Even today, their mission is to provide a "platform that encourages the cultural, intellectual, political, and social growth of the Boston College student body."

Therefore, it is not surprising that in 2014 members of the Black Student Forum penned a letter to the senior administration of Boston College. In part, the letter reads:

> We, as Black students of Boston College...are extremely disappointed by this institution's failure to acknowledge the injustices that have been taking place throughout the country and the lack of judicial accountability. We are particularly frustrated because Boston College is a Jesuit institution committed to social justice. As students who are receiving an education based on the principles of St. Ignatius of Loyola, we expect more from our school. We interpret the administration's silence as a sign of neutrality and, as Desmond Tutu states, "If you are neutral in situations of injustice, you have chosen the side of the oppressor. If an elephant has its foot on the tail of a mouse and you say that you are neutral, the mouse will not appreciate your neutrality." (Black Student Forum, 2014)

The students charge that the institution is part of a "failing system" that has "turned a blind eye" to the realities of oppression faced by its Black students, despite the college's motto: For here all are one. They situate their letter as part of the international #BlackLivesMatter movement founded in 2012 following the murder of Trayvon Martin, and "rooted in the experiences of Black people in this country who actively resist our de-humanization" (Black Lives Matter, 2015). The #BlackLivesMatter call to action was taken up by millions of Black and racially diverse people seeking freedom for Black people from the violence of systemic oppression. The movement highlights the ongoing violence perpetuated onto Black people of all genders, abilities, social statuses, and ages—violence that is often state-sponsored, via police involved shootings and mass incarceration. The Black Student Forum letter contends that Boston College institutionally avoids discussions on race and actions against racism—again, an avoidance that goes against its stated Jesuit principles of transformational engagement in the world.

Academically, members of the forum claim that the history and current realities of Black students and communities in the United States and across the African diaspora are nearly absent from major course offerings. In fact, they write that, currently they "cannot major in African and African Diaspora Studies.... In our non-African and African Diaspora Studies, our professors do not incorporate Black history or issues or create a space for students to discuss, learn, and foster an appreciation of our heritage" (Black Student Forum, 2014). As such, they demand from the college's administration, at the least, a public statement regarding the "New Civil Rights Movement," ongoing discussions on race and racism, integration of Black and African studies more fully into the curriculum, and more Black faculty and administration across the college. Meeting these demands, they assert, can represent one step in the college's "willingness to support the greater discussion on race in America, and the personal experiences of race at Boston College" (Black Student Forum, 2014).

By writing this letter, and posting it on the Internet, the Black Student Forum languaged their concerns about the college's silence on racism and its lack of curricular investment in Black students. The letter is a counter-narrative because it proves that Black students are present on campus and aware that institutional structures have ignored their histories, cultures, and academic interests (for more information, see the complete open letter). Furthermore, the letter's chastising of the administration's failure to uphold its own values exposes the hypocrisy of the college's majoritarian story, which purports that Boston College is a place concerned with "transformation of the world" (Black Student Forum, 2014, para. 3). Insofar as language is concerned, the students decided to write their letter by utilizing dominant academic English (DAE), a choice that is itself a counternarrative inasmuch as it uses the *master's tools* to critique the master, himself. In using DAE to speak about aspects of the Black experience at the college and in America, the students recognize the reality of their "two-ness" (DuBois, 1903/2007): being "an American, a Negro; two souls, two thoughts, two unreconciled strivings; two warring ideals in one dark body" with a "longing to attain self-conscious[ness]" (p. 8). Thus, the languaging practices of the Black Student Forum reflect a level of self-consciousness—with full claims made to Blackness and Americanness—and an attempt to counter how racism materializes even in silence and inaction.

Case 3: On Rendell and Not Being a Statistic

Rendell's sentiments about public perceptions of Black youth who attend urban schools and his insistence that we "tell our stories" are important to recall. He says:

> I'm a Black male who went to urban schools. I grew up with a working single parent. People want you thinking Black kids aren't smart and capable of success. That's not true. We gotta work against that; tell our stories about who we are.

In telling his own story about who he is and about his involvement in a critical service-learning project, Rendell languaged his experiences during a series of interviews, in team meetings, and at various conferences. That is, he voiced his rejection of public narratives and policies that portray Black males in a negative light (e.g., see the racist implications of the "stop-and-frisk" law, the zero-tolerance policy, and the push-out to prison efforts, especially directed at Black people). Rendell also languaged his resistance to feelings of alienation and failure projected onto him (e.g., the widespread exclusion of Black cultural practices in the curricula; the predominance of White monolingual and monocultural norms throughout society). In fact, he used the opportunity at the Raise Your Hand event to reflect on his lived conditions. He explained:

> Coming into high school and being a young Black male coming from a single parent home in a city school, I honestly didn't know what my purpose was 'cause, I mean, with a single parent...no father, no [male] guidance.

His reflections led him to question whether he "was going to go to college or not," given the ways Black males are often positioned in schools as academically underprepared, and in society as deviant. However, Rendell shared with the audience an important turning point in his life: "But then I...found my teacher, Ms. [Tori] Washington, I got involved with the [service-learning] group, and she showed me that involvement was the best thing that you could do in high school to be successful."

Throughout the majority of his K–12 schooling experiences, Rendell was often made to question his academic acuity, as he regularly received admonitions from peers and adults alike about the "struggles of Black males" and the "hard times Black people in single-parent homes, growing up poor in city neighborhoods" experience. During high school, Rendell realized the value of languaging as a strategy to produce counternarratives that reject one-sided representations of Black males, Black family structures, and urban communities. In an interview, Rendell asserted: "You grow up hearing those things. A lot of us believe 'em and start acting on what they say about

Black people. But I opened my eyes. See, I know that's not who we are. I don't listen to those stories anymore." Instead of continuing to listen to those stories, Rendell resists White normative expectations that have long been imposed upon him. And like many other Black youth, Rendell's rejection of such expectations—as well as the support he receives from "my mother and my teacher, and, um, from my Black role models"—has encouraged him to "believe I can do something and achieve something."

Additionally, Rendell's languaging of his experiences in ways that counter dominant narratives about his racial, gendered, linguistic, and academic identities encouraged him to examine "the statistics of young Black males who don't graduate from high school or who don't go to college." He admitted to being discouraged by the statistics because they tell an incomplete story about Black males, and the academic and social barriers (e.g., educational inequity, racial disparity, systemic racism, the hidden curriculum) that work to (de)limit their success. Rendell shared:

> my mentality was messed up from coming in [to high school] as a freshman . . . looking at the statistics of young Black males that don't graduate. But then the empowerment of my teacher had helped me get over that and had got my mentality right, now I wake up every morning. Look at success right in the eye.

Undoubtedly, Rendell languaged his story by acknowledging his Black role models and by recognizing his potential for success.

THE EXAMPLES: LANGUAGING AND COUNTERNARRATIVE PRODUCTION

Collectively, the three examples discussed in this chapter—the case of Rachel Jeantel, the Black Student Forum of Boston College, and Rendell's refusal to be a statistic—point to some of the ways Black people language their experiences with racism, inequity, and marginalization. They reject White, middle-class expectations related to the utility of language and the exclusion of Black intellectual traditions from the curricula. Also, they refuse to ignore the realities of oppression and violence that many Black people have endured (and continue to endure). In so doing, the examples represent conscious attempts by Black youth to language their experiences in a variety of contexts that are often not welcoming of their humanity, that are often dangerous for their spirits, and that are often not protective of their civil rights. And yet Black people still stand tall and enter bravely into these environments. Thus, there is an urgency to engage in languaging and counternarrative production that center blackness. Equally important is the need to complicate blackness in ways that counter oppressive representations of people, their cultural practices, and their intellectual traditions.

Thus, Rachel Jeantel and her use of Black English represent powerful forms of resistance against a racist legal state that too readily persecutes Black youth for being Black (e.g., Rekia Boyd, Michael Brown, Aiyana Stanley-Jones, Trayvon Martin, Tamir Rice, and many others). Similarly, the Black Student Forum highlights the tendency of institutions to remain silent on the exclusion of Black traditions from White dominated spaces, and on the state-sanctioned violence directed toward many Black youth. The case of Rendell offers a counternarrative to negative depictions of Black youth in schools and society that paint them as uneducated and as statistics. All three examples speak to the importance of encouraging Black people to language their experiences in ways that produce counternarratives, which can serve as forms of resistance to dominant ideologies that undermine Black lives, Black identities, Black intellectual traditions, and Black cultural practices.

LANGUAGING, COUNTERNARRATIVE PRODUCTION, AND LESSONS OF PRAXIS

As we consider practical implications of Black youth languaging and producing counternarratives, we briefly return to the case of Rachel Jeantel. In May of 2014, she graduated from high school, an accomplishment with special importance to Jeantel because it made good on her promise to Trayvon Martin. Her graduation also pleased the cadre of mentors who joined together as a "village" during the trial to support Jeantel's educational trajectory. She transferred to an alternative high school "with smaller classes and intense staff involvement" because her mentors felt that her court testimony evidenced how the Miami-Dade public school system had "failed" Jeantel (Thompson & Parker, 2014). However, in their article on the politics of Jeantel's village, Thompson and Parker question the attempt to standardize Jeantel's language and behavior because it reifies that who she is, is simply not good enough. It also suggests that she must conform to dominant linguistic and cultural expectations to be seen as a success. For example, Tom Joyner's offer to pay for Jeantel's college education did not extend to fashion school—the career path Jeantel initially chose. Wanting her to attend a 4-year college, Joyner believed he took her "to the water," but she refused to "drink." In other words, in eschewing a predetermined and narrow path toward respectability, some in Jeantel's village believed she failed them. According to Michaela Angela Davis, the village held Jeantel to the standards of middle-class Black values that insist, in part, that "we can't perform the full range of blackness in public" (cited in Thompson

& Parker, 2014). Performing this "full range of blackness" is impossible, especially if students can only rely on village support when their career paths and educational desires align with respectability politics and defer to whiteness. We share this follow-up to Jeantel's story because, on the one hand, it is important to consider how her village might have supported her differently (and, by extension, how other villages might effectively support Black youth). On the other hand, and for the purposes of this chapter, it is also necessary to consider how teachers can create learning environments that encourage Black youth to language their experiences and produce counternarratives as they learn to enact their own blackness.

Instead of deciding for Black youth the shape their lives must take, we believe teachers, teacher educators, school administrators, educational researchers, parents, and policymakers (and other members of students' villages) should ask them to share their stories, concerns, and convictions in whatever languages and modes that are available to them. Insofar as schools are concerned, we believe that classrooms should be supportive spaces for students to disrupt the status quo, engage in storytelling, and learn to resist oppression. In fact, we agree with Hemmings (2006), who argues that Black students' sense of agency can be bolstered if they understand the collective struggle against contemporary injustices that are rooted in historical inequalities. Their understandings are also affected by the "daily activities in classrooms and corridors as well as social interactions with teachers, peers, and others" (Hemmings, 2006, p. 91).

Therefore, our recommendation—that all educators and educational leaders support students in critiquing and resisting structural inequalities—requires changes in practices, pedagogies, and policies that typify schools in the 21st century United States of America. These changes are as necessary as they are difficult to enact. And with the overwhelming pressures teachers and administrators face with standardization (e.g., teaching, testing, and disciplining of students; see also Gonzalez, McIntyre, & Rosebury, 2001; Sleeter, 2005), changing course is not without unforeseen consequences. Yet we remind educators that oftentimes Black students' lives are hanging in the balance of a racist, sexist, and unjust society. It is important, then, to recognize the efforts of Black youth and adults across the world who understand that Black lives matter.

Rendell demanded to be seen not as a statistic or an object of study, but as a complex individual. Likewise, Rachel Jeantel and the Black Student Forum at Boston College rejected systemic oppression and exclusion directed toward Black people. These examples are important to recognize, for they reveal the value of Black people languaging their experiences to counter the narratives of failure and inferiority that regularly get enacted upon them. They also reveal the importance of Black youth having a supportive village that encourages them to critique racism, inequities, and other forms of marginalization.

Thus, we offer the following starting points for educators to create learning environments that support Black students' languaging and counternarrative production inside classrooms.

- Engage in open dialogue with administrators, policymakers, and parents about the impact of standardization on teaching and learning, and how the pressures of standardization affect Black students from state to state and district to district.
- Invite students to grapple with the realities of race by historicizing and contextualizing discussions of race, racism, and oppression in the curricula. One practical way to do this is by asking students to consider how the nature and demographics of contexts (e.g., classrooms, schools, neighborhoods, and other nonschool spaces) help them understand historical and/or contemporary events, stories, and rights' movements. Questions might include: What do you know about a specific context; who's included and/or excluded from the context; and how does the context impact your understanding of race, racism, oppression, and equity?
- Rely on teaching practices that are neither pervasive nor "too closely aligned with linguistic, literate, and cultural hegemony." Such practices should not be concerned "with the seemingly panoptic 'White gaze' (Morrison, 1998) that permeates educational research and practice with and for students of color, their teachers, and their schools" (Paris & Alim, 2014, p. 86). Thus, teaching practices should connect to who Black students are, and to what they *already* know and need to know. Teachers can invite students' languages and cultures into the classroom in ways that allow students themselves to determine what aspects of their lives they are willing to share. In this way, teachers can work to avoid essentialist notions of who students are and what constitutes their realities.
- Design lessons and extracurricular activities that attend to local and global realities, struggles, and activist practices involving Black people. In addition to teachers working with students to co-construct the culture of the classroom, teachers can also collaborate with them to examine social and political realities of which they might be unaware. Students can listen to radio programs, watch and critique news shows from around the world, research texts about educational issues, and connect with classrooms in other communities. These experiences can increase their awareness of multiple realities, histories, and lives.

- Engage in reflexive action that examines teachers' knowledge of the histories and contexts that shape Black students' lived experiences. In this way, listen to students and to other teachers to determine the pedagogical practices, instructional content, and action that are important to center in classrooms. In other words, we believe that teachers must always be learners who willingly study the world around them in ways that can contribute to the work of social justice.
- Support student engagement in social action and invite students to take on leadership roles inside classrooms in ways that foster learning as collaborative and action-oriented. Examples of this can be found in films, such as *Precious Knowledge* (Palos, 2011), and *Un Poquito de Tanto Verdad* (Freidberg, 2007).
- An important policy implication of this work involves diversifying the teaching force. Therefore, we believe administrators, school leaders, and policymakers must be intentional with their hiring practices (who they hire and for what purposes), particularly with respect to hiring individuals who are in charge of teaching, evaluating, and assessing Black students.

We do not view this list as exhaustive or definitive. In fact, we believe that it is necessary for educators to be supported by other teachers and teacher educators, administrators, researchers, parents, and policymakers in order to engage in teaching that speaks to students and not to standardizations. And in this belief, we argue that languaging and counternarrative production can disrupt deficit-oriented perspectives about the lives, literacies, languages, and identities of Black youth. This work must happen inside schools and it must also extend to nonschool contexts. Indeed, Black lives matter.

REFERENCES

Black lives matter. (2015). About us. Retrieved from http://blacklivesmatter.com/about/

Black student forum of Boston College. (2014). In *Facebook* [student forum page]. Retrieved from https://www.facebook.com/BlackStudentForum

Black student forum open letter. (2014). http://bcheights.com/opinions/2014/letter-black-student-forum-bc-administration/

Cooper, B. (2013). Dark skinned and plus sized: The real Rachel Jeantel story. *Salon* http://www.salon.com/2013/06/28/did_anyone_really_hear_rachel_jeantel/

Delgado, R., & Stefancic, J. (2012). *Critical race theory: An introduction.* New York, NY: New York University Press.

DuBois, W. E. B. (2007). *The souls of Black folk.* Oxford, England: Oxford University Press. (Original published in 1903).

Freidberg, J., Van, L. J., Patterson, L., & Alvarez, Q. F. (2007). *Un poquito de tanta verdad.* Seattle, WA: Corrugated Films & Mal de Ojo TV.

García, O. (2010). Languaging and ethnifying. In J. Fishman & O. García (Eds.), *Handbook of language and ethnicity: Disciplinary and regional perspectives,* (2nd ed., pp. 519–535). New York, NY: Oxford University Press.

Gonzalez, N., McIntyre, E., & Rosebury, A. S. (Eds.). (2001). *Classroom diversity: Connecting curriculum to students' lives.* Portsmouth, NH: Heinemann.

Haymes, S. (1995). *Race, culture, and the city: A pedagogy for Black urban struggle.* Albany, NY: State University of New York Press.

Hemmings, A. (2006). Shifting images of blackness: Coming of age as black students in urban schools. In E. McNamera Horvat & C. O'Connor (Eds.), *Beyond acting white: Reframing the debate on black student achievement.* Lanham, MD: Rowman & Littlefield.

hooks, b. (1989). Talking back: Thinking feminist, thinking Black. New York, NY: South End Press.

Jordan, J. (1989). Nobody mean more to me than you and the future life of Willie Jordan. In J. Jordan (Ed.), *Moving towards home: Political essays* (pp. 175–189). London, England: Virago.

Jørgensen, J. N. (2008). Introduction: Polylingual languaging around and among children and adolescents. *International Journal of Multilingualism,* 5(3), 161–176.

Kinloch, V. (2005). Revisiting the promise of students' right to their own language: Pedagogical strategies. *College Composition and Communication* 57(1): 83–113.

Knouzi, I., Swain, M., Lapkin, S., & Brooks, L. (2010). Self-scaffolding mediated by languaging: Microgenetic analysis of high and low performers. *International Journal of Applied Linguistics,* 20(1), 23–49.

Lado, R. (1979). Thinking and "languaging": A psycholinguistic model of performance and learning. *Sophia Linguistica,* 12, 3–24.

Matsuda, M. J. (1987). Looking to the bottom: critical legal studies and reparations. (Minority critiques of the critical legal studies movement; selected papers written for a panel discussion at the 10th National Critical Legal Studies Conference, January 7, 1987). *Harvard Civil Rights-Civil Liberties Law Review,* 22(2), 323–399.

McLaren, P., & Hammer, R. (2007). Media knowledges, warrior citizenry, and postmodern literacies. In D. Macedo & S.R. Steinberg (Eds.), *Media literacy: A reader* (pp. 116–139). New York, NY: Peter Lang.

Morrison, T. (1998). Toni Morrison refuses to privilege white people in her novels: Interview on *Charlie Rose* (Video). *Public Broadcasting Service.* Retrieved from http://www.youtube.com/watch?v=F4vIGvKpT1c

NAACP (2015). *Criminal justice fact sheet.* Retrieved from http://www.naacp.org/pages/criminal-justice-fact-sheet

Palos, A. L., McGinnis, E., & Fifer, S. J. (2011). *Precious knowledge* (Video). In Bricca, J., Amor, N., Dos Vatos Productions, Independent Television Service, Corporation for Public Broadcasting. Tucson, AZ: Dos Vatos Productions.

Paris, D., & Alim, S. (2014). What are we seeking to sustain through culturally sustaining pedagogy? A loving critique forward. *Harvard Educational Review, 84*(1), 85–100.

Quigley, R. (2013, June 27). "That's retarded, sir": Trayvon Martin trial's star witness cracks when her credibility is questioned and is forced to admit she could not read letter she allegedly wrote. *The Daily Mail.* Retrieved from http://www.dailymail.co.uk/news/article-2349794/George-Zimmerman-trial-Rachel-Jeantel-Trayvon-Martin-prosecutions-star-witness-dragged-coals-defense.html

Sleeter, C. E. (2005). *Un-standardizing curriculum: Multicultural teaching in the standards-based classroom.* New York, NY: Teachers College Press.

Solórzano, D. G., & Yosso, T. J. (2002). Critical race methodology: Counter-storytelling as an analytical framework for education research. *Qualitative Inquiry, 8*(1), 23–44.

Smitherman, G. (1977). *Talkin and testifyin: The language of Black America:* Detroit, MI: Wayne State University Press.

Swain, M. (2006). Languaging, agency and collaboration in advanced second language learning. In H. Byrnes (Ed.), *Advanced language learning: The contributions of Halliday and Vygotsky* (pp. 95–108). London, England: Continuum.

Swain, M., Lapkin, S., Knouzi, I., Suzuki, W., & Brooks, L. (2009). Languaging: University students learn the grammatical concept of voice in French. *The Modern Language Journal, 93*(1), 5–29.

Thompson, K., & Parker, L. (2014, June 4). For Trayvon Martin's friend Rachel Jeantel, a 'village' of mentors trying to keep her on track. *The Washington Post.* http://www.washingtonpost.com/lifestyle/style/for-rachel-jeantel-travyon-martins-friend-the-journey-continues/2014/06/04/0135d5a2-ec11-11e3-93d2-cdd-4be1f5d9e_story.html

CHAPTER 3

UNDOCUMENTED YOUTH, AGENCY, AND POWER

The Tension Between Policy and Praxis

Leticia Alvarez Gutiérrez
University of Utah

Patricia D. Quijada Cerecer
University of California, Davis

> *When Mexico sends its people, they're not sending their best. They're not sending you. They're sending people that have lots of problems, and they're bringing those problems with us. They're bringing drugs. They're bringing crime. They're rapists. And some, I assume, are good people.*

—Donald Trump, GOP presidential candidate (June 16, 2015)

The reality television host Donald Trump stated the above during his announcement that launched his presidential campaign (Lee, 2015). Rather than his xenophobic rhetoric being a liability to his campaign, it instead had the opposite effect and propelled him as the Republican front-runner. The more egregious Donald's remarks become about undocumented immigrants, particularly Mexicans, the more momentum his campaign gained. It is deplorable that in 2015 citizens of the United States

Educational Policies and Youth in the 21st Century, pages 39–56
Copyright © 2016 by Information Age Publishing
All rights of reproduction in any form reserved.

39

are supporting an individual spouting xenophobic statements and whose biggest campaign weapons include kicking out the estimated 11 million undocumented immigrants residing in the United States and building a 2,000-mile border wall that would prevent immigrants from south of the border from entering the country. To surpass the remarks by Mr. Trump, GOP presidential candidate Ben Carson started to gain traction in his campaign when he horrendously proposed to use drone strikes along the southern border to stop the flow of illegal immigration. Why are many voters applauding this rhetoric? Are Latino immigrants really posing a threat to U.S. citizens and the economy? Why is the browning of America posing such a fear for mainstream folk?

The GOP presidential candidates have reignited racist and violent sides of the anti-immigrant national discourses, which have often resulted in physical acts of violence toward Latinos across the country, regardless of an individual's documentation status, because if one fits the profile of being undocumented one easily becomes a target. Hateful attitudes and violence toward undocumented or unauthorized,[1] particularly Mexican immigrants, pervade the airwaves, social media, and blogosphere. Media headlines continuously showcase repulsive statements criminalizing and violently attacking hard-working unauthorized Latino families, innocent young people, children, and communities. One such violent act includes the 2015 decision made in Texas by a federal judge to deny birth certificates to the U.S. born children of undocumented immigrants. This decision has negative ramifications for these children and families, as these children will not be able to be vaccinated, enroll in school, or hold legal documents identifying them as U.S. citizens. Another example is the "voluntary return" documents that thousands of noncitizens in southern California signed, but were denied their day in court to petition for re-entry into the United States after being expelled to Mexico. Judge John A. Kronstadt concluded that immigration enforcement officers used deceptive tactics to convince immigrants to sign the voluntary return forms and denied them their right to see a judge and reapply for their return into the country. Gabriela Rivera, ACLU attorney of San Diego and Imperial counties said:

> Now we can begin the process of reuniting some of the families who could have remained together in the United States but were driven apart by government practices that rely upon misinformation, deception, and coercion. (ACLU, 2015)

These anti-immigrant, anti-Latino policies are not isolated policies against undocumented immigrants. Historically there have been many policies against the presence of immigrants. In most recent years Alabama, Georgia, Indiana, South Carolina, and Utah passed Arizona's SB 1070 style copycat laws, which have resulted in family separations, deportations, and detentions. In 2014 approximately 43 states across the country approved 171 immigration-related laws and voted on 117 resolutions related to anti-immigration (NCSL, 2016), and Mr. Trump making racist and criminalizing remarks about Mexicans suggests that anti-immigration sentiments continue to be strong and unrelenting.

While immigration reform has been a dominant (and contentious) issue in the United States, the discourse purposefully centers on characteristics of immigrants rather than the structural issues or policies that frame the broken immigration system. Rather than examine the legal barriers to citizenship or deconstructing the economic and social factors prompting immigration patterns, policymakers are keen to blame immigrants as corrupt and immoral people engaged in criminal activity. The terms used to describe undocumented immigrants are dehumanizing (e.g., illegals, illegal alien, and illegal immigrant) and exacerbate and perpetuate deficit perspectives and help to sustain anti-immigrant attitudes and policies (Alvarez Gutiérrez, 2013; Negrón-Gonzales, 2014). Policymakers strategically use these terms as a way to garner public support for anti-immigration positions (see Chapter 10) by referring to immigrants with dehumanizing identities (illegals) and automatically position them as immigrants who are inherently criminal, which has often resulted in xenophobic policies and resistance from undocumented youth (Alvarez Gutiérrez, 2013; Negrón-Gonzales, 2014).

In spite of these ongoing negative characterizations and labels suggesting an overwhelmingly rejecting view of immigrant populations, there has been legislation passed founded on a more positive and supportive orientation. More specifically, over the last 3 years, President Obama has supported actions to endorse unauthorized students to pursue postsecondary education in the United States. The federal Deferred Action for Childhood Arrivals (DACA) initiative provides temporary lawful residence to undocumented youth and young adults. This initiative provides new opportunities to undocumented youth who came to the United States before the age of 16, have lived in the United States continuously for at least 5 years, and have graduated from high school or obtained a GED. In November 2014, President Obama expanded DACA to allow individuals born prior to June 15, 1981, to apply for DACA for 3 years instead of 2. During this time, President Obama also introduced Deferred Action for Parents of Americans (DAPA) and lawful permanent residents, which has been on hold for now. Twenty-six states are taking Obama's executive orders to court because they want to overturn both DACA and DAPA. In January 2016 the Supreme Court agreed to take the case of the *United States v. Texas* and a final decision is expected to be made in June 2016. More specifically, more than half of the states are involved in a lawsuit to halt President Obama's executive actions. These executive orders present a "two-steps forward, two-steps back" scenario; therefore, alone they will not lead to structural changes needed to transform immigration policy in the United States.

The push for greater recognition of undocumented youth's rights is positive; however, offering only temporary resident status creates unchartered, challenging terrain for undocumented young people and their pursuit of higher education (Abrego, 2006). For these youth, negotiating the "politics of inclusion" presents social and emotional obstacles. As Patel (2013) argues,

> Immigration, and more so policy and rhetoric about immigration, is in many ways about inclusion—the terms of who is included and on what conditions exclusion is based. These policy initiatives provide young people with a temporary, imminently revocable, and liminal status in the United States. (Patel, 2013, p. xvi)

Undocumented youth are forced to navigate uncomfortable and confusing spaces of simultaneous acceptance and rejection with little guidance and support, which leads young people to learn how to become undocumented as they become aware of losing their protected status as students just as they transition to adulthood (Gonzales, 2009).

Hostile policies impacting undocumented children and young people raise several concerns for their development, especially as it pertains to their experiences in public educational institutions. From our work, we have learned from undocumented young people that keeping families together, working hard, and putting forth effort in school can come to a complete and abrupt halt when legislations impose boundaries and create roadblocks to pursue career aspirations made available by attending college. These imposed obstacles are not the all-too-common road bumps that many exaggeratedly assert can be overcome by "working harder" or "putting more effort in one's studies." Instead of these meritocratic ideologies, anti-immigrant and educational policies impact everyday lives by halting dreams of future education and career prospects by often making it impossible to navigate or overcome challenges that come along with their undocumented status. We are particularly concerned with how these legally imposed anti-immigration laws and policies disrupt, alter, and hurt the development of these students' academic dispositions toward learning (Suárez-Orozco, Yoshikawa, Teranishi, & Suárez-Orozco, 2011).

One goal of our chapter is to discuss how anti-immigration sentiments impact academic and social emotional identities of undocumented young people as they navigate school spaces. How do young people make meaning of their lives as youth when they are "positioned in a liminal space by policymakers [whose policies] provide minimal assurance that their identities will not be used to pursue, detain, and deport them" (Patel, 2013, p. xvi)? In other words, how do educational leaders in and out of schools mediate the impact of immigration policies on the emotional well-being and academic identities of young undocumented students? In this chapter we share qualitative narratives from undocumented youth to show the nuanced way(s) immigration policies and educational practices impact their identities as students and as young people "coming of age" in the United States and the roles adults play in this process (Alvarez Gutiérrez, 2013).

We begin this chapter with an overview of the demographics of immigrant young people in the United States. Then, we provide a brief overview of immigration policies impacting K–12. Next, we share stories from undocumented students who share the ways in which they have navigated educational spaces and the impact it has on their identities as immigrant youth and as students. We conclude with a discussion of the implications these youths' experiences have for teachers, administrators, and educational policies.

DEMOGRAPHIC TRENDS

Currently, approximately 11 million undocumented immigrants, representing up to 3.5% of the nation's population, reside in the United States. Of these, slightly more than 1.5 million are under the age of 18 with about 25% enrolled in public elementary school and approximately 20% in high school (Pérez, 2012). Immigrant demographic trends indicate 60% of unauthorized immigrants reside in the following six states: California, Florida, New York, Texas, Illinois, and New Jersey (Passel & Cohn, 2009). Between 2009 and 2012 there was an increase of unauthorized individuals in the following states: Florida, Idaho, Maryland, Nebraska, New Jersey , Pennsylvania, and Virginia (Krogstad & Passel, 2015). These demographic trends indicate that the distribution patterns are changing, and that policy prescriptions affect unauthorized families throughout the United States (Krogstad & Passel, 2015).

While approximately 65,000 to 80,000 undocumented students become high school graduates every year, only 49% of these students will enroll in postsecondary institutions, primarily in community colleges (Pérez, 2012). College attendance increases slightly to 62% if immigrant students arrived in the United State and were enrolled in a school before the age of 14. By 2050 immigrant youth will make up close to one third of U.S. school children (Passel, 2011).

There are substantial numbers of mixed-status families in the United States. Mixed-status families are defined as having at least one unauthorized parent/guardian and at least one U.S. born child (Passel, 2006). Roughly 7% of K–12 students in 2012 had at least one unauthorized immigrant parent/guardian (Krogstad & Passel, 2015). Children of mixed families are under almost constant threat of one (or more) of their family members/parents/guardians being deported. Indeed, close to 4.5 million U.S. children have had at least one parent/guardian deported in the last decade (Passel, 2011). The social and emotional costs of these sudden deportations for children and youth are worsened when their family members are transferred to a detention 300 miles away (Wessler, 2011). To compound these effects, children are also not allowed to remain with family members who are not legal guardians. Instead, these children get placed in foster care or are put up for formal adoption without parent/guardian permission. And, on top of it, detainees (parents/guardians) are not kept informed of the situation with their children and end up labeled as neglectful when they fail to show up for scheduled court dates about which they were completely unaware. Immigration reform must include provisions that preserve and protect family unity, as well as begin to address and lessen the harm caused by current immigration policies and deportation raids.

The social and emotional health and educational outcomes of immigrant status in the United States are significant. Importantly, they are not isolated to immigrant status, but also to "perceived" immigrant status. Arguably, all Latina/o students (or students perceived to be of Latina/o descent) are likely targets of hostile attitudes. Given the growing numbers of Latina/o students in our schools, the potential effects of these policies and attitudes toward immigrant students are potentially detrimental (Chaudry et al., 2010). During the school year, students spend a great deal of time in schools and therefore with their teachers (e.g., upwards of 8 hours a day or one third of their total time); therefore, it is important that our educators be equipped to mediate the external (and hostile) policy climate with the needs of their students (Alvarez Gutiérrez, 2013; Suárez-Orozco, Yoshikawa, Teranishi, & Suárez-Orozco, 2011). Educators must be trained on everyday worries, stressors, and familial structure so that they will have the necessary skills to best support undocumented students and children of immigrants in order to ensure them with more educational opportunities that can result in overall well-being and educational successes. Children's and youth's sense of safety is essential for their healthfulness and well-being. More specifically researchers have found that the threat of detention and deportation have negative health outcomes for these youth and children (Satinsky, Hu, Heller, & Farhang, 2013). Approximately 100,000 U.S. Citizens show withdrawal after a parent/guardian has been detained and/or in process of deportation. Such daily stressors can result in poorer health, behavioral problems which can then result in anxiety and withdraw. Such stressors facilitate low school performance and challenging developmental outcomes (Stinsky, et al., 2013).

RACIALIZED IMMIGRATION POLICIES

The 1982 Supreme Court case of *Plyer v. Doe* established that undocumented children and youth are legally entitled to the same K–12 educational opportunities that states provide to those who are citizens or legal residents. This includes eligibility for free and reduced-price meals, special education services, and school sponsored events and activities. However, since then this legal mandate has been offset by increasingly hostile anti-immigrant attitudes made more visible and salient as the Latina/o population nearly tripled (from 14.6 million in 1980 to 52 million in 2011). This has made present day K–12 school leaders' jobs even more complicated as they work to preserve the integrity of students' rights as stipulated in *Plyer v. Doe*, while also negotiating statewide measures and deeply rooted anti-immigrant sentiments that often seep into the school culture.

This backdrop includes a succession of statewide bills aimed at restricting and often denying educational opportunities to children of immigrants and undocumented immigrant youth. For example, bilingual education was dismantled in California following the 1998 passage of Proposition 227. This legislation was immediately mirrored in Arizona by the 2000 passage of Proposition 203. Then there was an attempt to deny public education, health care and other "public" services to individuals who were undocumented via California's Proposition 187, which was passed in 1994. Elsewhere, there have been anti-immigration bills that withhold support and resources from immigrant youth while at the same time racially profile unauthorized (and authorized) Latinos (e.g., Alabama's HB 56, Arizona's SB 1070, Georgia's HB 87 and Montana's referendum LR 121) (see Chapter 7 for a more in-depth discussion of these policies). These initiatives introduce impenetrable barriers and roadblocks for students and families who come to the United States seeking the Sueños Americanos (American Dreams) in order to have more educational and social mobility.

The good news is that in spite of these restrictive policies, there has been some measured progress that alleviate some of these barriers. The passage of DACA, for example, offers a safety net for undocumented young people attending and graduating from 4-year colleges and universities. The 2- to 3-year temporary residency permit provides liberation to students to pursue internships, postsecondary education, work–school opportunities, and engage in daily routines without the fear of being detained or deported in the short run. However, it has also placed lives on hold. For example, a 2- to 3-year reprieve is such a short term that it does not provide a reasonable amount of time for youth to complete a bachelor's degree. Further, congressional inactivity (e.g., failure to formalize the law) and the bureaucracy involved in gaining approval (e.g., the time it takes to get temporary status) has left many youth uncertain about their futures (Abrego, 2006).

The immigration process and policies such as DACA place many of our undocumented young people and families in a legal and social status that is liminal, ambivalent, and oftentimes in flux and in between status (Torres & Wicks-Asbun, 2014) that affects the individual's "different spheres of life—the immigrant's immediate sphere of social networks and family, the community-level place of religious institutions in the immigrants' lives, and the broader domain of artistic expression" (Menjívar, 2006, p. 1,000). Living in this "in between" status or liminal legality ambivalent state, not surprisingly, presents unique and confusing challenges to families and individuals. Many undocumented and children of immigrants, for example, have spent the bulk of their educational experiences in U.S. schools, and have acquired fluency in both their native language as well as English, and have come to identify as cultual U.S. citizens. However, these executive orders may suddenly and abruptly shift their status in ways that are difficult to understand—especially without adult support and guidance. In some cases, students may receive a temporary "stay," whereas in other situations impending deportation (of them or family members) may become more or less possible and immediate. These youth are forced to navigate a citizenship status that teeters in the gray area, between certainty and ambivalence, which is not a secure place for their learner, ethnic, and social identities.

As activist-scholars-educators, how do we make meaning of these policies and their impact on undocumented students throughout the P-20 systems? And how can we educators disrupt the anti-immigrant rhetoric and practices that encourage stereotypes while being inclusive of those who are most marginalized? In the next section, we discuss how we conceptualize young peoples' identities. Such a theoretical grounding provides an understanding of youths' academic identities and the multiple ways youths view their academic identities in school contexts. Understanding youth development provides a way for educators to better understand how anti-immigrant policies impact youths' identities as learners. This becomes central since the exclusion of immigrant students is heightened by White normative socialization and educational practices that often contribute to racial inequities (Alvarez Gutiérrez, 2014).

UNDOCUMENTED YOUTH: IDENTITY, AGENCY, AND VOICE

We argue that the links among cultural practices, language, learner identities, and civic participation are central to understanding the impact that anti-immigrant (Mexicans) educational policies and practices have on children of immigrants and undocumented youths' health (e.g., anxiety, fear, stress). We view identity as active, fluid, and constantly changing based upon context (Holland Lachiotte, Skinner, & Cain, 1998). Holland and colleagues assert that individuals are actors who engage in social practices, and through these practices continuously form their own identities and "new ways of being in the world" (Holland et al., 1998, p. 5). This perspective of identity disrupts traditional paradigms that situate identity formation as being an individual process where one moves through stages and toward becoming a unified sense of self (Erikson, 1968). Traditional developmental paradigms tend to privilege whiteness as the dominant race and middle to upper socioeconomic class. In doing so, race and class as central social constructs are ignored as are the nuanced ways social practices are formed and enacted upon in different settings.

Building upon the work of scholars who examine the social identity of youth, we find that the relationship between an individual and her or his environment as mediated through educational institutions is particularly challenging for youth of color and immigrant students. For example, research asserts that educational institutions embody cultural norms and expectations defined by a White middle-class paradigm. In so doing, educational institutions automatically construct students of color and immigrant students as the "other." In other words, "Race is *invisibilized* when applied to whites [and] usually the 'Other' refers to people-of-color who are 'racially marked'" (Leonardo, 2000, p. 113), thus the importance of addressing challenging discriminatory practices.

For immigrant youth, then, the deficit ways that educators view the intersectionalies of social constructs (i.e., race, immigration status, class, gender, and sexual orientation to name a few) can inevitably impact how educators treat, teach, and interact with children of immigrants, immigrant students, and their families. The type of interactions educators develop with students can often be the deciding factor in the success or the end of an immigrants' educational trajectory. The "racialized politics embedded in the macro society regulate student identities for youth of color and often undervalue their social and learner status in educational institutions" (Alvarez Gutiérrez, 2014, p. 311); thus such limited conceptualizations of immigrant youth often leads to essentializing immigrant young people. Patel (2013) reminds us "in the context of schooling, assumptions about age, stage, and what is 'developmentally appropriate' predominate. As such, a one-size fits all perception spurs adults to set limitations that do not always reflect the immediate circumstances accurately"(p. 36). In other words, educators' conceptualizations of immigrant students who are more or less capable or deserving are exhibited in the type of relationships educators form with them. Therefore, colorblind policies and practices serve only to limit the academic potential of students and perpetuate deficit ideologies about the learning abilities of children of immigrants and undocumented children. Regardless of immigration status, Latina/o immigrant youth are "challenged to navigate between achieved identities (e.g., sense of belonging) and ascribed identities (e.g., imposed) ... with achieved identity [being] the extent to which an individual achieves a sense of belonging—'I am a member of this group.' An ascribed identity is imposed either by co-ethnics—'You are a member of our group,' or imposed by members of the dominant culture—'You are a member of that group'" (Suárez-Orozco, 2004, p. 177). That is, identities developed through cultural and social norms and ability to act on one's own behalf as a learner and civic participant are extremely important and can serve to support the ethnic, cultural and learner identities of immigrant youth and children of immigrants (Alvarez Gutiérrez, 2014, p. 311–312). These forms of identities are dynamic and fluid; thus it is important to change how educators understand how young people experience particular identities through social macro-micro inclusions and exclusions.

Importantly, youth play an active role in constructing their identities. Youth don't just "receive" their identity from more knowledgeable or powerful others. Instead, youth participate in social activities (classroom exchanges, etc.) through which they discover new meanings about self and other. In some cases, this self-discovery process occurs in safe places among teachers who are supportive and helpful. But for many undocumented youth, we find that identity-based explorations occur under more contentious, ambivalent, and unsupportive situations. Next we offer a few voices from undocumented high school students that illustrate one way undocumented youth of color have appropriated through their personal agency identity features that resist and challenge the dominant paradigm being foisted onto them.

Youth and Agency

Undocumented students are forced to navigate two fractured systems (the immigration system and the educational system) without any benefit of security or certainty of their status (Gándara & Contreras, 2009). In this section, we share narratives from four undocumented youth[2] (Marco, Santiago, Catalina, and Mia) who emerged from a larger, multiyear ethnographic study that centered on youth, parents or families, and educators in the mountain West. These youth shared the ways they negotiated their immigration status, language, and racial or ethnic identities as students and academic learners in one high school.

We know that teachers' preconceptions of learners (i.e., who is competent, who is not) may be influenced by preconceived notions of the ethnicity, culture, class, language, and immigration status of the student (Valenzuela, 1999). For example, we know that deficit ideologies associated with students of color are communicated in various ways and play out in the form of educators having low expectations of students (Steele, 2007, Valencia & Solórzano, 1997; Valenzuela, 1999). In fact, 62% of new teachers feel unprepared to meet the needs of linguistically and cultural diverse students (U.S. Department of Education, 2011). This pattern was evident in our experiences with these students who attended a school served by majority White female educators. In this high school context, teachers did not view the students' funds of knowledge as a resource for learning (Moll, Amanti, & Gonzalez, 1992). By ignoring students' "funds of knowledge," such as the "historically accumulated and culturally developed bodies of knowledge and skills essential for household or individual functioning and well-being" (Moll, Amanti, Neff, & González, 1992, p. 33), teachers marginalized and silenced students' individual experiences that may be sustainable for learning (Paris & Talim, 2014). In fact, most of the teachers in our study perceived students' funds of knowledge as impediments to rather than resources for learning. This had the result of limiting students' access and use of their cultural knowledge. Our students also experienced low expectations in the form of teachers discounting their abilities to perform academically, contribute to classroom dialogue, and potential for college. Levinson (2012) found that there are huge discrepancies of "civic empowerment gaps" in the United States and schools are the primary institutions that contribute to these gaps (p. 816).

We argue that participatory civic engagement is helpful in supporting and building students' ethnic, linguistic, and academic identities. As our theoretical positioning predicts, these youth were not passive recipients of educators' low expectations. Rather, they engaged with educators and other students in ways that demonstrated agency and helped to shape their identities in positive and proactive ways. Marco, for example, developed strong relationships with a few teachers throughout his first and second year of high school. He put forth much effort in his classes, earned high grades, and perceived himself as college bound. As a junior in high school he confided to a few teachers that he was undocumented. His decision to disclose such personal information was not a hasty one as the topic was delicate, challenging, and risky. Marco understood the risk of sharing his immigration status with his most trusted teacher. Yet to Marco's disappointment, the teacher ended their relationship. She not only stopped talking to Marco and his family, but also ceased supporting him with scholarship applications. For Marco, sharing his status with his teacher would hopefully elicit more help to understand the complex and often confusing college admission policies and scholarship opportunities. Unfortunately, this was not the case. As a result of confiding his situation, the relationship with his teacher grew tense and contentious.

It was also clear that this trusted teacher had shared his status with others who used it against him. We learned from Marco's mother how a teacher had "told him that he should give up researching the university because he didn't qualify to go to the university because he was undocumented." Marco described the emotional impact he experienced when teachers began to ignore him in the classroom once he came out as undocumented. Marco shared,

> My teacher made me feel really bad because she was always helping me, but when she found out I was undocumented, the help stopped. I didn't think

that this was going to bother her. Now I just go to class and we never talk about scholarships or the university.

For Marco, Catalina, and Mia as well as for other students in our study disclosing their immigration status to their teachers was a risk they were willing to take. Because they had built strong supportive relationships with them. Students trusted their teachers and anticipated teachers would be supportive of their status. Unfortunately, this was not the case. Catalina shared:

> I saw how this teacher treated Marco differently. I felt bad for him because she used to help him in class with our assignments, but then she stopped talking with him and barely would look at him. I know Marco felt bad because he thought the teacher thought he had educational potential, but we realized that she is racist against us undocumented students and our families. I don't trust anyone in the school, only you because we meet twice a month and see one another 3 times a week and I see how you treat me and my family. You would not treat us differently just because we are undocumented, you have family who is undocumented and you understand, somethings are not easy to explain that is why we like when we talk with you.

Upon learning of their immigration status, teachers ceased their ongoing relationship with students and began to withhold support and guidance. We also learned that teachers toyed with students' emotions with threats to end certain dimensions of the teacher–student relationship. For example, Marco's teacher stopped helping him to develop career goals and withdrew her support in identifying postsecondary opportunities. For Marco, this was a painful turn of events that deeply challenged his confidence and sense of self as a learner.

Youths' Perceptions of Their Teachers

Teachers' actions convey powerful messages to students about their academic and social potential. When it came to our undocumented youth, they noticed how teachers grew increasingly unsupportive and critical of their cultural backgrounds by ignoring racist bullying by their White peers. Santiago, an eleventh grader shared: "We are constantly being teased for being Mexican and not speaking English." Another student, Marielena, shared: "They [White peers] make fun of us for not speaking English, the way we dress, because we don't wear fancy expensive name brands like North Face or Ugg boots and for not answering questions in class."

Santiago confirmed what Marielena shared about attire and class participation:

Sometimes I think the teachers don't think there is anything wrong with pushing Mexican students around and that is why they don't say anything. You see this in the school and outside the school, in TV, newspapers, that we [Mexicans] are criminals and are taking jobs, and are not smart. Teachers blame us for their [White students] behavior by telling us we Mexicans have to be more friendlier with them [White students].

However, for students in our project being 'friendlier' placed undocumented students in precarious situations. These often resulted in physical or verbal altercations. Teachers, however, were in positions to mediate and encourage cross-cultural relationships. Rather than teachers facilitating and fostering healthy peer relationships students were expected to initiate and make structural changes.

Powerfully, the young people in our study learned how to negotiate these racialized social practices embodied by those who held power over them. Our students stood up and used their funds of knowledge to respond to these incidents. For example, Catalina shared how her family and friends were "involved in several marches that protested anti-immigrant laws because this was affecting us in school and in the community." She further detailed the importance of uplifting her younger siblings and community members: "I protest because I want to promote change, not just for me, but also for my younger siblings and other immigrant students. That is why we try to achieve in schools because it is also for all the sacrifices my parents have made." For Catalina, educational success is constructed as both a familial and community achievement, not an individual one.

Mia, an eleventh grader, shared how despite being teased by peers she and her friends "do our best in school so that we can prove them wrong and return someday with my college degree and show them that we [Mexicans] are smart and can contribute to the community in good ways." Catalina, an eleventh grader shared,

We felt that we were constantly threatened in the school and not able to succeed in education, and outside of the school with being deported...so we joined the movement for our rights, and that somehow seemed to help us feel we were part of a larger group of people experiencing similar things in school and in the community.

Marco, Catalina, and Mia each demonstrated how they managed relationships with peers and teachers who had preconceived biases and stereotypes regarding what it meant to be an "undocumented" student and their acceptance as learners and active participatory citizens in and outside of the school.

IMPLICATIONS FOR POLICY AND PRACTICE

In this chapter, we provided examples of the ways a few undocumented high school students resisted being silenced and marginalized by teachers, who upon learning of their undocumented status grew more hostile and rejecting. Through their narratives, these youth demonstrated agency and engagement in the production of knowledge as students and as young people. As noted through the students' narratives, teachers have immense power in school contexts, particularly in the formation of student–teacher relationship. Teachers are actively involved in the construction of high school students' academic identities in schools and classrooms. In the formation of student–teacher relationships, teachers have more power than students given their roles and the organizational structure of traditional school contexts. Yet, we learned immigrant youth also have agency and are able to resist the ways teachers construct their identities or accept them.

In our data, students were able to redirect the once friendly turned hostile relationships with their teachers into productive and proactive activities and outlets. It is important to note, however, that not all students in similar situations would react similarly. Although it was disheartening to see how these students managed to navigate the hateful rhetoric and actions toward them, these students are likely the exception. Most undocumented students live in the shadows and experience bias and prejudice without having safe opportunities to speak out and voice their experiences. For them, being hidden and then also experiencing ambivalent immigrant status presents unique challenges that educators must be ready and willing to face and learn from.

In light of this discussion, we offer a few implications for policy and for practice. As it relates to policy, there needs to be greater efforts to recruit and train teachers of color as well as to prepare White teacher candidates on the impact that anti-immigrant rhetoric and educational practices have on the children of immigrants or undocumented youths' well-being (e.g., to help them navigate their fears, anxieties, and consequences of the sudden deportation of parents/family members). Boser (2014) reports that students of color who are taught by educators of color perform better academically and relate to teachers of color as role models. Oftentimes teachers of color have sociocultural knowledge of students lived realities that serve to strengthen teacher–student relationships. In so doing, student-learning opportunities can be enhanced as can students' academic identities. There must be equitable efforts by universities to enlist preservice teachers of color who can help to transform school cultures.

Student narratives from our study also demonstrate the need for preservice training and professional development for teachers surrounding the effects of anti-immigration attitudes and policies on children of immigrants, undocumented and U.S. Latina/o people (Alvarez Gutiérrez, 2013). Our data revealed a troubling pattern of teacher bias against undocumented students. Even after teachers had developed positive and supportive relationships with their students, the revelation that those same students were undocumented radically shifted how they engaged with them. From this we learn that it wasn't that students were Latina/o, but rather their undocumented status that led to the change in the teacher–student–family relationships. Teachers must be better trained to be mindful of these intense biases that might damage their relationships with students.

Educational leaders and teachers must also understand the ways immigration policies impact students' overall well-being (Alvarez Gutiérrez, 2013). In this complex policy environment, undocumented youth live under quite varied legal statuses that may be confusing to educators. Some undocumented youth may be temporary legal, whereas others may exist in liminal status of uncertainty. By contrast, some may have experienced family member deportation, whereas others may live with the ongoing threat of deportation. These varied statuses render varied social and emotional outcomes for youth. At the core, these students require and deserve our support, guidance, and assistance throughout their educational journeys.

Educators' professional development in schools should focus on providing educators with current literature and discussion forums that grapple with understanding the racial and ethnic identities of diverse student learners. These professional development opportunities must be continuous and provide time for educators to reflect upon, grapple, and unpack, preconceived racial or ethnic biases that educators may bring to schools and into the classroom (Quijada Cerecer, 2013). These reflections must also include biases toward recent immigrants, undocumented students, and their respective families. These biases when not deconstructed impact teacher–student relationships, student learning opportunities, and school racial climates.

As it relates to educational practice, teachers should actively work to understand students' lived experiences. We recommend engaging teachers in professional development training where teachers have opportunities to reflect upon the ways they may have internalized the majoritarian narrative of what constitutes student–family civic engagement and support needed that results in academic success. For example, how do teachers learn about the students' cultural practices and their respective communities without essentializing students' ethnic identities? (Quijada Cerecer, 2013). Aside from calling home or parent–teacher conferences, how do teachers involve families in students' education? Teachers may unintentionally position immigrant students as liminal learners and not capable to succeed academically while not validating the knowledge students and their respective families bring into the school context. This creates distance among teachers and students. Such preservice training and professional development opportunities assist teachers reflect on the complex and multidimensional ways students learn and produce knowledge without essentializing students of color and their respective communities (Quijada Cerecer, 2013).

In sum, we return to the most critical issues that we anticipate this chapter advances. We advocate for policy development that seeks to strengthen the P-20 educational pathway for children of immigrants and undocumented students. Second, we advocate for the continued active recruitment of teachers of color. We also seek policy development that mandates professional development opportunities for educators in K–12 focused on unpacking immigration bias. We recognize that in conducting these trainings, subsequent professional development opportunities will also have to include preparations centered on educators' biases toward students based on linguistic or cultural backgrounds. These policy developments manifest in practice by providing educators with knowledge that improve their pedagogy to better work effectively with all students, especially those in difficult situations, such as undocumented young people.

NOTES

1. The terms alien, illegal, and criminal are often used interchangeably to perpetuate xenophobic ideologies. We use the term undocumented and unauthorized interchangeably and challenge aforementioned inferences made based on immigration status. Policymakers stridently avoid more "neutral" labels such as "unauthorized" or "undocumented" since they might offer a more positive framing, making it possible to see the social, linguistic, and cultural contributions of immigrants to the United States.
2. All names are pseudonyms.

REFERENCES

Abrego, L. J. (2006). "I can't go to college because I don't have papers": Incorporation patterns of Latino undocumented youth. *Latino Studies, 4(3)*, 212–231.

ACLU. (2015). *Families separated by coercive immigration practices may be reunited in U.S.* Retrieved on September 15, 2015, at https://www.aclu.org/news/families-separated-coercive-immigration-practices-may-be-reunited-us

Alvarez Gutiérrez, L. (2013). Costo alto de política anti-imigrante sobre la familia y educación: The adverse consequences of anti-Latino immigration laws. *Theory Into Practice, 52(3)*, 169–179. doi: 10.1080/00405841.2013.804308

Alvarez Gutiérrez, L. (2014). Youth engagement in social justice educational movements in the face of Anti-Latina/o immigrant legitimacy. *The Urban Review, 46(3)*, 307–323. doi: 10.1007/s11256-013-0269-y

Boser, U. (2014). Teacher diversity revisited: A state-by-state analysis. *Center for American progress.* Retrieved from https://cdn.americanprogress.org/wp-content/uploads/2014/05/TeacherDiversity.pdf

Chaudry, A., Capps, R., Pedroza, J., Castañeda, R. M., Santos, R., & Scott, M. M. (2010). *Facing our future: Children in the aftermath of immigration enforcement.* Washington, DC: Urban Institute.

Erikson, E. (1968). *Youth and crises.* New York, NY: Norton.

Gándara, P. C. & Contreras, F. (2009). *The Latino education crisis: The consequences of failed social policies.* Cambridge, MA: Harvard University Press.

Gonzales, R. G. (2009). Learning to be illegal: Undocumented youth and shifting legal contexts in the transition to adulthood. *American Sociological Review, 76*(4), 602–619. doi: 10.1177/0003122411411901

Holland, D., Lachiotte, W. J., Skinner, D., & Cain, C. (1998). *Identity and agency in cultural Worlds.* Cambridge, MA: Harvard University Press.

Krogstad, J. M. & Passel, J. S. (2015). *5 facts about illegal immigration in the U.S.* Washington, DC: Pew Research Center.

Lee, M. (2015). Donald Trump false comments connecting Mexican immigrants and crime. *The Washington Post.* Retrieved from https://www.washingtonpost.com/news/fact-checker/wp/2015/07/08/donald-trumps-false-comments-connecting-mexican-immigrants-and-crime/

Leonardo, Z. (2000). Betwixt and between: Introduction to politics of identity. In C. Tejeda, C. Martinez, & Z. Leonard (Eds), *Charting new terrain in Chicana(o)/Latina(o) education* (pp. 107–129). Creskill, NJ: Hampton Press.

Menjívar, C. (2006). Liminal legality: Salvadoran and Guatemalan immigrants' lives in the United States. *American Journal of Sociology, 111(4)*, 999–1037.

Moll, L., Amanti, C., Neff, D., & González, N. (1992). Funds of knowledge for teaching: Using a qualitative approach to connect homes and classrooms. *Theory into Practice, 31*(2), 132–141.

National Conference of State Legislatures (NCLS). (2016). *Immigration Policy Report. Report on 2015 state immigration laws.* Retrived from http://www.ncsl.org/documents/statefed/ImmigrationReport2015Final_Feb2016.pdf

Negrón-Gonzales, G. (2014). Undocumented, unafraid and unapologetic: Re-articulatory practices and migrant youth "illegality." *Latino Studies, 12*(2), 259–278. doi:10.1057/lst.2014.20

Paris, D., & Alim, H. S. (2014). What are we seeking to sustain through culturally sustaining pedagogy? A loving critique forward. *Harvard Educational Review, 84*(1), 85–100.

Passel, J. S. (2006). The size and characteristics of the unauthorized migrant population in the U.S. *Pew Hispanic Center.* Retrieved from http://www.pewhispanic.org/files/reports/61.pdf

Passel, J. S. (2011). Demography of immigrant youth: Past, present, and future. *Future of Children, 21*(1), 19–41. doi: 10.1353/foc.2011.0001

Passel, J. S., & Cohn, D. (2009). A portrait of unauthorized immigrants in the United States. *Pew Hispanic Center.* Retrieved from http://www.pewhispanic.org/files/reports/107.pdf

Patel, L. (2013). *Youth held at the border: Immigration, education, and the politics of inclusion.* New York, NY: Teachers College Press.

Pérez, W. (2012). *Americans by heart: Undocumented Latino students and the promise of higher education.* New York, NY: Teachers College Press.

Quijada Cerecer, P. D. (2013). Independence, dominance, and power: (Re)examining the impact of school policies on the academic development of indigenous youth. *Theory Into Practice, 52*(3), 196–202. doi:10.1080/00405841.2013.804313

Satinsky, S., Hu, A. Heller, J., & Farhang, L. (2013). *How family-focused immigration reform will mean better health for children and families.* Retrieved from http://www.familyunityfamilyhealth.org/

Steele, C. M. (2007). Stereotype threat and African American student achievement. In D. Grusky & S. Szelenyi (Eds.), *The inequality reader* (pp. 252–257). Boulder, CO: Westview Press.

Suárez-Orozco, C. (2004). Formulating identity in a globalized world. In M. Suárez-Orozco & D.B.Q Hillard, (Eds.), *Globalization: Culture and education in the new millennium* (pp. 173–202). Berkeley, CA: University of California Press and the Ross Institute.

Suárez Orozco, C., Bang, H. J., & Kim, H. Y. (2010). I felt like my heart was staying behind: Psychological implications of family separations and reunifications for immigrant youth. *Journal of Adolescent Research, 26*(2), 222–257. doi:10.1177/0743558410376830

Suárez-Orozco, C., Yoshikawa, Y., Teranishi, R., & Suárez-Orozco, M. (2011). Growing up in the shadows: The developmental implications of unauthorized status. *Harvard Educational Review, 81*(3), 438–472. doi: http://dx.doi.org/10.17763/haer.81.3.g23x203763783m75

Torres, R., & Wicks-Asbun, M. (2014). Undocumented students' narratives of liminal citizenship: High aspirations, exclusion and 'in-between' identities. *Professional Geographer, 66(2),* 195–204. doi:10.1080/00330124.2012.735936

U.S. Department of Education. (2011). *Our Future, our teachers: The Obama administration's plan for teacher education reform and improvement.* Washington, D.C.

Valencia, R., & Solórzano, D. (1997). Contemporary deficit thinking. In R. Valencia (Ed.), *The evolution of deficit thinking in educational thought and practice* (pp. 160–212). New York, NY: Falmer.

Valenzuela, A. (1999). *Subtractive schooling: U.S.-Mexican youth and the politics of caring.* New York, NY: State University of New York Press.

Wessler, S. F. (2011). *Thousands of kids lost from parents in U.S. deportation system.* New York, NY: Colorlines.com. Retrieved from http://colorlines.com/archives/2011/11/thousands_of_kids_lost_in_foster_homes_after_parents_deportation.html

CHAPTER 4

SEXUAL ORIENTATION AND GENDER IDENTITY IN EDUCATION

Making Schools Safe for All Students

Charlotte J. Patterson
University of Virginia

Bernadette V. Blanchfield
University of Virginia

Rachel G. Riskind
Guilford College

In recent years, public discourse has increasingly focused on the concerns of lesbian, gay, bisexual and transgender (LGBT) youth. Antigay harassment has been widely publicized in the media. Programs intended to support LGBT youth, such as school-based gay-straight alliances, have engendered considerable debate. Public discussions of these issues have attracted commentary across the entire spectrum of opinion. Some religious and political

Educational Policies and Youth in the 21st Century, pages 57–80
Copyright © 2016 by Information Age Publishing
All rights of reproduction in any form reserved.

figures have been vociferous in their opposition to LGBT communities. On the other side, many openly LGBT or allied writers, politicians, religious leaders, and celebrities have voiced their support. In one particularly high-profile example, President Barack Obama was the first U.S. president to voice his support for LGBT people in an inaugural address, and his administration has continued to advance the cause of equal rights for LGBT citizens of all ages. In addition, school administrators, teachers, parents, and students themselves are increasingly joining the debate. Why is there so much discussion of LGBT youth today?

One reason is surely news coverage of the shocking, high-profile deaths of LGBT youth. For example, 15-year-old Lawrence King was shot to death in 2008 by a 14-year-old classmate at his California school because the classmate believed Lawrence to be gay; this story was heavily reported in the news media (e.g., Cathcart, 2008). There have also been well-publicized cases of LGBT youth who were harassed by other students, fell into despair, and took their own lives. One such youth was Tyler Clementi, a 19-year-old whose college roommate secretly videotaped his intimate activities with a same-sex partner, and shared the tapes with his friends (Parker, 2012). After Tyler learned that this had happened, he jumped to his death from New York City's George Washington Bridge leaving a Facebook message that read, "Jumping off the gw bridge sorry" (Parker, 2012). Another case involves the suicide in 2014 of 17-year-old Leelah Alcorn, a transgender student in Ohio (Johnston, 2014). When Leelah's conservative parents learned that peers at her local high school were embracing her transition, they enrolled her in a "re-education" program and prohibited her from communicating with her friends. Socially isolated and desperate, Leelah wrote a heartbreaking suicide note, which she intended for publication after she died after walking in front of a truck on a highway three miles from her home (Johnston, 2014). Tragic deaths such as these have been widely reported in the media, and have drawn considerable attention to the issues of LGBT youth.

Another reason that public discussion of LGBT youth has emerged is that some LGBT students have responded to school-based harassment by fighting back. Best known among those who have fought back successfully is a man named Jamie Nabozny (Ball, 2010; Mezey, 2009). Growing up in rural Wisconsin, Nabozny suffered years of harrowing attacks in high school and he attempted suicide multiple times. School administrators refused to intervene or to stop the harassment. Later, Nabozny sued the school for its failure to provide him with a safe environment, and won; he was ultimately awarded $962,000 in damages (Ball, 2010). Nabozny's case was by no means an isolated incident. In another case, a California school district was ordered to pay $750,000 for having failed to protect a student from harassment (Potts, 2014). As these and related cases have established, a school's failure to protect the safety of its LGBT students can prove costly.

School districts have responded to these developments in many ways (Mayo, 2013). Some have revised school nondiscrimination policies to ensure that policies prevent discrimination on the basis of sexual orientation, gender identity, and/or gender expression. Others have established antibullying programs to reduce harassment in general, have added specific programs aimed at reducing antigay harassment, or encouraged students to form gay-straight alliances (Vaccaro, August, & Kennedy, 2012). Such changes have often generated controversy within and beyond school communities (Cianciotto & Cahill, 2003, 2012; Mayo, 2013).

Social science research can inform responses to many of the questions these debates have raised. Who are the LGBT students in our schools? How do school policies affect LGBT and other students? What are the best ways to encourage positive youth development among LGBT and other students? In what follows, we begin with a demographic portrait of sexual minority youth, we then summarize findings from research on the concerns of LGBT students; finally, we present findings from research on emerging responses to problems experienced by many LGBT youth at school. Many of these concerns have attracted public attention only in recent years, and much of the research in this area has been conducted within the last decade. Although there are many questions in this area that have not yet been addressed, there is enough high-quality research to suggest some steps that can be taken to encourage positive development among LGBT youth.

WHO ARE LGBT STUDENTS?

Sexual orientation and gender identity are "invisible identities," meaning that it is often difficult or impossible to identify sexual orientation or gender identity based on appearance. Because identification of LGBT students requires their self-disclosure of gender identity, sexual identity, attractions, and/or sexual behaviors, it can be difficult to provide an accurate demographic portrait of LGBT students in the United States. Given that school settings can be hostile to sexual minority individuals, many LGBT students may choose not to identify themselves as such. Furthermore, LGBT youth are a diverse group; each student experiences his or her sexual and gender identities together with other important aspects of identity, including race, ethnicity, religion, and social class. LGBT students may thus experience stress and/or support in multiple domains.

How Many LGBT Students Are There?

Most estimates suggest that in the United States, anywhere from 3% to 10% of today's teenagers are LGBT (Ciancatto & Cahill, 2003, 2012). This is a very broad range of estimates, much wider than is usually found in estimates among adults (Gates, 2011, 2013). Why is it so difficult to estimate the numbers of LGBT youth in the United States today?

Part of the reason it is difficult to give a decisive answer is attributable to the methodological challenges involved in studying young sexual and gender minority populations (Savin-Williams, 2008). Researchers measure sexual orientation by assessing one or more of three aspects of this concept: identity, attraction, and behavior (Berg-Kelly, 2003; Diamond, 2008; Thompson & Morgan, 2008). Identity refers to one's self-descriptions with regard to sexual orientation (usually lesbian, gay, bisexual, or heterosexual). Attraction refers to the gender of the object of one's sexual, romantic, and emotional feelings (i.e., same-sex, opposite-sex, or both sexes). Sexual behavior refers to the gender of one's partners in sexual activities (Savin-Williams, 2006). Thus, the concept of sexual orientation is itself complex, and some researchers focus on one aspect while others may assess another one. Moreover, assessments of attractions, behaviors, and identities may yield disparate results (Rosario & Schrimshaw, 2013).

Assessment of sexual orientation is a challenge for any researcher studying human sexuality, but it is particularly complex for those who work with youth. The potential for variation over time in all aspects of sexuality is particularly great during adolescence, when youth are still actively forging their identities (APA, 2008). For example, youth who experiment with same-sex sexuality during adolescence may be captured in behaviorally-based estimates even though they may see themselves as heterosexual (Savin-Williams, 2008). Conversely, youth who identify as lesbian, gay or bisexual, but who are not yet sexually experienced may not be identified. In other words, assessments of attractions may be inconsistent with those focused on identity and behavior (APA, 2008). Moreover, some adolescents may not yet be aware of same-sex attractions, or may be in the process of questioning their sexuality; they may come to identify as lesbian, gay, or bisexual after assessments have been done, and thus not be picked up by school-based survey methods (Savin-Williams, 2008).

When considering the welfare of LGBT students, it may be important to remember that no single aspect of sexual orientation is necessarily more important than another. Although youth who identify as LGBT are often thought of as the group of greatest interest to educators and policymakers, others—such as those who are involved in risky sexual behavior with same-sex partners—may also be at risk. The best path for researchers, educators, and policymakers may often be to take into account any and all aspects of youth's sexuality and gender identity.

When research has taken the multidimensional nature of sexuality into account, the results have been revealing. Results from the 2001 Massachusetts Youth Risk Behavior Survey indicated that 5% of participants self-identified as gay, lesbian, or bisexual, or reported same-sex sexual experiences (MDOE, 2002). Nationally representative data from the 2002 National Survey of Family Growth indicated that 11% of female youth and 4% of male youth (ages 15–21) reported same-sex sexual activity—though only 6% of the female and 3% of the male youth identified as lesbian, gay, or bisexual (McCabe, Brewster, & Tilman, 2011). Thus, estimates based on behavior alone and those based on identity alone may identify different groups of sexual minority youth.

It is also worth noting that gender and sexual identity are not unrelated. Girls are more likely than boys to identify as bisexual, and the difference is sizable. For instance, in a large representative sample of adolescents in the United States, Mustanski and his colleagues (2014) reported that while more than 5% of girls 16–18 years of age identified as bisexual, only about 2% of their male peers did so. The same is true of adult men and women; adult women are more likely than adult men to identify as bisexual (Gates, 2013). Taken together, results of research suggest that bisexual identities are more common among girls and women than among boys and men.

Bisexually-identified girls may be at greater risk than their lesbian or heterosexual peers, both in terms of mental health and physical health. For instance, in a recent study drawing on a nationally representative sample of 15 to 20-year-old girls and young women in the United States, bisexual girls reported an earlier sexual debut, more male partners, more use of emergency contraceptives, and higher rates of pregnancy termination than did same-aged, lesbian-identified, or heterosexually-identified girls (Tornello, Riskind & Patterson, 2014). In another study of a representative sample of U.S. high school girls, both lesbian and bisexual girls reported riskier sexual behaviors and more negative reproductive health outcomes than did their heterosexual peers (Riskind, Tornello, Younger, & Patterson, 2014). Overall, sexual minority girls—and especially those identifying as bisexual—appear to be at higher risk in many areas when compared with their heterosexual peers (Riskind et al., 2014; Tornello et al., 2014).

The above discussion does not include transgender youth, for whom gender identity rather than sexual orientation is the characteristic of interest. Gender identity refers to the sense of oneself as male or female, independent of biological sex (Diamond, 2002). If one's gender identity and biological sex coincide, one may be called "cisgender." This term is derived from the Latin *cis*, which means "on this side of," or "on the same side." If one's gender identity and biological sex are different, the individual may identify as "transgender." Also derived from the Latin, the term *trans* means "on the other side." Thus, cisgender and transgender labels refer to the extent to which a person's gender identity is or is not aligned with that individual's assigned (or biological) sex.

In recent years, transgender youth may have come more and more into the public eye, but population-based data documenting gender-identity trends remain rare. Analysis of the 2007 and 2009 Massachusetts Behavioral Risk Factor Surveillance Survey indicated that 0.5% of adults identified as transgender (Gates, 2011). Results from the 2003 California LGBT Tobacco Survey, indicated that 3.2% of all LGBT individuals in California identified as transgender—suggesting that approximately 0.1% of Californians identified in this way (Gates, 2011, 2013). Calculations based on these figures yield the estimate of approximately 700,000 transgender people in the United States today. There are currently no data on the numbers of transgender youth (GenIUSS Group, 2014). Thus, it is not surprising that the needs of transgender youth are often overlooked in schools.

Racial Diversity Among LGBT Youth

LGBT youth are a varied group from a diverse array of backgrounds. A survey of more than 10,000 LGBT-identified teenagers ages 13 to 17 years in the United States revealed that approximately 65% identified themselves as White or Caucasian, 6% as Black or African American, 20% as Latino or Hispanic, 3% as Asian or Pacific-Islander, 1% as Native American, and 5% as something else (HRC, 2012). Another recent study suggests that Black or African American youth may be more likely, and Asian or Pacific Islander youth less likely than White or Caucasian youth to identify as members of sexual minorities (Mustanski et al., 2014). The intersections of sexual identity and other aspects of identity, such as race, ethnicity, education, and income can result in important differences among LGBT youth.

In the United States today, many youth of color face special challenges and heightened risks compared to their White peers (Bridges, 2007). For example, non-White LGBT youth may be less likely to disclose sexual orientation or gender identity to parents and hence may be less likely to have strong support from parents. One study found that 80% of White youth (ages 18–24) were "out" to their parents, compared to only 71% of Latinos, 61% of African Americans, and 51% of Asian or Pacific-Islanders (Grov, Bimbi, Nanin & Parsons, 2006). Non-White youth may experience less social support in other domains as well. A large-scale survey of Black Pride attendees indicated that many Black LGBT youth were members of churches that describe homosexuality is "wrong and sinful" (Bennett & Battle, 2001). The prevalence of Catholicism and *machismo* sensibilities in Latino communities may prevent some LGBT youth from seeking resources to cope with stressors prompted by LGBT identities (Bridges, 2007). Likewise, many LGBT youth of Asian and Pacific-Islander descent face pressures to conform to heterosexual lifestyles so as not to shame their families (Bridges, 2007). These results and others like them suggest that many diverse elements of youth identities are strongly intertwined. When assessing the safety of students in school settings, it may be useful to keep these issues in mind, because risks to LGBT youth may vary as a function of students' other identities.

ARE LGBT YOUTH SAFE AT SCHOOL?

Research has revealed that schools are often astonishingly hostile environments for LGBT adolescents. Of course, some LGBT adolescents have the support of their parents and other family members, attend welcoming schools, and encounter little or no hostility among teachers or peers. On average, however, LGBT adolescents are more likely than their heterosexual and cisgender peers to encounter dangerous environments at school and are more likely to feel unsafe and disconnected from others (HRC, 2012). Relatedly, LGBT students are more likely than heterosexual and cisgender peers to suffer from depression and to use alcohol and tobacco, and they are much more likely to attempt suicide (IOM, 2011). In sum, although many LGBT youth are developing well, LGBT adolescents are far more likely than their heterosexual and cisgender peers to experience mental and physical health difficulties.

Schools as Stressful Environments

Antigay remarks, threats, and harassment seem to be pervasive in many American schools today (HRC, 2012). National surveys of LGBT adolescents in the United States have found that three quarters, including roughly 80% of transgender adolescents, reported distress from hearing antigay remarks or antitrans language used regularly at school (HRC, 2012; Kosciw & Diaz, 2006; Kosciw, Greytak, Palmer, & Boesen, 2014; McGuire, Anderson, Toomey, & Russell, 2010). In a national survey of more than 7,000 youth in the United States (Kosciw et al., 2014), most LGBT adolescents reported that they had been harassed or threatened at school. Fully one in three reported that they had been physically harassed (i.e., pushed or shoved) because of their sexual orientation or gender expression, and approximately 15% reported that they had been physically assaulted (i.e., punched, kicked, or injured with a weapon). Half of the students also reported being bullied via social media on the Internet. LGBT students who identified as multiracial were at increased risk compared to their peers of single ethnicities; White LGBT students typically reported lower rates of harassment than did their non-White peers (Kosciw et al., 2014).

These studies cited were not based on representative samples, but the findings do not seem attributable to sampling bias. In a representative sample of more than 13,000 Wisconsin high school students, LGB students reported experiencing more antigay teasing than did heterosexual students (Espelage, Aragon, Birkett & Koenig, 2008). Students who were questioning their sexual orientation seemed to be at highest risk for victimization compared to their LGB or heterosexual counterparts; the questioning students reported experiencing more victimization through antigay teasing and general peer harassment than did LGB or heterosexual students (Espelage et al., 2008).

Many if not most incidents of antigay teasing and harassment apparently go unreported at school (Mayo, 2013). LGBT students may fear that reporting will make the situation worse or that reporting will not result in effective support from teachers or administrators (Kosciw et al., 2014). These students may have good reason to avoid reporting: more than 50% of students surveyed reported hearing homophobic remarks or negative remarks about gender expression from teachers or other school staff (Kosciw et al., 2014).

It is easy to understand, then, why more than half of LGBT adolescents in a nationwide survey reported feeling unsafe at school due to their sexual orientation, and why more than a third of these students reported feeling unsafe due to their gender expression (Kosciw et al., 2014). In this study, more than one third of LGBT students reported that—whether from fear or discomfort—they avoided gender-segregated spaces at school, such as bathrooms and locker rooms. Furthermore, students who reported having experienced harassment also reported missing more days of school, receiving lower grades, and harboring more modest educational aspirations than did other students. These general findings have been replicated in several studies (e.g., Kosciw & Diaz, 2006; McGuire, Anderson, Toomey, & Russell, 2010; Toomey, McGuire, & Russell, 2012). Understandably, such victimization and feelings of being unsafe at school are associated with truancy and poor academic achievement among affected students (IOM, 2011).

Coping With Stressful School Environments

How do LGBT adolescents cope with being required to attend schools that feel unsafe and dangerous to them? Some literally fight back, engaging in physical conflict at school (Russell, Franz, & Driscoll, 2001; IOM, 2011). Without adequate support, and in the face of hostility and victimization, many feel lonely and experience distress (Russell, 2002; IOM, 2011).

Sexual and gender minority adolescents are more likely than other youth to report symptoms of depression, anxiety, and eating disorders (IOM, 2011). Many skip school because they feel unsafe (Peter, Taylor, Ristock & Edkins, 2015). Bisexual and transgender youth are more likely to experience such difficulties than their lesbian and gay peers; evidence suggests that they also experience more victimization than do lesbian and gay youth (IOM, 2011).

Feelings of exclusion and hopelessness may lead to unsafe behavior, such as the use of alcohol and other drugs (IOM, 2011). Statewide surveys based on representative samples of high school students in Massachusetts and in Vermont have revealed that those with same-sex sexual experience were more likely than their peers to report having used alcohol and other drugs (Massachusetts Department of Health, 2012; Vermont Department of Health, 2012). Especially among girls, reports of alcohol and drug use were also associated with reports of sexual minority status in national samples of adolescents (Russell, Driscoll & Truong, 2002). Alcohol and drug use may themselves be linked in multiple ways with other problem behaviors, such as delinquency and risky sexual behavior (IOM, 2011).

As one might expect, based on other problems experienced by LGBT youth, sexual and gender minority youth are at heightened risk of suicidal thoughts and actions (Hatzenbuehler, Birkett, van Wagenen, & Meyer, 2014; IOM, 2011). Information from large-scale, population-based studies has demonstrated that sexual and gender minority adolescents are considerably more likely than others to report having attempted suicide. For example, in a national sample of American high school students, those who reported same-sex attractions and/or same-sex sexual experiences were at least twice as likely as other youth to report having made a suicide attempt (Russell & Joyner, 2001). Recent research suggests that Latino and American Native LGBT youth are the most likely to attempt suicide, compared to their White, Black, and Asian LGBT peers (Bostwick, et al., 2014). Students who report uncertainty about their sexual identities may also be more likely to attempt suicide, compared with heterosexual peers (Zhao, Montoro, Igartua, & Thombs, 2010).

Middle School Students and Transgender Students

Until recent times, most LGBT individuals did not disclose their sexual orientation or gender identity until late adolescence or early adulthood, if at all. In recent years, however, many LGBT individuals have come out in early adolescence or even in childhood (IOM, 2011). Research on the experiences of sexual minority individuals before they enter high school is still sparse, but a few studies have examined the lives of LGBT middle school students.

66 ▪ C. J. PATTERSON, B. V. BLANCHFIELD, and R. G. RISKIND

In one study of more than 600 self-described LGBT middle school students, 81% reported experiencing verbal harassment and 39% reported experiencing physical assaults by other students (GLSEN, 2009). Of those who informed teachers or administrators about such difficulties, only a minority believed that any effective intervention had resulted. Students who reported experiencing harassment were also more likely than others to say that they had been absent from school due to concerns about safety. Similarly, in a representative county-wide sample of almost 4,000 Wisconsin middle school students, LGBT youth were at elevated risk for a variety of mental, physical, and educational problems, including suicidal ideation, suicide attempts, victimization by peers, and unexcused absences from school (Robinson & Espelage, 2011). The risk of negative outcomes was particularly high among bisexual students. Thus, elevated risk for sexual and gender minority youth does not begin in high school. It is important to remember, however, that despite their elevated risk, some students who identified themselves as LGBT came from supportive families, attended safe schools, and were developing well.

Transgender and gender nonconforming youth have been explicitly studied less often than lesbian and gay youth, but some studies have included measures of both sexual orientation and gender identity. One such study, based on a sample of high school seniors in rural New York, demonstrated that gender nonconformity was a better predictor of psychological well-being among youth than was sexual orientation (Rieger & Savin-Williams, 2011). It appears that transgender and gender nonconforming youth are at least as likely as cisgender and gender-conforming lesbian and gay students to face hostile environments at school. In fact, transgender and gender nonconforming youth seem to be victimized more and show more depressive symptoms than do their cisgender and gender-conforming classmates (IOM, 2011). In one study, heightened levels of depressive symptoms among transgender and gender nonconforming youth were fully accounted for by their elevated likelihood of victimization (Toomey, Ryan, Diaz, Card, & Russell, 2010). To improve our understanding of links between sexual orientation, gender identity, gender nonconformity, and psychological and educational outcomes, further research is needed.

Conclusions About Safety of LGBT Youth in Schools

School environments are generally more hostile for LGBT youth than they are for heterosexual and cisgender youth. Rates of victimization and problem behaviors are also higher among LGBT youth than among heterosexual and cisgender youth. However, even though the risks are elevated overall, not all LGBT youth encounter hostile environments, and many

LGBT youth are developing well (IOM, 2011). Some LGBT youth experience little or no harassment, while others demonstrate resilience, developing in healthy ways despite victimization experiences. Overall, much remains to be done to improve school safety for LGBT students.

HOW CAN SCHOOLS BE MADE SAFER FOR LGBT STUDENTS?

Many approaches have been taken to the problem of how to minimize difficulties that LGBT students encounter at school (Cianciotto & Cahill, 2012; Mayo, 2013; Vaccaro et al., 2012). One strategy has involved efforts to pass "safe schools" laws that prohibit discrimination in schools on the basis of sexual orientation or gender identity. Such measures often stipulate that administrators and teachers undergo training to understand, identify, and prevent harassment of LGBT students. In the absence of federal or state laws, some individual districts and schools have chosen to enact safe schools policies. Another strategy has been to incorporate LGBT-related resources into the school curriculum or school-sponsored social events and programs. Yet another approach has been to establish gay-straight alliances and other school-based clubs that provide support and advocacy for LGBT students (MacGillivray, 2007). To what extent do these steps make schools into more welcoming environments for LGBT students? In this section, we summarize research evidence that addresses this question.

"Safe Schools" Laws and Policies

Some attempts to make schools safer for LGBT students have involved legislative action. Although a federal safe schools improvement act has been considered, it has not yet been passed into law by Congress (Russell, Kosciw, Horn, & Saewyc, 2010; HRC, 2015). At the time of this writing, 17 states and the District of Columbia have safe schools laws that prohibit discrimination or harassment in schools on the basis of sexual orientation or gender identity (GLSEN, 2015a). For example, in New York, the Dignity for All Students Act protects students from discrimination or harassment based on sexual orientation, among other characteristics, and it also provides for training of administrators, teachers, and other school employees on how to discourage harassment. Many other states have nondiscrimination laws that do not specifically mention LGBT issues or that include sexual orientation but not gender identity (Russell et al., 2010).

LGBT students in states with safe schools laws that include sexual orientation report to researchers that they feel safer and experience less harassment than do their peers in states without these protections. In one national study, Kosciw and his colleagues (2008) found that students in such states heard fewer antigay remarks at school and reported lower levels of harassment than did those in other states. Moreover, when harassment did occur, students in safe schools states reported that teachers were more likely to intervene.

Even within a single, relatively progressive state, the climate for LGBT students can vary as a function of safe schools policies. In a stratified random sample of more than 1,500 Massachusetts high school students attending 33 different schools, those who attended schools with inclusive antidiscrimination policies reported that the school had a more welcoming environment for LGBT students than did those attending schools without such policies (Szalacha, 2003). Interestingly, the result was replicated within both heterosexual and LGBT subsamples, and it remained true despite the fact that 65% of the students were unaware of their school's policy. A similar study involved more than 2,400 California students (Russell, et al., 2010), and found that students who reported that their schools had explicit policies protecting LGBT students felt safer, reported less LGBT harassment, and described their schools as safer for LGBT students. An Oregon study also examined the impact on LGBT students of school district antibullying policies that were inclusive of sexual orientation (Hatzenbuehler & Keyes, 2013). Results showed that students living in areas that had fewer inclusive policies were twice as likely as students living in areas where inclusive policies were common to say that they had made a suicide attempt in the past year (Hatzenbuehler & Keyes, 2013).

Associations between school policies and student outcomes strongly suggest that policies shape the experiences of LGBT youth. It is, however, not yet clear whether the policies have an impact on school environments or merely reflect preexisting school climates surrounding LGBT issues. Because the studies to date have employed cross-sectional designs, causality cannot be inferred from the results. As Hatzenbuehler and his colleagues have suggested, however, longitudinal studies could clarify issues of causality by studying the impact of policies over time (Hatzenbuehler & Keyes, 2013).

LGBT Content in Academic Curricula

A second approach to creating safer schools has been to include LGBT-relevant material in the school curriculum (Mayo, 2013). This might include relatively minor revisions to existing curricula. For example, an English teacher might mention that many scholars believe that Emily Dickinson loved both women and men. A history teacher might give a lesson about nonbinary gender roles in American Indian cultures. A health teacher might discuss how sexual partners of the same sex can avoid sexually transmitted infections. Issues of sexual orientation and gender identity could be integrated into many areas of the standard curriculum.

Limited evidence suggests that inclusion of LGBT content in curricula is associated with LGBT students' feeling of safety. One researcher reported that, when LGBT issues were included in school curricula, students said that they felt safer in school environments (Szalacha, 2003). Another group of researchers found that, when students knew where to find information and support relevant to LGBT issues at school, they felt safer (Russell et al., 2010). When schools' sex education lessons included material relevant to same-sex relationships, Blake and colleagues (2001) found that gay male students reported less sexual risk-taking behavior. Again, it is not clear whether these curricular changes influenced or merely reflected school climates surrounding LGBT issues.

Early in 2012, a California law went into effect requiring that the accomplishments of LGBT Americans be taught in public schools (Lovett, 2011). However, its impact on students has not yet been studied. Overall, less is known about the influence of curricular material than about legislative and policy responses to the problems of LGBT students in schools. Available evidence, however, suggests that both legislative and curricular changes may make schools safer or reflect a more positive school climate for LGBT students.

Inclusion of LGBT Students in Extracurricular Activities

It is not only within the classroom curriculum that schools can make an impact on LGBT students' functioning, but in school-sanctioned extracurricular programs or events as well. For example, there have been numerous instances in which schools have made headlines for instituting policies that prohibit same-sex couples from attending school dances (Eckes, DeMitchell, & Fossey, 2013). In these situations, litigation (or the threat of it) has sometimes been the only recourse for LGBT students wishing to participate in what are very important social events in the lives of many American adolescents. In one such instance in Missouri (Owens, 2013), the Scott County Central School District repealed a discriminatory prom policy only when the Southern Poverty Law Center threatened a lawsuit on behalf of a gay student who wished to attend the school's dance with his boyfriend. In another case, a transgender student sued the Gary (Indiana) School Corporation after being barred from her high school prom. The school authorities saw her as male, and would allow her to attend the prom only in male attire, but she saw herself as female and wanted to wear a dress. Eventually, the case was settled out of court (Robson, 2013). In another Indiana case, after learning that a gay couple planned to attend the local high school's prom, a community group started a "traditional prom" exclusively for straight couples (Eckes et al., 2013). In response, the Southwest School Corporation of Southern Indiana issued statements emphasizing the school prom's inclusivity to all students (Eckes et al., 2013).

The legal grounds for inclusion of LGBT students and their dates at school dances have long been established but continue to be challenged, largely due the fact that sexual orientation and gender identity remain unprotected by federal law. Courts instead often defer to arguments concerning students' First Amendment rights. For example, in 2010, the Itawamba School District in Mississippi canceled their prom when a student said she would attend with her girlfriend, and that she intended to wear a tuxedo. In *McMillen vs. Itawamba School District* (2010) the court held that the school's refusal to allow her to attend the prom in a tuxedo violated the girl's First Amendment right to self-expression. This was consistent with a decision many years earlier in *Fricke v. Lynch* (1980) against a Cumberland, Rhode Island, school district that did not wish to allow a male student to bring a male date to his prom (Fricke, 1981).

In addition to promoting LGBT-inclusive social events, schools have made efforts to engage pupils in LGBT awareness outside of the academic curriculum. For example, some schools take the lead from a national organization called the Gay, Lesbian, and Straight Education Network (GLSEN). GLSEN works specifically with students, teachers, and parents to promote LGBT-positive school environments through national events and year-round programs. Some of GLSEN's events and programs include a National Ally Week (which aims to identify, support, and recognize LGBT allies in America's schools), a ThinkB4YouSpeak program (aiming to reduce and prevent the use of anti-LGBT language), a National Day of Silence (which raises awareness about the silencing effect of LGBT harassment and discrimination), a Safe Space Kit (which helps educators establish safe and positive learning environments for LGBT students), a No Name-Calling Week (which aims to reduce many aspects of teasing, including bullying grounded in LGBT prejudices), and other school- or district-specific training modules (GLSEN, 2015b).

GLSEN's interventions have grown out of research on the needs of LGBT youth. They are easily accessible online and include instructions for implementation; however, the events and programs rely on school administrators, faculty, and/or students to self-select into participation. Moreover, GLSEN has published formal program evaluations for only two of its initiatives: a 1- and 4-year evaluation of its No Name-Calling Week (Kosciw, Diaz, Colic, & Goldin, 2005; Greytak, Kosciw, & Jerman, 2008), and a 1-year evaluation of a two-day LGBT-sensitivity training for staff representatives of schools served by the New York City Department of Education (Greytak &

Kosciw, 2010). The No Name-Calling Week evaluations indicated that, after program interventions, staff perceived school climates to have improved, including fewer instances of harassment and increased reporting of bullying (Kosciw, Diaz, Colic, & Goldin, 2005; Greytak, Kosicw, & Jerman, 2008). Likewise, the NYC DOE evaluation found that teachers who participated in the training were more knowledgeable about and effective in dealing with LGBT issues than were teachers who did not take the training—even six months after the training program had ended (Greytak & Kosciw, 2010). These positive program outcomes suggest that concerted efforts to promote LGBT-awareness and sensitivity—among students and teachers alike—may improve school climates.

Gay–Straight Alliances

Gay–straight alliances (GSAs) provide another important response to the challenges facing LGBT students. GSAs are student clubs that advocate to improve school climates for sexual and gender minority youth, and that provide support for LGBT and allied students (GLSEN, 2007). Since the first GSA was founded in 1988, the movement has grown rapidly, and there are now more than 4,000 GSAs nationwide (Mayo, 2013). Under the 1984 Federal Equal Access Act, any school that allows one extracurricular club must allow all others, including GSAs (MacGillivray, 2007). Thus, in the United States today, the right to form a GSA is protected by federal law.

LGBT students seem to experience more positive educational and psychological outcomes in schools with GSAs, compared to schools without them. In schools with GSAs, LGBT students report higher grade-point averages (Toomey & Russell, 2011). At schools with GSAs, LGBT students are less likely to report feeling unsafe (Kosciw & Diaz, 2006; Szalacha, 2003), and all students describe the climate as more favorable (Goodenow, Szalacha & Westheimer, 2006; Peter et al., 2015; Szalacha, 2003). Moreover, at schools with GSAs, all students report healthier behavior in a number of ways; they report less truancy, less tobacco and alcohol use, less suicidality, and less risky sexual behavior (Poteat, Sinclair, DiGiovanni, Koenig, & Russell, 2013). LGBT students at schools with GSAs may hear fewer antigay remarks, experience less peer victimization, and feel a greater sense of belonging (Kosciw & Diaz, 2006; Palmer, Kosciw, & Bartkiewicz, 2012; Toomey & Russell, 2011; but see Poteat et al., 2013 for a nonreplication).

Retrospective studies suggest similar conclusions. In a community sample of LGBT young adults, those who recalled their high schools as having GSAs reported fewer depressive symptoms and higher self-esteem than peers who did not recall their high schools as having GSAs (Toomey, Ryan, Diaz, & Russell, 2011). LGBT young adults who recalled their high school as having a GSA were also more likely to report college-level educational attainment (Toomey et al., 2011). Similarly, in a study of LGBT college students currently involved with LGBT organizations, those who recalled their high school as having a GSA reported significantly better school experiences, less alcohol use, and less psychological distress (Heck, Flentje, & Cochran, 2011). Thus, the presence of a GSA in a school is both retrospectively and prospectively associated with positive outcomes for LGBT students.

LGBT students who participate in GSAs may experience more positive outcomes than peers who do not participate. For example, in a sample of LGBT students in California middle and high schools, GSA membership was associated with greater feelings of school belongingness (Toomey & Russell, 2011). Moreover, participation in GSA-related social justice activities was associated with better academic performance (Toomey & Russell, 2011). Membership and involvement in GSAs has also been found to be associated with greater self-efficacy and openness about sexual orientation among LGBT students (Kosciw, Greytak, Diaz, & Bartkiewicz, 2010; Russell, Muraco, Subramaniam, & Laub, 2009). However, the mere presence of a GSA in a school may be more strongly associated with positive school experiences than GSA membership (Walls, Kane, & Wisneski, 2010). In short, LGBT students who participate in GSAs seem to be better off than those who do not participate, but the mere presence of a GSA is also associated with positive school experiences.

While the presence of GSAs seems to be associated with favorable outcomes for students, it remains unclear whether GSAs are actually the cause of positive outcomes. It is possible that the existence of GSAs may be a marker for school climates that are favorable for LGBT students. Are GSAs associated with positive outcomes because they tend to take root in school climates that are already welcoming to LGBT youth? Or can GSAs actually improve school climates for LGBT students? Definitive answers to these questions are not yet available, but researchers have begun to address them.

Interviews with students who have participated in GSAs seem to support the latter view. For example, one student commented, "going to Gay Straight Alliance... you don't feel alone... there's others out there to support you" (Russell et al., 2009, page 899). A second student shared, "Being the president of a Gay Straight Alliance is really empowering to me, it gives me a lot of control... I've devoted a lot of time to it, and that's empowering, knowing that like I have the power to make this change in my school" (Russell et al., 2009, page 903). A third student stated, "We all need a sanctuary. I'm extremely grateful I was involved since [the GSA] helped me come to terms with being different" (Fetner, Elafros, Bortolin, Dreschler, 2012, page 199). Whether the association is causal or not, the presence of a GSA in a particular school is clearly associated with greater feelings of safety and support among sexual minority youth (GLSEN, 2007).

Research has also begun to analyze the possible impact of different elements of GSAs. In a study that examined student, advisor, and structural factors associated with positive outcomes of GSA involvement among LGBT and heterosexual students, Poteat and his colleagues studied 146 youth in 13 different GSAs in Massachusetts (Poteat et al., 2015). They found that youth whose GSA advisers had served longer, felt more control, and were in more supportive school contexts reported more positive experiences, such as feelings of mastery, purpose and self-esteem. Overall, structural factors as well as individual and advisor characteristics were important predictors of student experiences in a GSA (Poteat et al., 2015).

SUMMARY AND CONCLUSIONS

Not all school environments are safe for LGBT youth. In fact, school environments are often shockingly hostile to LGBT students. As a result of their disproportionate likelihood of being victimized, LGBT students are more likely than their peers to report mental and physical health difficulties, as well as academic problems at school (IOM, 2011). Despite these realities, many states lack safe schools laws that protect LGBT students, and many schools lack nondiscrimination policies that include sexual orientation, gender identity, and gender expression. Moreover, LGBT issues remain underrepresented in most curricula, and not all schools offer LGBT-inclusive extracurricular events and groups.

Inclusive nondiscrimination policies show real potential for improving school climates. Especially when such policies include training for school personnel and monitoring of school climates, positive outcomes may be maximized (Cianciotto & Cahill, 2012; Mayo, 2013). School districts in many states do not, however, have inclusive nondiscrimination policies of any kind, and much work remains to be done in this area.

Gay-straight alliances (GSAs) have also emerged as a useful response to pervasive hostility against LGBT youth in schools. GSAs provide support for LGBT students and their allies, and they foster efforts to improve school climates. Results of research to date suggest that membership in a GSA, participation in the activities of a GSA, and even the mere existence of a GSA at a school are all associated with positive outcomes for LGBT students. Whether positive social climates allow GSAs to flourish, whether GSAs improve the social climates of schools in which they operate, or whether both are true is not yet clear. Full understanding of these issues awaits the results of future research.

If the social climates of schools are important to the well-being of LGBT students, how much more significant might broader social climates be? We need to know more about the impact of changing legal and policy environments on LGBT students. Our ability to create safer schools will depend upon school-based initiatives, to be sure, but schools exist within school districts, and districts are supported by taxes that are paid by voters. Making schools safer for LGBT students will thus require the efforts of many people. With politicians, citizens, and educators working together, schools can become safe places where all students can succeed.

Recommendations for Teachers, Administrators, and Lawmakers

Teachers have much to contribute in providing a safe and supportive environment for LGBT youth at school. Teachers can articulate their support for diversity, can use inclusive language, and can refuse to assume that every student is heterosexual. Teachers can furnish their classrooms with images and symbols (such as rainbow flags) that affirm their support of sexual minority students. Teachers can oppose, and if necessary intervene against, bullying or harassment of LGBT students in their school environments. Teachers can agree to sponsor GSAs, and they can support revision of school lessons so as to make them more inclusive of LGBT concerns. In all these ways, teachers can make school environments safer for the LGBT youth who attend them.

Administrators also have an important role in creating safe, supportive schools. Those in administrative roles can conduct school-wide or district-wide assessments of the climate for LGBT students, and can organize professional trainings in areas where they are needed. Administrators can support GSAs, advocate for LGBT-inclusive library resources, and support LGBT-inclusive curricular changes in their schools and districts.

The role of lawmakers is also important. Safe schools laws that prohibit discrimination and harassment on the basis of sexual orientation or gender identity can protect students' access to safe and secure educational environments. Legislators can also go further, as they have in California, to require inclusion of LGBT issues and concerns in the school curriculum. Whether they work at federal, state, or local levels, lawmakers can also insist that school policies and practices are as inclusive of sexual minority students as they are of heterosexual students. With laws and policies to protect their safety, LGBT students are more likely to feel safe at school.

Conclusion

In the United States today, school environments are not always safe for sexual minority students. Despite real progress, much more work remains to be done to create truly inclusive environments in which LGBT students can be as free as their heterosexual peers to grow and learn. In the effort to create LGBT-affirmative environments in the schools, legislators at all levels must work together with teachers and administrators. When lawmakers, teachers, and administrators coordinate their work with that of parents and students, the result can be an improved and enriched experience for all students.

REFERENCES

American Psychological Association. (2008). *Answers to your questions: For a better* Retrieved from www.apa.org/topics/sorientation.pdf

Ball, C. A. (2010). *From the closet to the courtroom: Five LGBT rights lawsuits that have changed our nation.* Boston, MA: Beacon Press.

Bennett, M., & Battle, J. (2001). "We can see them, but we can't hear them": LGBT members of African American families. In M. Bernstein & R. Reimann (Eds.), *Queer families, queer politics: Challenging culture and the state.* New York, NY: Columbia University Press.

Berg-Kelly, K, (2003). Adolescent homosexuality: We need to learn more about causes and consequences. *Acta Paediatrica, 92,* 141–144.

Blake, S., Ledsky, R., Lehman, T., Goodenow, C., Sawyer, R., & Hack, T. (2001). Preventing sexual risk behaviors among gay, lesbian, and bisexual adolescents: The benefits of gay-sensitive HIV instruction in schools. *American Journal of Public Health, 91,* 940–946.

Bostwick, W. B., Meyer, I., Aranda, F., Russell, S., Hughes, T., Birkett, M., & Mustanski, B. (2014). Mental health and suicidality among racially/ethnically diverse sexual minority youths. *American Journal of Public Health, 104,* 1129–1136.

Bridges, E. (2007). The impact of homophobia and racism on GLBTQ youth of color. *Washington, DC: Advocates for Youth.* Retrieved from http://www.lgbt. ucla.edu/documents/Impactof HomophobiaandRacism_000.pdf

Cathcart, R. (2008, February 23). Boy's killing, labeled a hate crime, stuns a town, *New York Times.* Retrieved from http://www.nytimes.com/2008/02/23/us/23oxnard.html

Cianciotto, J., & Cahill, S. (2003). *Education policy: Issues affecting lesbian, gay, bisexual, and transgender youth.* New York, NY: The National Gay and Lesbian Task Force Policy Institute.

Cianciotto, J., & Cahill, S. (2012). *LGBT youth in America's schools.* Ann Arbor, MI: University of Michigan Press.

Diamond, L. M. (2008). Female bisexuality from adolescence to adulthood: Results from a year longitudinal study. *Developmental Psychology, 44,* 5–14.

Diamond, M. (2002). Sex and gender are different: Sexual identity and gender identity are different. *Clinical Child Psychology and Psychiatry, 7,* 320–324.

Eckes, S., DeMitchell, T., & Fossey, R. (2013, March 29). Commentary: A white sport coat and a pink carnation: Protecting the legal rights of LGBT students to attend the prom. *Teachers College Record.* Retrieved from http://www.tcrecord.org/content.asp?ContentID=17072

Espelage, D. L., Aragon, S. R., Birkett, M., & Koenig, B. W. (2008). Homophobic teasing, psychological outcomes, and sexual orientation among high school students: What influence do parents and schools have? *School Psychology Review, 37,* 202–216.

Fetner, T., Elafros, A., Bortolin, S., & Drechsler, C. (2012). Safe spaces: Gay-straight alliances in high schools. *Canadian Review of Sociology/Revue Canadienne de Sociologie, 49,* 188–207.

Fricke, A. (1981). *Reflections of a rock lobster: A story about growing up gay.* Boston, MA: Alyson Press.

Fricke v. Lynch, 491 F. Supp. 381 – Dist. Court, D. Rhode Island 1980.

Gates, G. J. (2011, April). *How many people are lesbian, bisexual, and transgender?* (Research brief). Los Angeles, CA: UCLA Williams Institute.

Gates, G. J. (2013). Demographic perspectives on sexual orientation. In C. J. Patterson & A. R. D'Augelli (Eds.), *Handbook of psychology and sexual orientation.* New York, NY: Oxford University Press.

GenIUSS Group. (2014). *Best practices for asking questions to identify transgender and other gender minority respondents on population-based surveys.* Los Angeles, CA: UCLA Williams Institute.

GLSEN. (2007). *Gay-straight alliances: Creating safer schools for LGBT students and their allies* (Research brief). New York, NY: Gay, Lesbian, and Straight Education Network.

GLSEN. (2009). *The experiences of lesbian, gay, bisexual, and transgender middle school students.* New York, NY: Gay, Lesbian, and Straight Education Network.

GLSEN. (2015a). *States with safe schools laws.* Retrieved from http://www.glsen.org/article/state-maps

GLSEN. (2015b). *GLSEN programs.* Retrieved from http://www.glsen.org/participate/programs

Goodenow, C., Szalacha, L., & Westheimer, K. (2006). School support groups, other school factors, and the safety of sexual minority adolescents. *Psychology in the Schools, 43,* 573–589.

Greytak. E. A., Kosicw, J. G., & Jerman, K. (2008). *No name-calling project: Year four evaluation.* Retrieved from http://www.glsen.org/sites/default/files/NNCW%20Year%204%20Eval.pdf

Greytak, E. A., & Kosciw, J. G. (2010). *Year one evaluation of the New York City Department of Education Respect for All training program.* Retrieved from: http://glsen.org/sites/default/files/NYC%20Respect%20for%20All%20Training%20Evaluation.pdf

Grov, C., Bimbi, D. S., Nanin, J. E., & Parsons, J. T. (2006). Race, ethnicity, gender, and generational factors associated with the coming-out process among gay, lesbian, and bisexual individuals. *Journal of Sex Research, 43,* 115–121.

Hatzenbuehler, M. L., Birkett, M., van Wagenen, A., & Meyer, I. H. (2014). Protective school climates and reduced risk for suicide ideation among sexual minority youths. *American Journal of Public Health, 104,* 279–286.

Hatzenbuehler, M. L., Hirsch, J., Parker, R., Nathanson, C., & Fairchild, A. (2014). The mental health consequences of anti-bullying policies. In P. Goldblum, D.

Espelage, J. Chu, & B. Bongar (Eds.), *The challenge of youth suicide and bullying.* New York, NY: Oxford University Press.

Hatzenbuehler, M. L., & Keyes, K. M. (2013). Inclusive anti-bullying policies and reduced risk of suicide attempts in lesbian and gay youth. *Journal of Adolescent Health, 53,* 521–526.

Heck, N. C., Flentje, A., & Cochran, B. N. (2011). Offsetting risks: High school gay-straight alliances and lesbian, gay, bisexual, and transgender (LGBT) youth. *School Psychology Quarterly, 26,* 161–174.

HRC (Human Rights Campaign). (2012). *Growing up LGBT in America.* Retrieved from http://hrc-assets.s3-website-us-east-1.amazonaws.com//files/assets/resources/Growing-Up-LGBT-in-America_Report.pdf

HRC (Human Rights Campaign). (2015). *Safe schools improvement act.* Retrieved from www.hrc.org/resources/entry/safe-schools-improvement-act

IOM (Institute of Medicine). (2011). *The health of lesbian, gay, bisexual, and transgender people: Building a foundation for better understanding.* Washington, DC: The National Academies Press.

Johnston, M. (2014, December 31). Transgender teen Leelah Alcorn: "My death needs to mean something." *Boston Globe.* Retrieved from: http://www.bostonglobe.com/lifestyle/2014/12/31/transgender-teen-leelah-alcorn-death-needs-mean-something/4hw6uPd8NtjIbn8kAdyAbM/story.html

Kosciw, J. G., & Diaz, E. M. (2006). *The 2005 national school climate study.* New York, NY: GLSEN.

Kosciw, J. G., Diaz, E. M., Colic, D. M., & Goldin, R. (2005). *No name-calling project: Year four evaluation.* Retrieved from: http://www.glsen.org/sites/default/files/NNCW%20Year%20One%20Evaluation.pdf

Kosciw, J. G., Diaz, E. M., & Greytak, E. A. (2008). *2007 National school climate survey: The experiences of lesbian, gay, bisexual, and transgender youth in our nation's schools.* New York, NY: GLSEN.

Kosciw, J. G., Greytak, E. A., Diaz, E. M., & Bartkiewicz, M. J. (2010). *The 2009 national school climate survey: The experiences of lesbian, gay, bisexual and transgender youth in our nation's schools.* New York, NY: GLSEN.

Kosciw, J. G., Greytak, E. A., Palmer, N. A. & Boesen, M. J. (2014). *2013 national school climate survey: The experiences of lesbian, gay, bisexual, and transgender youth in our nation's schools.* New York, NY: GLSEN.

Lovett, I. (2011, July 14). California to require gay history in schools. *New York Times.* Retrieved from www.nytimes.com/2011/07/15/us/15gay.html.2

MacGillivray, I. K. (2007). *Gay-straight alliances: A handbook for students, educators, and parents.* New York, NY: Routledge.

Massachusetts Department of Education. (2002). *2001 Massachusetts youth risk behavior survey results.* Malden, MA: Author. Retrieved from http://www.doe.mass.edu/hssss/yrbs/01/results.pdf

Mayo, C. (2013). *LGBTQ youth and education: Policies and practices.* New York, NY: Teachers College Press.

McCabe, J., Brewster, K. L., & Tillman, K. H. (2011). Patterns and correlates of same-sex sexual activity among U.S. teenagers and young adults. *Perspectives on Sexual and Reproductive Health, 43,* 142–150.

McGuire, J. K., Anderson, C. R., Toomey, R. B., & Russell, S. T. (2010). School climate for transgender youth: A mixed method investigation of student experiences and school responses. *Journal of Youth and Adolescence, 39,* 1175–1188.

McMillen v. Itawamba County School District. 2010 U.S. Dist. LEXIS 27589 (N. D. Miss. 2010).

Mezey, S. G. (2009). *Gay families and the courts: The quest for equal rights.* Boston, MA: Rowman & Littlefield.

Mustanski, B., Birkett, M., Greene, G. J., Rosario, M., Bostwick, W., & Everett, B. G. (2014). The association between sexual orientation identity and behavior across race/ethnicity, sex, and age in a probability sample of high school students. *American Journal of Public Health, 104,* 237–244.

Owens, E. (2013, February 19). High school will change policy so gay student can bring boyfriend to prom. Washington, DC: *The Daily Caller.*

Palmer, N. A., Kosciw, J. G., & Bartkiewicz, M. J. (2012). *Strengths and silences: The experiences of lesbian, gay, bisexual and transgender students in rural and small town schools.* New York, NY: GLSEN.

Parker, I. (2012, February 6). The story of a suicide. *The New Yorker.* Retrieved from http://www.newyorker.com/magazine/2012/02/06/the-story-of-a-suicide

Peter, T., Taylor, C., Ristock, J., & Edkins, T. (2015). Pride and prejudice: Factors affecting school attachment among lesbian, bisexual, and heterosexual girls. *Journal of Lesbian Studies, 19,* 249–273.

Poteat, V. P., Sinclair, K. O., DiGiovanni, C. D., Koenig, B. W., & Russell, S. T. (2013). Gay-straight alliances are associated with student health: A multischool comparison of LGBTQ and heterosexual youth. *Journal of Research on Adolescence, 23,* 319–330.

Poteat, V. P., Yoshikawa, H., Calzo, J. P., Gray, M. L., DiGiovanni, C. D., Lipkin, A., . . . Shaw, M. P. (2015). Contextualizing gay-straight alliances: Student, advisor, and structural factors related to positive youth development among members. *Child Development, 86,* 176–193.

Potts, A. (2014, June 5). California school district pays out $750,000 over bullied teen's suicide. London, England: *Gay Star News.*

Rieger, G., & Savin-Williams, R. C. (2011). Gender nonconformity, sexual orientation, and psychological well-being. *Archives of Sexual Behavior, 39*(6), 611–621.

Riskind, R. G., Tornello, S. L., Younger, B. C., & Patterson, C. J. (2014). Sexual identity, partner gender, and sexual health among adolescent girls in the United States. *American Journal of Public Health, 104,* 1957–1963.

Robinson, J. P., & Espelage, D. L. (2011). Inequities in educational and psychological outcomes between LGBTQ and straight students in middle and high school. *Educational Researcher, 40,* 315–330.

Robson, R. (2013). *Dressing constitutionally: Hierarchy, sexuality, and democracy from our hairstyles to our shoes.* New York, NY: Cambridge University Press.

Rosario, M., & Schrimshaw, E. W. (2013). The sexual identity development and health of lesbian, gay, and bisexual adolescents: An ecological perspective. In C. J. Patterson & A. R. D'Augelli (Eds.), *Handbook of psychology and sexual orientation.* New York, NY: Oxford University Press.

Russell, S. T. (2002). Queer in America: Citizenship for sexual minority youth. *Applied Developmental Science, 6,* 258–263.

Russell, S. T., Driscoll, A. K., & Truong, N. (2002). Adolescent same-sex romantic attractions and relationships: Implications for substance use and abuse. *American Journal of Public Health, 92,* 198–202.

Russell, S. T., Franz, B. T., & Driscoll, A. K. (2001). Same-sex romantic attraction and experiences of violence in adolescence. *American Journal of Public Health, 91,* 903.

Russell, S. T., & Joyner, K. (2001). Adolescent sexual orientation and suicide risk: Evidence from a national study. *American Journal of Public Health, 91,* 1276–1281.

Russell, S. T., Kosciw, J., Horn, S., & Saewyc, E. (2010). Safe schools policy for LGBTQ students. *SRCD Social Policy Report, 24*(4).

Russell, S. T., Muraco, A., Subramaniam, A. & Laub, C. (2009). Youth empowerment and high school gay-straight alliances. *Journal of Youth and Adolescence, 38,* 891–903.

Savin-Williams, R. C. (2006). Who's gay? Does it matter? *Current Directions in Psychological Science, 15,* 40–44.

Savin-Williams, R. C. (2008). Then and now: Recruitment, definition, diversity, and positive attributes of same-sex populations. *Developmental Psychology, 44,* 135–138.

Szalacha, L. A. (2003). Safer sexual diversity climates: Lessons learned from an evaluation of Massachusetts Safe Schools Program for gay and lesbian students. *American Journal of Education, 110,* 58–88.

Thompson, E. M., & Morgan, E. M. (2008). "Mostly straight" young women: Variations in sexual behavior and identity development. *Developmental Psychology, 44,* 15–21.

Toomey, R. B., McGuire, J. K., & Russell, S. T. (2012). Heteronormativity, school climates, and perceived safety for gender nonconforming peers. *Journal of Adolescence, 35,* 187–196.

Toomey, R. B., & Russell, S. T. (2011). Gay-straight alliances, social justice involvement, and school victimization of lesbian, gay, bisexual, and queer youth: Implications for school well-being and plans to vote. *Youth and Society, 45*(4), 500–522.

Toomey, R. B., Ryan, C., Diaz, R. M., Card, N. A., & Russell, S. T. (2010). Gender-nonconforming lesbian, gay, bisexual, and transgender youth: School victimization and young adult psychosocial adjustment. *Developmental Psychology, 46,* 1580–1589.

Toomey, R. B., Ryan, C., Diaz, R. M. & Russell, S. T. (2011). High school gay-straight alliances (GSAs) and young adult well-being: An examination of GSA presence, participation, and perceived effectiveness. *Applied Developmental Science, 15,* 175–185.

Tornello, S. L., Riskind, R. G., & Patterson, C. J. (2014). Sexual orientation and sexual and reproductive health among adolescent young women in the United States. *Journal of Adolescent Health, 54,* 160–168.

Vaccaro, A., August, G., & Kennedy, M. S. (2012). *Safe spaces: Making schools and communities welcoming to LGBT youth.* New York, NY: Praeger.

Vermont Department of Health Office of Alcohol and Drug Abuse Programs. (2002). *2001 Vermont youth risk behavior survey.* Burlington, VT: Author. Retrieved from http://www.state.vt.us/health/adap/pubs/2001/yrbs2001.pdf

Walls, N. E., Kane, S. B., & Wisneski, H. (2010). Gay-straight alliances and school experiences of sexual minority youth. *Youth & Society, 41,* 307–332.

Zhao, Y., Montoro, R., Igartua, K., & Thombs, B. D. (2010). Suicidal ideation and attempt among adolescents reporting "unsure" sexual identity or heterosexual identity plus same-sex attraction or behavior: Forgotten groups? *Journal of the American Academy of Child & Adolescent Psychiatry, 49,* 104–113.

CHAPTER 5

YOUTHS OF POVERTY

Bruce J. Biddle
University of Missouri (Professor Emeritus)

This chapter concerns what is now known about two huge, closely related but widely ignored social problems that create a disaster for America and its educational system. In brief, the United States generates an enormous amount of youth poverty: each year more than a fifth of all young Americans experience poverty. Such a poverty rate is far higher than comparable poverty rates for adults and the elderly in the United States, and the American youth poverty rate greatly exceeds those for youths in all other advanced nations. Because serious burdens are associated with poverty, youth impoverishment is the key factor responsible for educational failure in America. It generates many of the apparent negative academic effects of student race and ethnicity, broken homes, lack of parental education, and the supposed failures of teachers and school administrators in the United States; ruins lives for millions of Americans; and creates serious, derivative problems for the country at large.

More than a thousand studies have now appeared focused on these closely-related problems and attracting sharply conflicting claims about their findings and implications from advocates representing the Left (who favor public efforts to alleviate social problems) and the Right (who do not). But so far these studies, findings, and claims have created little media

Educational Policies and Youth in the 21st Century, pages 81–102
Copyright © 2016 by Information Age Publishing
All rights of reproduction in any form reserved.

interest in the issues they represent; no full-scale, public discussions of them have yet appeared; and current American policies bearing on youths and educational "reform" reveal little understanding of the astounding scope of youth poverty in the country and the key role it plays in generating educational failure.

This ignorance greatly distorts thinking about success and failure. Americans have long believed that their country offers "opportunities for all," that youths in their country can succeed if they have sufficient talent, motivation, and access to education, and that, when appropriately conducted, American public schools provide a "level playing field" where students can acquire the knowledge and qualifications needed for success. These beliefs reflect admirable goals, but they do not describe the world inhabited by America's impoverished youths and the educators who serve them. And unless thoughtful citizens become aware of the facts concerning the country's astounding rate of youth poverty and its harmful effects in public schools, they will continue to tolerate social policies that perpetuate or worsen the youth-poverty-generated disaster that now besets the United States.

I write, therefore, to provide brief summaries of findings that have appeared concerning these problems and to discuss implications of those findings. Of necessity, my coverage of such issues is sketchy in this brief chapter. Those seeking further information should consult my recent book on the topic (Biddle, 2014) or thoughtful summary works that have focused on key aspects of the disaster, such as those of Bergmann (1996), Berliner & Biddle (1995), Books (2004), Bracey (2003), Carter & Welner (2013), Children's Defense Fund (2002), Darling-Hammond (2010), Duncan & Brooks-Gunn (1997), Duncan & Murnane (2011), Gornick & Meyers (2003), Huston (1991), Iceland (2003), National Commission on Children (1991), Polakow (1993), Rainwater & Smeeding (2003), Ravitch (2013), or Sherman (1997).

YOUTH POVERTY IN AMERICA: HOW SERIOUS IS IT?

Although many good-hearted Americans seem not to be aware of it, youth poverty poses an enormous problem for their country. Controversies have arisen over how to define and assess poverty, but all measures used for this purpose indicate that each year during the past decade, at least a fifth of Americans under the age of 18 years—thus 15 million, or more realistically 20 million or more infants, toddlers, children, and adolescents—lived in impoverished families or households, and this huge, ongoing problem was tolerated in the "World's Most Successful Nation."

There are several ways to think about America's astounding youth poverty rate. For one, more youths in the United States currently suffer from poverty than from all known diseases plus other physical and social disadvantages combined. Again, during at least the past three decades, the country's poverty rate for youths has been roughly twice its poverty rates for adults and the elderly. This was not always the case. Prior to the mid 1970s, the elderly were America's most impoverished age group, but poverty among retirees was thereafter slashed by the effects of Social Security, Medicare, and other federal programs that provide supports for this vulnerable age group; whereas America's youth poverty rate shot upwards during the 1970s, and comparable support programs have never been provided for America's youngsters.

Another way is to ask whether, as common stereotypes would have it, youth poverty in America is largely the result of fecklessness among African Americans and other supposedly "deficient" minority groups or is the product of dangerous urban slums in America's major cities. But it turns out that neither of these ugly beliefs is accurate. True, African American youths do have somewhat higher rates of poverty, as do Hispanic youths and those from other disadvantaged communities, but the bulk of America's youths are currently White, and roughly two thirds of all American youths who currently experience poverty are of White, Anglo-Saxon origin. And although slightly less than half of all youth poverty cases appear in America's central cities, nearly a third come from the suburbs, and fully a quarter are to be found in rural towns, southwestern barrios, Appalachian "hollows," Indian reservations, and other ex-urban venues. Truly, youth poverty is an all-American problem.

Some have also argued that poverty may not be "all that bad" in affluent America; indeed it may provide a needed incentive to work harder and improve one's lot in a society where individual enterprise is rewarded. But these arguments are astoundingly off base when it comes to America's youths. Poverty is not a benign experience for those who are young and impoverished, for they are subject to a huge span of serious problems that blight their lives.

Many of these problems reflect serious issues in the homes or other venues where impoverished youths live. To illustrate:

- During each of recent years, roughly 2.5 million impoverished young Americans experienced family homelessness—were forced to "double up" temporarily with other families in crowded quarters, to live in cars or "on the street," and/or to face frequent, disruptive relocations in their lives.

Those lucky enough to escape homelessness often lived in houses that were older, overcrowded, dilapidated, poorly heated, and vermin-infested where

they were exposed to serious toxins that create asthma and can permanently damage their minds or bodies. For example:

- At present, roughly half a million impoverished American youngsters between 1 and 5 years of age suffer from elevated levels of lead
  poisoning (generated by dust from aging, uncovered wall paint)
  that are known to cause learning disabilities, hyperactivity, behavioral disorders, metabolic and kidney damage, and mental retardation.

As well, hunger and inadequate nutrition are all-too predictable experiences for impoverished American youngsters. Again:

- Each year, some 8 million impoverished American families suffer from
  at least monthly "food insufficiency," which means that youngsters in
  those families are subject to the ravages of hunger, lassitude, vitamin
  deficiencies, stunted growth, and the diseases of malnutrition.

Preventive health care is also expensive in America, so by comparison with
middle- or upper-income youngsters, those who are impoverished are more
likely to suffer from chronic, untreated physical, mental, dental, visual, and
auditory problems. Their parents and caregivers are also more likely to be
undereducated and to be stressed by the demands of insecure, low-paying
jobs, and this means that they often can provide only "limited linguistic
environments" in their homes, which lead in turn to restricted vocabulary
acquisition and retarded brain development among impoverished infants
and toddlers. And if these problems were not sufficient, impoverished
homes are plagued by chronic shortages of books, writing materials, and
even the basic clothing needed for "making it" in America's neighborhoods
and schools.

Other problems appear in the ghettoed neighborhoods where those
youths often live: environments in which poverty and despair are endemic,
basic social services are missing, adult role models who portray legal success
images are in short supply, and deadly violence fueled by gang warfare may
be daily experiences. And still other problems are created by conditions in
the schools they often attend: academic environments in which the overwhelming bulk of students are also impoverished and alienated; per-capita
support for student education is a third or less of that provided for education in more-affluent neighborhoods; and tracking or other discriminatory
practices, traditional in American education, persist.

Few impoverished youths encounter the full panoply of these problems,
of course, but all have to face at least some of them, and those experiencing longer-lasting and deeper poverty will be brutalized by many of them.
And this means that America has organized its society so that impoverished

youths must bear a host of often-serious burdens not borne by youths from middle-income or affluent homes. As a result:

> Poverty stacks the odds against [American] children.... It stunts their physical growth and slows their educational development; frays their family bonds and wears down their resilience and emotional reserves; saps their spirits and sense of self; and subjects them over time to physical, mental, and emotional assault and indignity. Poverty even kills. Low-income children are [far more likely to die, and poverty] stalks its survivors down every avenue of their lives. It places them at greater risk of hunger, homelessness, sickness, physical and mental disability, violence, educational failure, teen parenthood and family stress, and deprives them of positive early childhood experiences that help prepare more affluent children for school and then college and work. (Edelman, 1994, pp. xvi-xvii)

Thus, by generating an enormous amount of youth poverty, the United States condemns literally millions of its youngest, most vulnerable citizens to experiences that will debase their lives and prevent them from ever making the badly needed contributions to science, the arts, industry, social services, and civic leadership that they might otherwise have made. And when America's teenagers respond to poverty by dropping out of school, engaging in early and unprotected sex, embracing illegal drugs, and joining violence-prone street gangs, they become major actors in dramas that generate the country's huge rates of unwanted pregnancy, venereal disease, drug addiction, murder, incarceration in prisons, and early death. These latter problems create mammoth costs for the society at large, and like others in the country, middle- and upper-income Americans pay dearly for these costs.

IS YOUTH POVERTY INEVITABLE?

Some Americans have been tempted to argue that high rates of poverty should be expected in advanced industrialized democracies, so that America's huge rate of youth poverty is more or less inevitable. But is this true? Answers for this question are available from leading international agencies such as the Luxembourg Income Study Group (LIS), the Organisation for Economic Co-operation and Development (OECD), and the United Nations Children's Fund (UNICEF), which regularly publish reports about problems in the industrialized world.

Some of these reports compare youth-poverty rates among advanced nations, and strikingly all of the latter conclude that the United States generates by far the highest national youth poverty rate in the advanced world. To illustrate, in a recent report which compared youth poverty rates among

22 advanced nations, UNICEF (2005) estimated that the American youth poverty rate was a whopping 21.9%; whereas those of the other English-speaking nations (Australia, Canada, Ireland, New Zealand, and the United Kingdom) ranged from 16.3% to 14.7%; those of Japan, as well as countries in central and southern Europe, varied from 16.6% to 6.8%; and the four Scandinavian nations (Denmark, Finland, Norway, and Sweden) generated vanishingly low rates of 4.2% to 2.4%.

Why on earth should America generate such a high youth poverty rate, and why are rates so much lower elsewhere? Impoverished youngsters come, of course, from impoverished households, so to find an answer we must examine how advanced nations differ in their treatment of the three crucial components of low-income households' net resources: the incomes those households earn, the taxes and fees they pay out for social benefits, and the social benefits they receive in return. When this is done, we discover that the United States comes up short in all three of these realms.

Household Incomes

For openers, many studies have found that low-income workers are paid sharply lower incomes in the United States than in other advanced nations. In part, this disparity reflects uniquely weak American customs bearing on minimal wages that can be paid to workers. (To illustrate, *in* America, the federal minimum wage is determined by occasional political haggling in Congress, applies only to workers in some industries, is not rigidly enforced, and is currently set at $7.25 per hour. Whereas in Australia, the federal minimum wage is reset annually by an independent tribunal, applies to all workers in the land, is rigidly enforced, and is currently set at about $16 per hour.) But also, the insufficient and shrinking wages of low-income Americans are a product of well-financed, political processes and corrupt congressional decision-making that, since the 1970s, have been transferring ever-larger shares of income and wealth, away from low- and middle-income Americans, and into the pockets of America's super-rich.

Thus, today

> the United States suffers from greater earnings and income inequality, higher poverty rates, and less movement out of poverty than almost every other OECD economy. Due to the highly unequal distribution of income in the United States, low-wage workers and low-income households are almost universally worse off in absolute terms than their low-wage, low-income counterparts in other less-affluent OECD countries. (Mishel, Bernstein, & Allegretto, 2005, p. 421)

Household Assessments

Unfortunately, the American picture does not improve when we turn to taxes and fees paid by low-income households. All advanced nations pay at least lip service to the notion that national governments should be responsible for aiding those who are truly needy, and in practice this means that resources must regularly be transferred from those who have to those who have not. Most advanced countries begin this process by collecting nationwide income taxes and fees for some services (such as retirement or unemployment benefits) that are progressive in nature—that assign higher rates to those who are affluent and lower or nil rates to those who are needy. But this simple and humane practice breaks down when it comes to the United States. In earlier years, America's federal income taxes were indeed progressive, but actions by Congress since the 1970s have inserted so many loopholes into the tax code that affluent Americans now pay federal income taxes at rates that are lower than those paid by low- and middle-income Americans. Most American earners also pay federal fees that help support Social Security and Medicare, but rates for these assessments are capped at the upper end, so those who are affluent again pay proportionately *less* to support these benefits. And unlike in most advanced nations, the bulk of Americans also pay additional income taxes to the state (and sometimes the city) in which they live, and many of these local taxes are either assessed at flat rates or are again capped so that high-income earners pay lower rates, and so it goes. Thus, low-income American workers and their families shoulder larger tax and fee burdens than low-income workers and families in other advanced countries.

Household Benefits

Nor does the picture improve when we examine benefits received by low-income households. For convenience, let us sort such benefits into those that do and do not involve cash payments.

The typical advanced country now supports low-income families by providing several types of nationally-funded cash benefits that respond to specific needs, but these customs vary from nation to nation. To illustrate:

- All advanced nations pay unemployment benefits to workers who have just lost their jobs—cash awards that are substantial and long-lasting in many countries, but are both skimpy and politically controversial in America.

- Many advanced nations have also set up national programs that provide housing benefits—cash assistance to support rental housing for low-income families—but the United States has not done so.
- All other advanced nations provide universal family allowance benefits—cash awards that are paid directly to all families with young children in the home—but America does not.
- Some advanced nations also provide dedicated child care benefits—cash assistance to support child care for low income families—but the United States does not.
- Some advanced nations also provide single-parent benefits—cash awards for single mothers (and/or fathers) who live with children—but the United States does not.
- All advanced countries except the United States also provide additional social assistance benefits—cash supports for needy people or families who lack access to other types of cash resources—whereas America currently provides only food stamps for impoverished families and school-based free or reduced-price lunches for impoverished kids, and even the latter supports are skimpy, controversial, and politically threatened.

Thus, the typical advanced nation has set up multiple programs that provide low-income individuals and their families with secure, supplemental cash supports, but such programs are absent, minimal, or threatened in the United States, and this means that low-income American youngsters are far more likely to live in anxiety-prone, cash-starved homes.

In addition, other advanced nations also provide low-income families with various forms of noncash benefits that are weak or missing in America. For example: All advanced countries support one of more forms of tax-supported daycare and preschool facilities that provide support for families, relief for frantic parents, and educational advantages for infants and toddlers. Such facilities are hugely popular among middle-income families, and they provide crucial help for those with low incomes, but advanced countries vary greatly in the strengths of their daycare and preschool programs. In some nations (France, Belgium, the Netherlands, and the Nordic countries, for example), such facilities tend to serve both infants and toddlers, to be conducted by trained and licensed personnel, to be available throughout the land and open to all children, and to receive generous support from taxes. But support for such facilities is far weaker in other countries, such as the United States. Tax support is not now available for the bulk of America's daycare and preschool facilities, which of necessity serve only families who can afford to pay for their services. America's few, tax-supported Head Start facilities—designed to serve toddlers from low-income families—are but weakly funded and are often staffed by unlicensed persons with minimal training and qualifications. Thus, the United States is one of several advanced nations where support for daycare and preschool facilities is minimal.

Again, most advanced countries also mandate various forms of paid leaves from work for needy parents or other adult caregivers. Outside of the United States, paid maternity leaves are always available, which help mothers with late-term pregnancies, parturition, childbirth, and care for newborn infants. In addition, some advanced nations also mandate paid paternity leaves so that fathers can help when births occur. Others countries require that paid emergency leaves be awarded to all adults who must cope with the illnesses or other serious crises of themselves, children, spouses, or partners; some nations make separate, extended leave provisions for workers with dependents who become disabled or chronically ill. Laws such as these generate benefits for all families, but these benefits provide crucially needed aid for low-income families who are often headed by single parents or parents who must work at demanding, inflexible, and insecure jobs. Alone among advanced nations, America has passed no national laws mandating such paid leaves—although the United States recently decided that mothers are entitled to at least unpaid maternity leaves—and this lack of support for paid leaves creates burdens for low-income American families that are unique in the industrialized world.

And again, alone among advanced countries, the United States does not now have a universal, tax-supported, national health care system, and this too creates problems that do not appear elsewhere. For one thing, Americans spend at least a third more per capita for health care than do persons from any other advanced nation. (Privately-owned insurance companies that provide no health services cumber up health care in the United States, and the American public pays dearly for the bureaucratic and profit-making costs they generate. Prescription drugs also cost far more in the United States because of corrupt decisions by Congress that have reflected interests of big pharmaceutical firms.) For another, America's modest tax-supported, healthcare programs (Medicare, Medicaid, SCHIP, and healthcare services for top-level federal employees) serve only limited groups, and most Americans must either fork out precious, post-tax dollars for health insurance, hope and pray that they don't get sick, or—when things get too bad—appear as indigent patients in the emergency rooms of public hospitals. As well, the American health "system" provides but few incentives to set up preventive healthcare facilities—common in other advanced countries—so Americans suffer from more preventable diseases, and average life expectancies are less for both men and women in the United States. And all these problems fall more heavily on low-income American families who are more often plagued by lack of preventive health care, serious but treatable diseases, chronic health problems, early deaths, and health-associated fiscal disasters than equivalent families in other advanced nations.

To summarize then, the huge American youth poverty rate is not inevitable. Rather, it is much higher in the United States than in other advanced nations because the low-income households in which those youths live suffer from uniquely low wages, uniquely high taxes, and uniquely weak supports in the forms of cash and noncash benefits. American youth poverty could be sharply reduced if the United States were to adopt even some of the poverty-reducing practices that are common elsewhere, but most Americans seem to be unaware that these boons are widely available in the rest of the advanced world.

HOME POVERTY AND EDUCATIONAL FAILURE

Given the many burdens associated with poverty, it is hardly surprising that youth poverty and educational failure are associated in America, but how strong is this association, and does youth poverty truly cause educational failure?

Over the years, many studies have claimed to examine the association between youth poverty and educational failure, but these have reported a surprising range of conclusions about the association, and this has generated both confusion and contradictory claims about the importance of youth poverty. On close examination, however, it turns out that many early studies did not assess youth poverty itself, but rather examined "convenient," proxy variables assumed to mirror that poverty—measures of general family "disadvantage" or socioeconomic status, parental education, reported family income, and the like—and findings of weak associations between poverty and failure generally came from these "convenience" studies. In contrast, recent, better-constructed studies have actually assessed youth poverty, and these have consistently reported strong associations between youth poverty and educational failure and higher failure rates when youth poverty is deeper and lasts longer. Thus, we may safely conclude that youth poverty and educational failure are, indeed, strongly tied.

But does poverty actually cause youths to fail in America's schools? A clear answer for this question is crucial. Although good-hearted Americans may believe that the evil effects of poverty are obvious and brutal, advocates for the Right have argued that poverty is nothing but a symptom of underlying, personal or ethnic deficiencies, and that any attempt to improve education by reducing poverty is equivalent to "throwing money out the window." But is this ugly argument tenable?

Impoverished youths come from homes that suffer from poverty, of course, and evidence from many types of studies support the claim that home poverty is, indeed, a strong cause of educational failure in America:

- Panel studies find that longer spells of family poverty, increasing severity of that poverty, and early poverty experiences are all associated with higher educational failure rates for students from those families.
- Studies using statistical controls find that ties between home poverty and educational failure are not eliminated when other major "risk" factors—such as single parenthood, minority racial status, or lack of parental education—are included in the picture. They find, instead, that poverty generates the strongest effects and often accounts for much the apparent impacts of other "risk" factors.
- Studies of potential pathways find that the link between home poverty and educational failure is generated, in part, by easy-to-understand problems associated with poverty, such as inferior housing, poor nutrition and lack of food, linguistic insufficiency, restricted resources for education in the home, parental stress reactions, or the outrageous costs of higher education in the United States.
- Field experiments find that when poverty in the home is alleviated, students are less likely to fail in education.

Given these many types of evidence, the countercausal arguments of advocates from the Right become laughable. Indeed, "denying the significance of poverty in schooling in the face of decades of research, testimony, and common sense requires profound naiveté or a frightening level of willed ignorance" (Books, 2004, p. 134).

NEIGHBORHOOD POVERTY AND EDUCATIONAL FAILURE

Unlike many other advanced nations, the United States has also long tolerated, indeed encouraged, the presence of ghettoed neighborhoods that are segregated by income (and often by race, ethnicity, religion, or national origin). This means that impoverished American youths are often forced to live in homes located in neighborhoods where they encounter additional, serious, poverty-associated problems.

To illustrate, poverty ghettos generate environments in which youths rarely encounter others who are not also impoverished; employment opportunities are restricted; alternative lifestyles are in short supply; vanishingly few adult role models are present who portray success in legally acceptable terms; and deadly violence, fueled by drugs and gang warfare, may be omnipresent. As well, basic social services—street cleaning, transportation facilities, police and fire protection, parks, libraries, and even shops that offer food and other necessities at reasonable prices—are often missing in poverty ghettos.

Although these problems are widely discussed, surprisingly little research has yet appeared on most of them and their effects. Good surveys and panel studies have appeared, however, which confirm that impoverished youths do better in education when their neighborhoods provide access to other persons who are advantaged, and that this effect is stronger when neighborhood poverty is extreme. As well, one or two field experiments have reported that educational prospects for impoverished youths improve when help is provided that enables their families to relocate out of poverty ghettos. These studies are promising, but a lot more research on impoverished neighborhoods is now needed.

POVERTY IN SCHOOLS AND EDUCATIONAL FAILURE

As well, impoverished youths also encounter several types of serious problems when they enter the doors of America's public schools, and extensive traditions of research have explored how these problems debase educational prospects for those youths.

Intense Poverty Concentration

Because American public schools serve their immediate neighborhoods, schools in poverty ghettos are often overwhelmed by large numbers of impoverished students, and this generates derivative effects. Schools with intense concentrations of impoverished students are often plagued by alienation and violence, disorganized classrooms, weak academic standards, and low morale as well as rapid turnover among the teaching staff. These effects create a predictable toll. As a rule, such schools generate low levels of academic success for all students, and crucial studies have shown that this effect piles additional burdens onto the backs of students who come from impoverished homes.

Concern about poverty concentration is widespread among America's educators, and Herculean efforts to reduce its vicious impact have appeared in some schools and school systems. To truly solve its problems, however, one must either set up busing programs that redistribute impoverished and nonimpoverished students among nearby schools or take steps to dismantle the ghettos that currently create high levels of scholastic poverty concentration in some of America's neediest neighborhoods.

Miserable School Funding

A second focus of research on school-based problems faced by impoverished youths concerns school funding. As it happens, the United States also differs from other advanced nations in how it funds education. Elsewhere public schools are supported by national, state, or provincial funds that are either awarded to all schools equally, throughout the land, based on the numbers of students they enroll, or are supplemented with "extra loadings" when schools must serve large numbers of "disadvantaged" students. But this humane picture breaks down when it comes to the United States In all but one American state (Hawaii), the bulk of funding for public schools comes from local school districts and is typically generated by taxes based on property values. But this means that, in mainland America, public schools in affluent districts receive three or more times as much per-student funding as schools in impoverished districts, and as a result, within America one finds some of the world's best-funded, most innovative, best equipped and staffed, highly attractive, public schools as well as far too many badly underfunded, unsafe and filthy, poorly staffed and equipped, depressing and dangerous, educational hovels—also public schools—that would not be tolerated in other advanced countries. And (surprise!) impoverished students are more often enrolled in the latter, miserably-funded schools.

American funding practices are controversial, of course, and educators as well as advocates for youths have long mounted state-level campaigns seeking greater funding equity. These efforts are resisted by the rich (and their advocates) who often see little reason why they should pay additional taxes to improve education for youths from "other" communities who may come from "the wrong" minority groups. This resistance takes several forms, but one of the strangest is to argue that the level of school funding really doesn't matter, that evidence does not support the claim that inadequate school funding throttles academic success! This argument makes little sense, but it surfaced in the 1980s in a set of articles by a young and inexperienced economist (who based his reasoning on a deeply-flawed "review" of early, poorly constructed studies). It was thereafter touted by Secretary of Education William Bennett in the Reagan administration, and has since become an unquestioned linchpin of far Right educational thought.

But what does research actually say about the issue? Not surprisingly, all subsequent, well-constructed studies and reviews of relevant research have concluded that levels of scholastic funding and academic success are strongly associated in America. As well, crucial evidence indicates that this association is also causal, and that inadequate school funding also creates additional burdens for impoverished students that add to those they bring with them when they enter the schoolhouse door.

Regarding the issue of causality, the strongest evidence has come from hundreds of studies that have found strong ties between funding-associated school resources and measures of educational success. To illustrate:

- Better funding allows schools to pay higher salaries to teachers and to recruit and retain those with more experience, stronger qualifications, and better teaching skills, and well-constructed studies have found that each of these factors is associated with academic benefits for students.
- Better funding can also allow schools to hire more staff, and multiple studies have found that a higher staff–student ratio is associated with better student outcomes.
- Better funding can allow schools to reduce the numbers of students taught in classrooms, and—although this issue was once controversial—impressive studies (including the largest field experiment ever reported for education!) now report that smaller classes generate substantial and long-lasting academic benefits for primary students, and that these benefits are stronger for students who suffer from poverty or other forms of educational disadvantage.
- Better funding can also be used to set up or enhance strong preschool programs in school districts, and abundant research indicates that such programs generate improved educational outcomes for both advantaged and (especially for) disadvantaged students.

Those concerned with equity in American education have strongly supported legal and political attempts to revise America's school funding practices, but to date the courts, the legislatures, and the school boards of the nation have often been more interested in preserving "tradition," honoring the nonsensical arguments of far-Right advocates, and serving the presumed needs and prejudices of the rich, so miserable funding for public schools that serve disadvantaged students has remained a tenacious feature of American education.

Multiply-Disadvantaged Schools

Extreme poverty concentration and miserable funding may not appear in the same schools, of course, and what are the effects when this happens? Very little research has yet addressed this question, but these two types of scholastic disadvantage are frequently imposed on the same hapless schools, and it is clear that vicious problems are created when this happens. Heartbreaking descriptions of these problems may be found in various sources such as the writings of Jonathan Kozol (1991, 1995, 2005), and needless to say, these problems create huge burdens for students.

As well, the fact that multiply-disadvantaged schools appear only in America bears on how one should interpret findings from studies that report national differences in student achievement. Scary reports from such studies often indicate that the United States does not generate the world's highest level of average student achievement—that average achievement levels are significantly greater in some other nations—and these reports have provoked alarms, stimulated calls for the reform of various features of American education, and provided fodder for far Right forces seeking to rubbish public schools.

But responses such as these all miss the point. When the United States tolerates the presence of multiply-disadvantaged schools, it generates huge differences in achievement among its public schools, an effect confirmed directly by data from at least one comparative study (Mullis, et al., 2001). This study reported average scores for 8th-grade mathematics achievement, not only for a host of nations, but also for selected American school districts, and—lo—these data showed that affluent American school districts where schools enjoy many advantages generated achievement scores that were among "the best in the world," whereas impoverished districts with multiply-disadvantaged schools earned achievement scores comparable only to those from third-world countries. So, although it may make sense to report average achievement scores for other advanced nations (where multiply-disadvantaged schools don't appear), it would make more sense if comparative studies always reported two sets of scores for America—those earned in schools that do and do not have to cope with multiple disadvantages.

Discriminatory Procedures

So far we've considered problems that appear only in poverty-ridden schools, but additional problems are created by procedures that are found widely in America's public schools, procedures that were once defensible but are now preserved for reasons that reflect discrimination and the interests of those who are affluent.

Consider tracking, enrichment, and remedial procedures in which students are sorted into rank-ordered groups that are treated differently in classrooms or schools. Tracking procedures originally appeared in America's comprehensive high schools that were tasked with offering appropriate curricula for students who were to pursue alternative career paths. Although the selection of tracks proffered varied among schools in differing locales, the following list was fairly typical: a college-preparatory track for students who were to pursue professional careers, an industrial track for boys who were to proceed from high school into the skilled trades, a commercial track for girls destined to become receptionists and secretaries, and a general education track for those who would shortly drop out of school to take jobs requiring only minimal education. Such tracks reflected conditions then prevalent in America's job market, but from the beginning they also reflected status distinctions between students who were and were not presumed to have "smarts," and these status distinctions were understood by both faculty and students in those schools.

Students who were to pursue each track were identified early in their high school careers using various criteria: student academic records and interests; parental occupations; teachers' judgments; and prejudices reflecting race, gender, and social class. Such criteria came under attack, however, and over time they were supplemented and often replaced by data from tests assessing general intelligence, specific skills, or handicaps. Such tests were presumed to provide "objective" information about students' native abilities, and as the job market changed and completion of high school became more important, they provided greater legitimacy for sorting students into groups that presumably differed in terms of academic potential. And as schools became larger and more bureaucratized, the impulse to sort students into test-based groups for "appropriate" education gradually spread downwards and is now widespread in both primary and secondary American schools. Given negative associations with the term "tracking," however, most such systems are now given new acronyms such as enrichment programs (for students thought to have general or specific "gifts") and remedial programs (for those not so blessed).

Unfortunately, all such systems suffer from two types of intransigent problems. First, even though the tests on which they are based are presumed to provide "objective" information about students' native abilities, those tests also reflect students' background experiences, and this means that average students from disadvantaged homes will always earn lower test scores. (To illustrate, when compared with the scores displayed by students from non-impoverished homes, the typical 5-year-old student from an impoverished home scores nine points lower on IQ tests when entering school at age 5.) Nor should this surprise us, since "at-risk" students bring burdens to those tests created by prejudice, discrimination, lack of language fluency, and, above all, poverty. And this means that students from privileged homes will thereafter appear more often in enhancement groups whereas remedial groups will more often be populated with students who come from disadvantaged homes. Thus, rank-ordering classification systems become tools for confirming prejudicial American suspicions about which students are truly "superior" and "inferior," and the burdens that disadvantaged students bring with them when they enter the schoolhouse door are reinforced by additional burdens imposed on them by classification systems that restrict their educational opportunities.

Second, the act of sorting students into rank-ordered groups is a public event. Once such decisions are made, students, parents, and teachers all know well which students are and are not thought to have academic ability, and this leads to responses that create derivative problems. For students from disadvantaged homes, the act of sorting generates negative conclusions about their own abilities, throttles ambition, and creates hostility to schooling; whereas students from advantaged families are more likely to decide that they are "truly gifted," that they should expand their efforts and plan for collegiate entry and professional careers. Worse, parents from advantaged families (who often serve on school boards) are likely to urge that extra resources should be provided for "gifted" students—such as "my own Johnny" or "my own Becky"—who will face tough competition if they are to gain entrance into high-status colleges and truly prestigious careers. And since it is more rewarding to teach students with "more ability," teachers with greater tenure, qualifications, and classroom skills will gravitate toward classrooms where such students are found; but classrooms serving students with "less ability" are likely to have teachers who are younger, have fewer qualifications, and lack classroom skills. And these processes nearly guarantee that early minor differences between students who were once thought to differ marginally in academic skills will expand over time, thus creating major differences in achievement between students who are "winners" and "losers."

And if these problems were not severe enough, consider those created by America's persisting commitment to a long summer educational "break" that often lasts 10 weeks or more, a far longer summer holiday than is common in other advanced nations. Although America's lengthy summer break once reflected needs in an economy dominated by agriculture, it has long since spawned collateral institutions, such as summer camps and "enrichment experiences" for students from affluent families as well as opportunities to earn higher-education qualifications for educators, so is widely popular today.

But what about the students? For some years it has been known that students tend to forget subject matter during the long summer break, and extensive research confirms that this effect is far worse for students from impoverished homes whose parents cannot afford to supply the extra food they will need to replace the school-based free or reduced price lunches they will no longer receive during the summer, let alone to provide them with enrichment experiences. So all students are handicapped by America's overly-long summer break, but for impoverished students the handicap is particularly severe.

ERRORS, EVIDENCE-BASED POLICIES, AND ADVICE

We turn now to some of the implications of findings concerning youths, poverty, and educational failure in America and begin with recent efforts designed to reform American public education.

Tragic Errors

For roughly the past three decades, the United States has been plagued by vigorous, well-organized efforts that are designed to reform or do away with public schools. Given massive evidence concerned with poverty-associated problems, it should come as little surprise to learn that a host of (impoverished) students do badly in America's public schools, and that this is particularly true in those schools suffering from intense poverty concentration and miserable school funding. Current reform efforts designed to improve the performance of America's public schools have ignored this evidence; instead, they have based their programs on the assumption that "failures" in schools reflect either the incompetence of teachers or the haplessness of administrators, and they have sought to improve education by requiring that all public schools exert effort or revise their procedures so that all of their students (including those known to be "at risk" for educational failure) earn "acceptable" scores on standardized tests or be punished by replacing their supposedly feckless educators, privatizing their procedures, or be closed down and replaced by "more promising" types of schools.

Responding to this reasoning, many new laws and administrative mandates have appeared during the past few years. Witness President George W. Bush's No Child Left Behind program; President Barak Obama's Race to the Top initiative; vigorous "enforcement" programs in such cities as Washington, DC, New York City, and Chicago; the privatizing of public school programs in other cities, such as Philadelphia; and the adoption of programs in many states authorizing publicly funded but unregulated charter schools or voucher programs that serve selected, advantaged students and are now transferring tax-dollar resources from public schools to private academies. And although once diffusely fueled by family-owned foundations that subscribed to individualistic and often racist ideologies, as well as hostility to unions and the public sector that surfaced during the Reagan years, this reform movement is now well-organized, well-funded by super-rich individuals, foundations, and powerful corporations that are ideologically driven or stand to profit greatly if their agenda prevails, and promoting it has become a key focus of organizations that promulgate the far-Right political agenda.

Although one would not know it from the incessant barrage of propaganda and faked reports of "research" (based on ideology) that are generated by far Right sources, none of the laws, mandates, or the assumptions on which this reform movement are based have ever reflected evidence from legitimate research, and many studies have since shown either that it has not achieved its stated goals or that it has truly harmed public education. (Among other effects, its reforms have distorted public-school curricula, depressed morale among educators, generated serious cheating associated with high-stakes testing, transferred funds previously available for public schools into the private sector, and distorted public-school student populations by funding charter-school and private-academy options for advantaged students.) Nor should we be surprised at such results. Since we now know that excessive youth poverty and the debilitating effects of poverty in education are the major drivers of educational failure in America, this vigorous reform effort makes no sense at all, indeed, its programs have unfairly brutalized educators who labor in public schools where concentrations of impoverished youngsters are excessive and funding for education is minimal.

Evidence-Based Policies

So much for what doesn't work. As findings I've reviewed also imply, many types of research-based programs could be set up that would usefully address problems associated with youths, poverty, and education in America. Most such programs would require legislative, administrative, or legal actions, of course, thus would likely provoke controversy and require well-planned, long-term, committed efforts from advocates. This does not mean that such efforts are doomed to fail. Far from it, two examples illustrate what might be done at the federal level: During the 1960s, and as part of President Lyndon Johnson's "War on Poverty," the federal Congress actually debated legislation that would have provided substantial cash awards, social assistance benefits then called "negative income taxes," to all families who were impoverished. But this initiative failed for various reasons (including insufficient support from advocates). Again, President Barak Obama has already proposed a program that would set up strong, tax-supported daycare and preschool facilities across the land. Such a program would be wildly popular, but like other proposals for new legislative action needed to address urgent national needs, this initiative will surely be ignored by Congress as long as it is dominated by far Right interests.

Other types of useful programs may be initiated at the state or local levels. To illustrate, vigorous advocacy has already forced more equitable funding of public schools within several states including California and Michigan, and serious efforts have also begun in some states to replace local funding with equal, per-student, state-level funding for all public schools. Again, some amalgamated school districts, such as that of Wake County/Raleigh, North Carolina, have begun to explore innovative programs that involve extra funding and "lighthouse programs" for central city schools as well as busing programs that promote more equal distributions of impoverished and nonimpoverished youngsters among schools in the district. And led in part by pioneering efforts in Montgomery County, Maryland, some American communities are now exploring ways to discourage or do away with poverty-based, residential ghettos.

Advice for Educators

But what advice should be given to the teacher or school administrator who sincerely wants to help educational prospects for America's many impoverished youths? First, it should be understood that public school students are far more likely to suffer from impoverishment than from any other form of disadvantage. For the first time ever, and reflecting in part the flight of affluent students into charter schools and private academies, last year more than half of all American public school students were eligible for free or reduced priced lunches. Thus, although student impoverishment may be harder to detect than other forms of student disadvantage for which visual cues are more obvious, educators should proceed on the assumption that many students they encounter will be impoverished and should take pains to identify such students early each school year.

Second, impoverished students bring a host of home- and neighborhood-created, often intransigent burdens with them as they enter the schoolhouse door. Many students will have responded to such burdens by becoming discouraged, sullen, "touchy," or violent; and even the best educational efforts cannot obliterate all of those burdens and their effects. So the best that can be done for these students is to plan educative experiences that respond sensitively to their burdens, encourage afflicted students to develop more adaptive responses, and urge all to "do their best" despite the burdens they bear.

Third, impoverished students differ sharply in the exact mix of burdens they bear, so getting to know each such student personally is crucial. This task requires sensitivity, patience, a willingness to understand and cope with defensive reactions, and often helping students deal with their immediate problems. To illustrate, some impoverished students will need safety pins to shore up ragged or hand-me-down clothing; others will need referrals to free or low-cost clinics for help with untreated physical, mental, dental, visual, or auditory problems; others will need to be provided with pencils, tablets, or reading materials that are missing from their homes; others will need help from collateral agencies to cope with housing or domestic violence problems; and many will benefit if their overworked, stressed-out, education-shy parents are contacted through supportive home visits.

Fourth, concerned educators can also help by becoming advocates for school-based programs that provide greater support for impoverished students. For example, a number of school districts have begun providing additional food for undernourished students either through free and reduced price breakfasts during the school year or nutritious meals during the summer break; and others are now providing in-school health services for students with medical problems; others have now instituted supplemental, late-afternoon or summer-time "enrichment" programs for students from low-income households. As well, others have replaced the practice of separating students into rank-ordered groups who will receive differentiated education with programs that bundle all students into common classrooms, cooperative learning is practiced, and "talented" students are taught to mentor and help "struggling" students—programs known to provide benefits for students at all skill levels. Prospects for impoverished students would improve if these and related programs were made available in more American schools.

Fifth, and above all, it should be understood that effective actions proceed from evidence and understanding. Although the public may not be aware of it, a great deal of research-based evidence has now appeared concerned with youths, poverty, and education in the United States, and as suggested earlier, excellent books have already been published that summarize portions of this evidence and discuss their implications. Thus, educators who truly want to improve educational prospects for impoverished youths will need to plunge into this literature and be prepared to keep up with the flow of new information from late-breaking, legitimate research bearing on the huge youth-poverty associated disaster that now afflicts America and its schools.

REFERENCES

Bergmann, B. R. (1996). *Saving our children from poverty: What the United States can learn from France.* New York, NY: Russell Sage Foundation.

Berliner, D. C., & Biddle, B. J. (1995). *The manufactured crisis: Myths, fraud, and the attack on America's public schools.* New York, NY: Longman.

Biddle, B. J. (2014). *The unacknowledged disaster: Youth poverty and educational failure in America.* Rotterdam, the Netherlands: Sense.

Books, S. (2004). *Poverty and schooling in the U.S.: Contexts and consequences.* Mahwah, NJ: Erlbaum.

Bracey, G. W. (2003). *On the death of childhood and the destruction of public schools.* Portsmouth, NH: Heinemann.

Carter, P. L., & Welner, K. G. (Eds.). (2013). *Closing the gap: What America must do to give every child an even chance.* New York, NY: Oxford University Press.

Children's Defense Fund. (2002). *The state of children in America's union: A 2002 guide to Leave No Child Behind.* Washington, DC: Author.

Darling-Hammond, L. (2010). *The flat world and education: How America's commitment to equity will determine our future.* New York, NY: Teachers College Press.

Duncan, G. J., & Brooks-Gunn, J. (Eds.). (1997). *Consequences of growing up poor.* New York, NY: Russell Sage Foundation.

Duncan, G. J., & Murnane, R. J. (Eds.) (2011). *Whither opportunity? Rising inequality, schools, and children's life chances.* New York, NY: Russell Sage Foundation.

Edelman, M. W. (1994). *Introduction.* In A. Sherman, *Wasting America's future: The Children's Defense Fund report on the costs of child poverty.* Boston, MA: Beacon Press.

Gornick, J. C., & Meyers, M. K. (2003). *Families that work: Policies for reconciling parenthood and employment.* New York, NY: Russell Sage Foundation.

Huston, A. C. (1991). *Children in poverty: Child development and public policy.* New York, NY: Cambridge University Press.

Iceland, J. (2003). *Poverty in America: A handbook.* Berkeley, CA: University of California Press.

Kozol, J. (1991). *Savage inequalities: Children in America's schools.* New York, NY: Crown.

Kozol, J. (1995). *Amazing grace: The lives of children and the conscience of a nation.* New York, NY: Crown.

Kozol, J. (2005). *The shame of a nation.* New York, NY: Crown.

Mishel, L., Bernstein, J., & Allegretto, S. (2005). *The state of working America 2004/2005.* Ithaca, NY: ILR Press.

Mullis, I. V. S., Martin, M. O., Gonzalez, E. J., O'Connor, K. M., Chrostowski, S. J., Gregory, K. D., et al. (2001). *Mathematics benchmarking report, TIMSS 1999– eighth grade: Achievement for U.S. states and districts in an international context.* Boston, MA: Boston College, Lynch School of Education, International Study Center.

National Commission on Children (1991). *Beyond rhetoric: A new American agenda for children and families.* Washington, DC: Author.

Polakow, V. (1993). *Lives on the edge: Single mothers and their children in the other America.* Chicago, IL: University of Chicago Press.

Rainwater, L., & Smeeding, T. M. (2003) *Poor kids in a rich country: America's children in comparative perspective.* New York, NY: Russell Sage Foundation.

Ravitch, D. (2013). *Reign of error: The hoax of the privatization movement and the danger to America's public schools.* New York, NY: Knopf.

Sherman, A. (1994). *Wasting America's future: The Children's Defense Fund report on the costs of child poverty.* Boston, MA: Beacon Press.

United Nations Children's Fund (UNICEF). (2005). *Child poverty in rich countries: 2005, innocenti report card no 6.* Florence, Italy: Innocenti Research Centre.

PART II

PROMINENT EDUCATIONAL
POLICIES AFFECTING YOUTH

CHAPTER 6

LANGUAGE EDUCATION POLICIES AND LATINO YOUTH

Francesca López
University of Arizona

*Bilingualism has a truly odd press in the United States today.
The common wisdom is that immigrant children in urban areas should be moved as
quickly as possible from their first language to English so they can join the mainstream and become "real Americans." Bilingualism is a good thing in the suburbs.
There children who acquire a second language are seen as substantially enhancing
their earning potential. And this good press is coupled with the school districts'
or the parents' ability to pay for language teaching.*
—Sander L. Gilman (2000)

There has been a steady increase in the Latino[1] English learner (ELs) population since 1965 (García & Frede, 2010; Krogstad & Keegan, 2014). Today, of the approximately 20% of students who speak a language other than English at home, 70% speak Spanish (García & Frede, 2010). Despite a growing presence of Latino ELs in schools for more than four decades and a Supreme Court decision (Lau v. Nichols, 1974) proclaiming schools' responsibility to ensure equitable instructional access for ELs, their educational experiences and outcomes vary widely. The variation in ELs' experiences stem from disparate state policies aimed at addressing their English proficiency.

Educational Policies and Youth in the 21st Century, pages 105–121
Copyright © 2016 by Information Age Publishing

Language education programs[2] implemented in schools are required to have empirical support. Overwhelmingly, research tends to favor approaches that use Latino ELs' native language; however, much of the research examining language education programs' effectiveness tends to focus on achievement, ignoring the psychological and emotional outcomes for Latino ELs. Nevertheless, the role of language in identity is salient. González (2001) explains,

> to speak of language is to speak of our "selves." Language is at the heart, literally and metaphorically, of who we are, how we present ourselves, and how others see us.... The ineffable link of language to emotion, to the very core of our being, is one of the ties that bind children to a sense of heritage. (p. xix)

The goal of this chapter is to provide an overview of empirical evidence that describes the relationship between schooling and psychological and emotional outcomes for Latino ELs. To contextualize this limited but growing body of research, however, I first provide an overview of the history detailing ways language education program policies have changed over time, as well as an overview of the different kind of language education programs presently used in the United States, I then turn to a brief review of some of the studies that have examined the relationship between language education programs and ELs' achievement before elaborating on the empirical evidence that highlights the psychological and emotional outcomes of Latino ELs. I conclude with recommendations for policy development, as well as implications for school leaders and teachers.

HISTORY OF U.S. LANGUAGE POLICIES FROM THE PAST TO THE PRESENT

The United States has varied substantially on its position on non-English speaking students. At times in its history, the United States has embraced policies that valued the heritage of linguistically diverse students. At other times, however, the United States has been hostile, endorsing policies that go to great lengths to prevent the maintenance of non-English languages among ELs.

Although never designated the official language,[3] English has been the dominant language in the United States since the 17th century. During the English colonial period (early to mid 1700s), the use of English as *lingua franca* was rooted in "the political and socioeconomic trade between England and colonial administrators, colonists, and traders" (Wiley & Wright, 2004, p. 144). Since then, English has generally coexisted with numerous other languages, but has remained the defining element of nationalistic loyalty. Historically, perceived threats to national loyalty led to language policies that were especially hostile towards non-English speaking communities. For example, some view Congress' enactment of an English language requirement for citizenship in the Naturalization Act of 1906 a response to the surge in the number of immigrants (Ovando, 2003).

Between 1839 and 1900, numerous states passed laws authorizing instruction in languages in addition to English. Among the earliest were German programs in Ohio; Spanish programs in the territory of New Mexico; and French programs in Louisiana. At the same time, states adopted bilingual education laws for European immigrants and Spanish-speaking populations native to colonized territories, while many private boarding schools were working toward eradicating other languages—specifically native languages of indigenous populations. The onset of World War I reversed the bilingual education trend, as German and other foreign languages were restricted in schools "until Grades 6 to 8, when it was less likely that children would draw on their native languages" (Wiley & Wright, 2004, p. 147). By the 1920s, bilingual education was virtually dissolved in U.S. schools until 1963, when a two-way bilingual education program was piloted at the Coral Way Elementary School in the Dade County, Florida, school system in response to a large number of refugees from Cuba (Logan, 1967).[4]

Despite numerous bilingual programs prior to World War I, the Bilingual Education Act of 1968 was the first federal legislation that focused on the rights of ELs in the United States. Although the law was voluntary and did not prescribe a specific language acquisition program, it provided funding for the support of educational resources and teacher training. In 1974, however, the Supreme Court decision in *Lau v. Nichols* asserted that the lack of language accommodations for students with limited English proficiency was a violation of Section 601 of the 1964 Civil Rights Act. Guidelines for assessing compliance with the Supreme Court's decision, known as Lau Remedies, have been used since 1975 by the Office of Civil Rights to determine whether education agencies were in compliance with Title IV of the Civil Rights Act and the Equal Educational Opportunity Act (EEOA) of 1974, which prohibited segregation of students based on race and national origin, while at the same time mandating school district action to overcome linguistic barriers. Underscoring these developments was the amendment of the Bilingual Education Act in 1974, which mentioned bilingual education explicitly and removed the voluntary status of participation.

Successive reauthorizations of the Bilingual Education Act between 1978 and 1988 evolved from mandating bilingual education strategies exclusively, to emphasizing the transitional nature of bilingual education, to including other strategies that could be classified as special alternative programs. Although it was not until 1994 that indigenous languages were included in the act, the 1990/1992 Native American Languages Act is "the only federal legislation that explicitly vows to protect and promote Indigenous languages" (McCarty, 2003, p. 160).

The Bilingual Education Act became the English Language Acquisition, Language Enhancement, and Academic Achievement Act with the passing of the No Child Left Behind Act of 2001 (NCLB, 2001). Under NCLB, all references to bilingual education were removed while the assessment of English proficiency and progress in English language acquisition were emphasized. NCLB mandates that states adopt some type of language education program, but left it up to the states what type of program they would adopt. As a result, there is wide variability in the ways states mandate language education programs (see Table 6.1). Many states continue to endorse language education programs that use ELs' native language in instruction (e.g., Texas and Wisconsin); however, the specificity of the linguistic provisions varies substantially, sometimes reflecting the availability of certified bilingual teachers and/or the density of ELs who share a native language within a geographical context. In Texas, for example, bilingual education is mandatory when a school district has at least 20 ELs who share

TABLE 6.1 Language Education Programs in 50 States and Washington, DC[a]	
No bilingual education or use of students' language is allowed. If there are waivers permitted, the waivers preclude the need for bilingual education.	AZ, AR, NH
No bilingual education or use of students' language allowed, but there are waivers and/or exceptions made with parental request.	CA, MA
Various language education programs are explicitly presented as options (e.g., ESL and SEI), but they exclude bilingual education.	GA, TN, VA, VT, WV
Any language education program can be used, but bilingual education is used rarely if at all.	AL, CT, IA, KY, ME, MD, NE, NV, SC, SD, WY
Any language education program can be used. Bilingual education is explicitly mentioned and/or used.	CO, DC, DE, FL, HI, ID, IN, KS, LA, MD, MN, MO, MS, MT, NC, OH, OK, OR, PA, RI, UT
Bilingual education is mandated in cases where staffing is available and/or a minimum number of students are enrolled in the same school.	IL, MI, NY, WI
Bilingual education is mandated in cases where a minimum number of students are enrolled in the district or individual education agency.	AK, NJ, TX, WA
Bilingual education is mandated for all students (including non-ELs).	NM

[a] States without an explicit language education program default to NCLB. For detailed information on states' policies, see López, McEneaney, and Nieswandt (2015).

a native language. Wisconsin, however, stipulates that bilingual education is mandatory when at least 10 ELs who share a native language in grades K–3 (20 in grades 4–8 or 9–12) are within the same school, as long as a certified bilingual teacher is available. There are also states that support various language education programs in their policies, including bilingual education, English as a Second Language (ESL), and Structured English Immersion (SEI) (e.g., Colorado and Nevada). Still other states have no mandates, deferring instead to NCLB requirements that omit any mention about the kinds of language education programs that should be used to meet the needs of ELs (e.g., Kentucky and Louisiana). In these states, decisions on language education programs are often left to each individual educational agency or school district. States are required to select language education programs that are supported empirically, but this provision has done little, if anything, to promote language education program policies that reflect best practices (see López, McEneaney, & Nieswandt, 2015).

Although most state policies on language education have not changed markedly since the BEA of 1974, three states[5] passed legislation replacing bilingual education programs with SEI (sheltered English immersion). California voters replaced bilingual education with SEI via Proposition 227 in 1998. In Arizona, Proposition 203 (2000) replaced bilingual education with SEI. Massachusetts eliminated bilingual education with the passage of ballot measure Question 2 in 2002. Although some researchers claim that bilingual education was to blame for the poor performance and high dropout rates among ELs (Rossell, 2002), in California, approximately 70% the students who qualified for linguistic support were not receiving it (Gándara, Rumberger, Maxwell-Jolly, & Callahan, 2003). Indeed, some have asserted that the push to eliminate bilingual education has little, if anything, to do with a desire to promote achievement for ELs and is instead a tactic to ensure assimilation of minority populations.

Language Education Programs

In some states, Latino ELs are largely educated in programs that use their native language to teach content as exposure to English is increased. In these settings, which are believed to provide students with additive approaches that view their linguistic backgrounds as strengths rather than obstacles, teachers are required to be certified in bilingual education, which often involves coursework on understanding the development of a second language and requires proficiency in Spanish. In other states, language education programs proscribe the use of ELs' native language because it is believed to limit English language development. In these subtractive settings, teachers are charged with ensuring ELs' equitable access to instructional materials with little more than 45 hours of professional development—inadequate training that teachers of ELs identify as "the number one gap in their preparation for teaching" (Herrera & Murry, 2006, p. 201). These disparities are rooted in the policies that determine *how* ELs will be provided with equitable instruction, which inform the type of training and support teachers receive (for a detailed discussion, see López, Scanlan, & Gundrum, 2013).

Schools use one or several of various language education programs (see Table 6.2). The most prevalent language education programs as reported by schools to the U.S. Department of Education are SEI, ESL, transitional bilingual, and developmental bilingual. Schools select the language education program based on the policies of their state as well as the feasibility of implementing a given program (e.g., availability of appropriately certified teachers). As such, although all education programs share the goal of promoting English fluency, they vary widely across and within states.

Structured English Immersion (SEI)

SEI is reported by 24 states. The empirical evidence that is used to claim support for SEI (e.g., Baker, 1999; Baker & de Katner, 1983) tends to reflect research conducted with majority language speaking students immersed in a minority language. These type of immersion programs are prevalent in the United States, but are critiqued as failing to adequately apply to language minority students in the United States. In addition to issues with the empirical support used to claim support for SEI, the version of SEI in Arizona, California, and Massachusetts is markedly distorted from researchers' original recommendations.[6]

ESL

Two types of ESL programs are used in U.S. schools. In the more prevalent pull-out version (used by 30 states), students are removed from their English-only classroom during a designated day (or days) and time, and are provided with focused English instruction in a small group setting. The lesser prevalent version focuses on English language learning in a specific content area (e.g., science) using various types of support (e.g., visual aids, and adapted texts). Although content-based ESL does not expressly inhibit the use of students' native language, it focuses on developing English proficiency. Pull-out methods tend to be used in school settings with relatively few ELs who share a native language, and where the feasibility of grouping ELs and providing other language education programs is problematic. In contrast, content-based ESL tends to be used in settings with a larger population of ELs (whether or not they share a native language).

Some scholars describe content-based ESL as a content area in and of itself, like science or mathematics, wherein a content area (e.g., science)

TABLE 6.2   State Information on the Kinds of Language Instruction Programs Used Reported to the U.S. Department of Education as Part of the Consolidated State Performance Report for State Formula Grants[7]

State	AK	AL	AR	AZ	CA	CO	CT	DC	DE	FL	GA	HI	IA	ID	IL	IN	KS
Structured English Immersion	X	X	X	X	X	X		X	X			X	X	X		X	X
Content Based ESL	X	X	X		X	X	X	X			X	X	X	X	X	X	X
Pull Out ESL	X	X	X		X	X	X	X	X		X	X	X	X	X	X	X
Transitional Bilingual	X				X	X	X	X	X			X		X	X	X	
Developmental Bilingual					X	X			X	X		X		X	X		
Two-way immersion					X	X	X	X	X	X		X		X	X		
Dual Language	X			X	X	X	X	X	X	X	X	X	X	X		X	X

State	KY	LA	MA	MD	ME	MI	MN	MO	MS	MT	NC	ND	NE	NH	NJ	NM	NV
Structured English Immersion	X	X		X	X	X	X	X	X	X	X	X	X		X	X	X
Content Based ESL	X	X		X	X	X	X		X		X	X	X	X	X	X	
Pull-out ESL	X	X		X	X	X	X	X	X	X	X	X	X	X	X	X	X
Transitional Bilingual		X	X	X		X	X	X	X		X		X		X	X	X
Developmental Bilingual						X	X		X						X	X	
Two-way immersion			X	X	X	X	X		X	•	•		X		X	X	X
Dual Language		X	X	X	X	X	X	X	X	•	X	X	X	X	X	X	X

State	NY	OH	OK	OR	PA	RI	SC	SD	TN	TX	UT	VA	VT	WA	WI	WV	WY
Structured English Immersion	X	X	X	X	X		X	X	X		X	X	X		X		X
Content Based ESL	X	X	X	X	X	X	X	X	X	X	X	X	X		X	X	X
Pull-out ESL	X	X	X	X	X	X	X	X	X	X	X	X	X		X		X
Transitional Bilingual	X	X	X	X		X				X		X		X	X		
Developmental Bilingual						X	X		X						X	X	
Two-way immersion		X		X	X					X	X	X	X	X		X	
Dual Language	X	X		X	X	X	X			X	X	X	X	X			

Note: Data compiled from 2010-2011 state reports available through the National Clearinghouse on English Language Acquisition. •No Response.

simply provides the necessary context to promote English development. Using this framework, Krashen (1985), asserts that the most effective transitional bilingual programs (see below) incorporate ESL to support students' English acquisition. Once students have reached an intermediate level of proficiency in English, students are placed in "sheltered" classes that are comprised of ELs with similar English proficiency across content areas, where they receive content-specific instruction in English. Content-based ESL is thus the emphasis of English-acquisition via content whereas sheltered English emphasizes content acquisition via increasing acquisition of English. Notably, other scholars diverge from this view of content-based ESL and assert that the specificity of academic language in each content area requires that content-based ESL deliver both content and its specialized English vocabulary for ELs to be successful (Quinn, Lee, Valdés, 2012). The belief is that sheltered English settings isolate ELs from their English-proficient peers, "thereby reducing opportunities for them to interact with English-speaking students who may be more academically prepared and, thus, denying them potential academic and linguistic resources" (Bunch, Abram, Lotan, & Valdés, 2001, p. 28).

Transitional Bilingual

Transitional bilingual programs are the most commonly implemented bilingual programs, but are not used as frequently as the language education programs already described. Of the two types of transitional bilingual programs, the early-exit model is the most widespread model provided in the United States, reported by 23 states. In these settings, ELs are transitioned to all-English instruction by the middle elementary grades (Ramirez, Yuen, Ramey, & Pasta, 1991). Only 12 states report using late-exit transitional programs, sometimes referred to as developmental bilingual education[8](DBE). In these settings, the transition to all-English instruction takes place by sixth grade or later. In both kinds of transitional bilingual programs, classrooms consist of children who share the same native language. Academic content is introduced in the native language, and concepts are expanded in English to promote English language development. As children progress through grade levels, a greater portion of academic instruction is presented in English, until eventually, children are transitioned to regular education programming in English.

There are many variations of DBE. Some programs initiate with 90% of instruction in students' native language and 10% in English during the first year of the program, gradually increasing the amount of English instruction each year. Other DBE programs may initiate the program with equivalent amounts of instruction in students' native language and English. In contrast to early-exit transitional bilingual education programs,

DBE emphasizes to a greater extent the promotion and maintenance of the home language while children learn English.

Two-Way Immersion

Two-way immersion implies that ELs and English speaking students (i.e., "two-way") are in classrooms where instruction occurs in both English and ELs' language. The programs are designed to promote bilingualism by bringing together a group of children who speak English as their native language and a group of children who share a non-English native language. Although two-way programs were not widely used in the past, they have become increasingly popular given their focus on promoting bilingualism for native English speaking students. Ideally, two-way immersion classrooms comprise equal numbers of students within these two groups and follow one of two models. In the first, referred to as 90:10, 90% of instruction is in the non-English language in kindergarten and English is incrementally introduced until a balance in the two languages is reached by the middle elementary grades. In the second, referred to as a 50:50 model, instruction is delivered in the two languages, equally, across grades. In two-way immersion programs, language learning is integrated with content instruction with goals to promote bilingualism, academic achievement, and cross-cultural understanding among all students.

Two-way immersion is reported by 24 states. Although two-way immersion is often interchangeably referred to as dual language or two-way bilingual immersion, some states distinguish between dual language and two-way bilingual programs. Arizona, for example, reports dual language programs, but not two-way bilingual. This reflects state policy that limits programs that promote bilingualism to students who are not ELs. Indeed, dual language is reported by 41 states—more than those reporting two-way immersion—but it is unclear whether the discrepancies reflect differences among states that use the terms interchangeably or conceptualize the two programs as distinct in terms of the students who enroll in the classes (even though the programs submitted to NCELA are meant to reflect programs for ELs).

EMPIRICAL EVIDENCE
OF LANGUAGE EDUCATION PROGRAMS

Language Education Programs and Achievement

Overwhelmingly, reviews of empirical studies have favored approaches that incorporate students' native language (August & Shannahan, 2006; Rolstad, Mahoney, & Glass, 2005; Slavin & Cheung, 2005)—particularly when effects are examined over time (e.g., Salazar, 1998). For example, in a reanalysis of a meta-analysis and longitudinal study, Salazar (1998) calculated the standardized mean difference in English reading achievement among ELs between English immersion and three distinct language acquisition programs: early-exit transitional bilingual, late-exit transitional bilingual, and dual language settings. Salazar found that there were negligible differences for the programs using native language support compared to English only settings in the early grades. Beginning in fourth grade, however, all three programs that used native language support had increasingly large, positive effects compared to English only. In early-exit transitional bilingual programs, the effects began steadily increasing in sixth grade, increasing from an effect size (ES) = .05[9] to ES = .28 by eleventh grade. For late-exit transitional bilingual, these effects were larger and began earlier, beginning with ES = .29 in fourth grade and increasing steadily to ES = .85 by eleventh grade. The most pronounced gains were associated with dual language settings: in fourth grade, the ES = .24, increasing to ES = 1.28 in eleventh grade.

Notably, the effects are substantially larger after students are no longer in the programs, with the most salient effects evident during high school. On the one hand, this finding could potentially be explained by research establishing the cognitive benefits of bilingualism. Students who speak two languages have been found to have higher levels of metacognitive awareness and problem-solving skills (Adesope, Lavin, Thompson, & Ungerleider, 2010). However, if the bilingual settings are beneficial only in terms of language, then the benefits would seem to decrease the longer students are not exposed to their native language in an academic setting. Moreover, despite equitable use of the non-English language and English in both late-exit and dual language program, data suggest dual language settings have the most marked effects—a 50% gain in the effect size compared to late-exit settings. Salazar's (1998) analysis adds to prior research supporting the long-term superiority of instruction that brings together language minority and language majority students (e.g., Gersten & Woodward, 1995).

Language Education Program Policies and Achievement

Rumberger and Tran (2010) analyzed reading and mathematics achievement gaps between ELs and non-ELs on the 2005 National Assessment of Educational Progress (NAEP) across all 50 states and the District of Columbia. They found that whereas only 15% to 20% of the variability in student achievement was attributable to state policies for non-ELs, state policies explained close to 40% of the variability in achievement gaps for ELs. Rumberger and Tran assert that,

This finding suggests that states have more control over the size of the EL achievement gap than over their overall achievement levels and that state policies—such as whether to provide EL students with specialized instruction ... could help reduce the gap. (Rumberger & Tran, 2010, p. 99)

Some scholars warn that a focus on achievement disparities ignores the problematic assumptions of gauging ELs' achievement against native English speakers' performance on assessments in English. That is, any assessment in English is a test of English and by definition, there will always be achievement gaps between ELs and non ELs. Nevertheless, Rumberger and Tran's (2010) research underscores that the magnitude of disparities are acquiescent. To illustrate, they point out that despite overall scores that are among the highest in the nation, the achievement gaps in Massachusetts (a state that replaced bilingual education with SEI in 2002) were among the largest in the United States. Accordingly, Rumberger and Tran assert that a rigorous curriculum that increases overall student achievement is insufficient to address the educational needs of ELs.

Other large-scale studies affirm the saliency of state language education program policies. In an examination of the relationship between state language education program policies and Latino (both EL and non-EL) achievement in states with some of the highest proportions of ELs in the United States, López and McEneaney (2012) found that state policies favoring bilingual approaches were associated with higher reading achievement on 2005 and 2007 NAEP among 4th-grade Latino ELs. In a more recent study, López, McEneaney, & Nieswandt (2015) used restricted use Grade 4 2009 NAEP achievement data in reading, mathematics, and science to evaluate the relationship between the degree to which state language education program policies emphasize bilingual methods and the academic achievement of 4th-grade Latino ELs across all 50 states and the District of Columbia, as well as the role of Latino population patterns. Although language education program policies emphasizing bilingual methods were negatively related to mean achievement in all subjects, the effect was conditional on the proportion of Latino residents in a state, becoming significantly positive in states with a high proportion of Latinos. Consistent with research conducted in settings that are densely populated with Latino ELs such as Arizona (e.g., Rolstad, Mahoney, & Glass, 2005) and Texas (e.g., Tong, Lara-Alecio, Irby, Mathes, & Kwok, 2008), bilingual emphasis does seem to play an important role in Latino ELs' achievement in states with high proportions of Latinos. Other states did not appear to mirror the relationships found in high-density states, although there was also a marked relationship between effectiveness of bilingual programs and the time since they had been implemented in policy. After examining population patterns over 40 years, López, McEneaney, and Nieswandt (2015) suggest the following:

> To ensure Title III funds are allocated in ways that will meet the needs of ELs, states should be required to comply with all three Castañeda prongs. First, states should be required to explicitly state the ways in which ELs will be provided with an equitable education (i.e., explicit LIEPs) and demonstrate that the LIEPs [Language Instruction Educational Programs] espoused at the state level have empirical support. Accordingly, the disbursement of Title III funds to support capacity building for LIEPs should be contingent on the extent to which a state's LIEPs reflect empirical, rather than ideological, evidence, as well as the extent to which states are providing support. To further ensure funding toward building capacity is aimed at LIEPs that demonstrate promise for ELs, the evaluation of the LIEPs used in school districts should be required. (López et al., 2015, p. 28)

Language Education Programs and Psychological and Emotional Outcomes for ELs

Notably, the value of using language education programs that incorporate ELs' native language is not only to ensure ELs acquire English. Rather, language education programs that use ELs' native language may be valuable to ELs because they offer something beyond linguistic scaffolding as they develop educational content knowledge. This is particularly evident not only in the distal effects found in longitudinal studies comparing different language education programs (e.g., Salazar, 1998), but also in the more recent research explicitly examining relationships between state-level language education program policies and ELs' achievement, as well as the evidence that teachers who are trained to incorporate students' native language in instruction can help buffer the constraints presented by subtractive state policies (López, 2014).

Scholars have found that ELs tend to have the most favorable achievement outcomes when they feel a sense of belonging in school (Valenzuela, 1999) and their ethnic identity relates positively to both their ethnic group and the mainstream group (Altschul, Oyserman, & Bybee, 2008). Considered together with the distal effects favoring dual language (Salazar, 1998), it is likely that language education programs influence factors beyond achievement. Unfortunately, there is a paucity of research focused on establishing a direct link between language education programs and both psychological and emotional outcomes among ELs. The scant evidence that does exist underscores a need to consider seriously students' emotional and psychological outcomes, as these are often closely linked with academic achievement. For example, ELs receiving bilingual education have been found to have substantially higher perceptions of their ability and educational opportunities than ELs receiving SEI; students receiving SEI had higher levels of acculturative stress, perceived discrimination, and substantially lower achievement than students receiving bilingual education (López, 2010).

Numerous scholars have documented that ELs who are members of the first or second generation in their families tend to have markedly better achievement outcomes than peers from the third generation and beyond, which is in direct contrast to the "upward mobility pattern historically evident among European-origin groups" (Valenzuela, 1999, p. 4). In short, immigrants who are newer to the United States tend to do better than those whose families have been around longer. Some have attempted to explain the phenomenon of downward mobility by alluding to deficiencies among later generations of traditionally marginalized immigrant youth when compared to European-origin groups or members of earlier generations (e.g., Matute-Bianchi, 1991). Instead of viewing the downward mobility through a deficiency perspective, Valenzuela asserts the need for researchers to consider that later generations of immigrant "youth are neither inherently antischool nor oppositional. They oppose a schooling process that disrespects them; they oppose not education, but *schooling*" (Valenzuela, 1999, p. 5). Here, Valenzuela refers to schooling as the ways schools inculcate immigrant youth with the notion that they should devalue their native language and culture. Notably, this is particularly evident in most language education programs that aim to replace ELs' native language with English. Thus, even though not directly examined with language education programs, the long-lasting effects of practices that devalue students' culture appear to have pervasively detrimental effects for linguistically and culturally diverse youth whose families have been in the United States for longer periods of time.

POLICY RECOMMENDATIONS

It is important to consider that the current antibilingual sentiment has targeted Spanish-speaking populations more than any other group (Wiley & Wright, 2004) and corresponds to the dramatic increase in the Latino population (García & Frede, 2010). Despite this dramatic growth, a review of the policies on language instruction programs for each of the 50 states and the District of Columbia reveals that to date 21 states have no mandate to ensure schools meet the needs of ELs. Most of the states that currently have no mandate are also among those that have experienced the largest growth of Latino EL student populations in the past decade. South Carolina and Kentucky, for example, have witnessed a growth of their EL population of more than 800% and 200%, respectively, since 1998, but have no language education policy to meet the needs of ELs. It is possible that states without policies have a paucity of resources to implement state language education programs that emphasize bilingual methods, limiting the extent to which these policies can be implemented. Nevertheless, it is important to consider that even in states with language education programs that emphasize bilingual methods, there is variability in implementation and resources. What seems to be most important—at least at the state level—is that the policies reflect an additive approach to meeting the needs of ELs. In doing so, policies can begin to address the achievement disparities that are not rooted in the acquisition of English alone, but rather the discrepancy view of Latinos that is promulgated by anti-native language policies, which in turn influence Latinos emotionally, psychologically, and academically.

Implications for Teachers

Given that ELs appear to benefit psychologically, emotionally, and academically when language education programs reflect an additive approach to English acquisition, it is important that teachers possess the knowledge necessary to support students' native language as they acquire English. For school leaders and teachers, this includes knowledge about language development, as well as effective practices and pedagogy to support language development (see López, Scanlan, & Gundrum, 2013). Possessing the knowledge that it takes several years for ELs to develop the English used in classrooms (Krashen, 1997; Lucas, Villegas, & Freedson-Gonzalez, 2008), which is distinct from the conversational English that takes 1 or 2 years to develop, allows practitioners to discern the claims made by proponents of English-only methods from empirical evidence. Namely, SEI proponents assert it takes only 1 year to achieve English proficiency—a claim that lacks empirical support. Practitioners who also possess knowledge about ways to support English proficiency by using visual aids, vocabulary instruction, and graphic organizers, for example, are better able to provide support to ELs to ensure they can access the curriculum. One way to ensure all teachers possess this knowledge is by requiring that they receive the necessary training to address the needs of ELs. This has been recommended by various scholars (e.g., Lucas et al., 2008), and holds promise to ensure all teachers are prepared to support ELs academically, emotionally, and psychologically—regardless of their working context.

NOTES

1. Although there are numerous languages other than English represented in the EL population of the United States, the majority (approximately 80%)

are Spanish-speaking ELs. Considering that Spanish is considered a low-status language and policies tend to target Spanish-speaking (i.e., Latino) populations, issues that are not necessarily found among the numerous languages represented by ELs in United States are introduced. As such, this chapter focuses on Latino ELs.

2. Researchers and states use various labels for the methods aimed at increasing English proficiency among ELs. Instructional models, language instruction educational programs, language acquisition models, language education instruction programs, and others are used interchangeably. Here, I use the terms language education programs and language education policies to reflect the focus on the language of instruction in policies.

3. Several states have passed Official English laws as early as 1812 (Louisiana) to as recently as 2010 (Oklahoma). As of now, 31 states have adopted English as the official state language (http://www.us-english.org/view/13).

4. The program was funded by a Ford Foundation Project award to the Dade County School system.

5. The three initiatives were authored by the same individual, Ron Unz.

6. For a detailed description of the various conceptualizations and inconsistencies reflected in SEI, see López and McEneaney (2012) and López, McEneaney, and Nieswandt (2015).

7. In cases where language education programs are not mandated by the state, they are determined by the local educational agency, school district, or school.

8. Although DBE is most often considered a late-exit transitional program, there are cases where it is conceptualized as a dual language program for ELs that spans grades K through 12.

9. Here, effect size reflects the magnitude of differences in standard deviation units.

REFERENCES

Adesope, O. O., Lavin, T., Thompson, T., & Ungerleider, C. (2010). A systematic review and meta-analysis of the cognitive correlates of bilingualism. *Review of Educational Research, 80,* 207–245.

Alschul, I., Oyserman, D., & Bybee, D. (2008). Racial-ethnic self-schemas and segmented assimilation: Identity and the academic achievement of Hispanic youth. *Social Psychology Quarterly, 71,* 302–320.

August, D., & Shanahan, T. (Eds.). (2006). *Developing literacy in second-language learners: Report of the National Literacy Panel on language-minority children and youth.* Mahwah, NJ: Erlbaum.

Baker, K. (1999). *Basics of structured English immersion for language minority students. Bilingual education: A focus on current research.* Retrieved from ERIC database. (ED432928)

Baker, K., & de Kanter, A. (Eds.). (1983). *Bilingual education: A reappraisal of federal policy.* Lexington, MA: Lexington Books.

Bunch, G. C., Abram, P. L., Lotan, R. A., & Valdés, F. (2001). Beyond sheltered instruction: Rethinking conditions for academic language development. *TESOL Journal, 10,* 28–33.

Gándara, P., Rumberger, R., Maxwell-Jolly, J., & Callahan, R. (2003). English learners in California schools: Unequal resources, unequal outcomes. *Education Policy Analysis Archives, 11.* Retrieved July 2007 from http://epaa.asu.edu/epaa/v11n36/

García, E., & Frede, E. C. (Eds.) (2010). *Young English language learners.* New York, NY: Teachers College Press.

Gersten, R., & Woodward, J. (1995). A longitudinal study of transitional and immersion bilingual education programs in one district. *Elementary School Journal, 95,* 223–240.

Gilman, S. L. (2000). Learning a foreign language in a monolingual world. *PMLA, 115,* 1032–1040.

González, N. (2001). *I am my language: Discourses of women and children in the borderlands.* Tucson, AZ: University of Arizona Press.

Herrera, S. G., & Murry, K. G. (2006). Accountability by assumption: Implications of reform agendas for teacher preparation. *Journal of Latinos and Education, 5,* 189–207.

Krashen, S. (1985). *Insights and inquiries.* Hayward, CA: Alemany Press.

Krashen, S. D. (1997). *A researcher's view of Unz.* Retrieved at http://www.language-policy.net/archives/Krashen1.htm

Krogstad, J. M., & Keegan, M. (2014.) *From Germany to Mexico: How America's source of immigrants has changed over a century.* Washington, DC: Pew Research Center. Available at www.pewresearch.org/fact-tank/2014/05/27/a-shift-from-germany-to-mexico-for-americas-immigrants.

Lau v. Nichols, 414 U.S. 563 (1974); Lau v. Hopp, U.S.D.C., N.D. Cal., No. C 70-627 LHB

Logan, J. L. (1967). Coral Way: A bilingual school. *TESOL Quarterly, 1,* 50–54.

López, F. (2010). Identity and motivation among English language learners in disparate educational contexts. *Education Policy Analysis Archives, 18.* Retrieved from http://epaa.asu.edu/ojs/article/view/717

López, F. (2014, November). *Addressing the need for explicit evidence on the role of culturally responsive teaching and achievement among Latino youth.* Paper presented at the 2014 annual meetings and fall retreat of the National Academy of Education, Washington, DC.

López, F., & McEneaney, E. (2012). English language learners and state language acquisition policies. *Educational Policy, 26,* 418–464.

López, F., McEneaney, E., & Nieswandt, M. (2015, April). Language instruction educational programs and academic achievement of Latino English learners: Considerations for states with changing demographics. *American Journal of Education, 121*(3).

López, F., Scanlan, M., & Gundrum, B. (2013). Preparing teachers of English language learners: Empirical evidence and policy implications. *Education Policy Analysis Archives, 21.* Retrieved from http://epaa.asu.edu/ojs/article/view/1132

Lucas, T., Villegas, A. M., & Freedson-Gonzalez, M. (2008). Linguistically responsive teacher education: Preparing classroom teachers to teach English language learners. *Journal of Teacher Education, 59,* 361–373.

Matute-Bianchi, M. E. (1991). Situational ethnicity and patterns of school performance among immigrant and nonimmigrant Mexican-descent students. In
M. A. Gibson & J. U. Ogbu (Eds.), *Minority status and schooling: A comparative study of immigrant and involuntary minorities* (pp. 205–247). New York, NY:
Garland.

McCarty, T. L. (2003). Revitalising indigenous languages in homogenising times.
Comparative Education, 39, 147–163.

No Child Left Behind Act of 2001 (NCLB), Public Law No. 107-110.

Ovando, C. (2003). Bilingual education in the United States: Historical development and current issues. *Bilingual Research Journal, 27*, 1–25.

Quinn, H., Lee, O., & Valdés, G. (April, 2012). *Language demands and opportunities
in relation to Next Generation Science Standard for English language learners: What
teachers need to know.* Paper presented at the 2012 Challenges and Opportunities for Language Learning in the Context of Common Core State Standards
and Next Generation Science Standards Conference, Stanford University. Retrieved at http://ell.stanford.edu/papers

Ramirez, J. D., Yuen, S. D., Ramey, D. R., & Pasta, D. J. (1991). *Final report: Longitudinal study of structured English immersion strategy, early-exit, and late-exit transitional bilingual education programs for language minority children.* Retrieved from
ERIC database. (ED330216)

Rolstad, K., Mahoney, K., & Glass, G. (2005). The big picture: A meta-analysis of program effectiveness research on English language learners. *Educational Policy,
19*, 572–594.

Rossell, C. (2002). *Dismantling bilingual education implementing English immersion: The
California initiative.* San Francisco, CA: Public Policy Institute of California.

Rumberger, R. W., & Tran, L. (2010). State language policies, school language prac-
tices, and the English learner achievement gap. In P. Gándara & M. Hopkins
(Eds.) *Forbidden language: English learners and restrictive language policies.* New
York, NY: Teachers College Press.

Salazar, J. J. (1998). A longitudinal model for interpreting thirty years of bilingual
education research. *Bilingual Research Journal, 22*, 1–12.

Slavin, R. E., & Cheung, A. (2005). A synthesis of research on language of reading
instruction for English language learners. *Review of Educational Research, 75*,
247–284.

Steele, C. M., & Aronson, J. (1995). Stereotype threat and the intellectual test performance of African Americans. *Journal of Personality and Social Psychology, 69*,
797–811.

Tong, F., Lara-Alecio, R., Irby, B., Mathes, P., & Kwok, O. (2008). Accelerating early
academic oral English development in transitional bilingual and structured
English immersion programs. *American Educational Research Journal, 45*,
1011–1044.

Valenzuela, A. (1999). *Subtractive schooling: U.S. Mexican youth and the politics of caring.* Albany, NY: SUNY Press.

Wiley, T. G., & Wright, W. E. (2004). Against the undertow: Language-minority education policy and politics in the age of accountability. *Educational Policy, 18*,
142–168.

CHAPTER 7

THE IMPACT
OF IMMIGRATION POLICY
ON EDUCATION

Sandra A. Alvear and Ruth N. López Turley
Rice University

Public education has a pivotal role in maintaining the fabric of our society and in
sustaining our political and cultural heritage; the deprivation of education takes an
inestimable toll on the social, economic, intellectual, and psychological well-being of
the individual, and poses an obstacle to individual achievement.
　　　　　　　　　　　　　　　—Plyler v. Doe, 1982, pp. 202–203

Like all school students, children of immigrants enter the classroom with a
set of unique perspectives, experiences, and preoccupations. In this chapter, we focus on the dramatic influence of recent, monumental shifts in
federal and state immigration policy on the schooling of children of immigrants. Notably, the most pervasive, politically-inciting immigration policies
do not target immigrants who move to the United States for postsecondary
education or high-paying jobs, they target immigrants with tenuous or undocumented legal status who are predominantly Latino. It is primarily their
children's experiences that are addressed in the following pages. Nearly
12 million children of immigrants and later-generation Latinos accounted
for 24% of the population of elementary and secondary students in the

Educational Policies and Youth in the 21st Century, pages 123–144

United States in 2011. These students will make up 30% of public school enrollment by 2023 (National Center for Education Statistics, 2014). The importance of these students' successful educational trajectories cannot be overstated.

Until recent years, research on the educational experiences of children of immigrants was not contextualized within broader analyses of immigration policy. Children of immigrants include young first generation immigrants, the 1.5 generation who is foreign born but raised primarily in the United States, and the U.S.-born second generation whose parents are immigrants.[1] As this chapter will highlight, when immigration policies are overly restrictive and intolerant, the negative repercussions to children's social-emotional well-being and sense of self, school engagement, and long-term educational opportunities can be dire. We call upon policymakers to halt restrictive immigration policies that not only wreak havoc in the lives of immigrant families, but place undue constrains on what should be boundless potential among children of immigrants. We also issue recommendations for school administrators and teachers to prioritize targeted student- and family-outreach efforts.

Children of immigrants have become the subject of extensive public discourse, political debate, and interdisciplinary academic research. In spite of this, there are few methodologically rigorous quantitative studies that examine how specific immigration policies relate to child/student outcomes (with the exception of Magaña and Lee's 2013 edited compilation). By contrast, numerous qualitative studies keenly demonstrate that immigration policies inflict severe tolls on student motivation and aspirations among undocumented children of immigrants (Abrego, 2006; Gonzales, 2011); and that children with detained immigrant parents undergo behavioral changes (from anxiety to withdrawal to aggression), and in some cases, a decline in academic performance (Chaudry, Capps, Pedroza, Castaneda, Santos, & Scott, 2010). However, these studies stop short of communicating practical guidance to school-site instructors and administrators for educating children of immigrants in a more inclusive way. This chapter seeks to bridge that gap by highlighting the specific dimensions of children's educational experiences that are likely affected by immigration policy, and extending the discussion to include practical implications for school teachers and administrators.

Although no state or federal immigration policy is uniformly positive or negative in its impact on the immigrant community, we use two broad policy categories to more clearly illustrate how policies shape schooling for children of immigrants. "Restrictive" immigration legislation effectively reduces rights, services, and resources available to immigrants and their families; these policies also enhance enforcement, deportation efforts, and criminal sanctions for immigrants who do not belong to high-priority enforcement groups.[2,3] Restrictive immigration policies are often motivated by fiscal concerns and are generally linked to conservative political affiliation (Espenshade & Hempstead, 1996). "Humanitarian" immigration policies offer civil liberties and resources to immigrants, including those with tenuous legal status. While both policy groups have social and financial implications for the broader society, their effects are especially salient for immigrant families and their school-aged children. We review the historical and social contexts that gave rise to the current immigration policy climate, and the important—in some cases troubling—effects of immigration legislation.

Specifically, we examine restrictive policies including House Bill (HB) 56 from Alabama (State of Alabama, 2011) and Senate Bill (SB) 2281 from Arizona (State of Arizona, 2010), as well as two humanitarian immigration policies, California's Assembly Bill (AB) 540 (State of California, 2001) and recent policies related to the proposed federal legislation, the Development, Relief, and Education for Alien Minors (DREAM) Act (United States Senate, 2011). Based on a review of multidisciplinary research, we contend that restrictive and humanitarian immigration policies impact the education of children of immigrants specifically through students' sense of identity and social-emotional well-being, which have tremendous implications for their school engagement, and children's real and perceived opportunity structures.

THE CONTEXT OF CONTEMPORARY IMMIGRATION POLICY

Contemporary immigration policy is cast against the landscape of a burgeoning, relatively young Latino population that has become more geographically dispersed, settling in nontraditional receiving communities across the United States (Diaz McConnell, 2013). Immigration policy has largely been swayed by increased media coverage of undocumented immigration and conservative Tea Party politics (Donnelly, 2013), an economic recession that scapegoated Latino immigrants (Massey & Sanchez, 2010; McDowell & Provine, 2013), and post-9/11 security concerns linking unauthorized immigration to terrorism (McDowell & Provine, 2013, p. 68). Unauthorized immigration has declined since its peak in 2007, but it remains at the heart of calls for restrictive immigration policies (Donnelly, 2013). Despite increases in budget allocations and border patrol agents, as well as an all-time high in deportations during the Obama administration, states and localities largely blame their depleted social service resources on a lack of federal enforcement of immigration law (McDowell & Provine, 2013).

The past two decades were among the most active times of congressional meetings on immigration legislation, and there was a substantial increase of state-based, anti-immigrant legislation (Chavez & Provine, 2009; McDowell & Provine, 2013). For example, changes in immigration policy started around 1990 when immigration policies shifted from regulating and restricting access to the United States to issuing increased controls on the everyday lives of immigrants already residing in the United States (Miller, 2005). Signs of this were evident at the federal level, including the Clinton administration's 1996 Anti-Terrorism and Effective Death Penalty Act (AEDPA, 1996), the Illegal Immigration Reform and Immigrant Responsibility Act of 1996, and its provisions for 287(g) agreements (IIRAIRA, 1996). Moreover, states have increasingly challenged the reach of federal plenary power by advancing a specter of restrictive immigration policies (Donnelly, 2013; McDowell & Provine, 2013). The trend in restrictive state-based immigration legislation began with California's Proposition 187 (approved by state voters in 1994; Jacobson, 2008), and it continued in 2010 with the landmark Arizona Senate Bill 1070 (State of Arizona, 2010; McDowell & Provine, 2013).[4,5] As we will discuss, HB 56 in Alabama (State of Alabama, 2011) and Arizona's HB 2281 (State of Arizona, 2010) further reinforced escalating trends in restrictive state immigration policy.

However, the trend toward restrictive immigration policy is not uniform: recent executive orders from the Obama administration and state-based legislation in California have challenged the restrictive orientation of immigration law. For example, The Development, Relief, and Education for Alien Minors (DREAM) Act (United States Senate, 2011), versions of which emerge at federal and state levels, sparked a national movement since it appeared in Congress in 2001. The DREAM Act framed undocumented students' restricted access to higher education and in-state tuition as a matter of human rights and social justice; segments of the American public and its leaders sympathized with the concept of young people being denied the tools to realize their full potential (Glenn, 2011). As we will address, President Obama issued executive orders in 2012 (United States Citizenship and Immigration Services, 2016; United States Department of Homeland Security, 2012) to allow a form of legal status and work authorization for undocumented immigrants who arrived in the United States as children, and provided similar protections for parents and spouses of American citizens and lawful permanent residents in 2014 (White House Office of the Press Secretary, 2014).

RESTRICTIVE IMMIGRATION POLICY

Immigration policies are often linked to broader political agendas and cultural trends across the United States. Amidst a backdrop of nationwide anti-immigration rhetoric came some of the most restrictive statewide policies to date. The first and most influential legislation came in 2010 through Arizona's SB 1070 (State of Arizona, 2010) that implemented a doctrine of "attrition through enforcement," requiring, among other things, that individuals produce legal status documentation upon request. In this chapter, we focus on two pieces of legislation that followed in the restrictive spirit of SB 1070 and are directly linked to educational settings. Alabama issued HB 56 in 2011 (State of Alabama, 2011), an exclusionary policy that mandated schools to screen the immigration status of students and their parents. Arizona's SB 2281 (2010) banned ethnic studies in state-funded schools (State of Arizona, 2010). Together, these policies evidenced two states' agendas of ethnic/cultural exclusion.

Alabama HB 56

In June 2011, the state of Alabama passed HB 56, known as the Beason-Hammon Taxpayer and Citizen Protection Act (State of Alabama, 2011), an incredibly hostile and intolerant piece of legislation mandating a host of provisions that threatens the very safety and security of undocumented citizens. For example, HB 56 voids any contract involving an undocumented immigrant if the other party had direct or constructive knowledge of the individual's legal status (impacting work and residential contracts, among others), and bars undocumented immigrants from any business transaction with the state government, including applications for motor vehicle licences and identification cards. Section 8 of HB 56 prohibits undocumented immigrants from enrolling in or attending any public postsecondary educational institution in Alabama. Of particular concern is Section 28 of HB 56, which requires parents/guardians to provide Alabama schools with documentation that confirms whether newly enrolling children were born in the United States, and further requires that school officials record parents' legal status. If materials attesting to a child's citizenship are not produced within 30 days, the child is presumed to be undocumented.

Section 28 operates under the pretext of collecting legal status data to more accurately account for the fiscal costs associated with serving undocumented children, and to assign children to English acquisition courses or any "other remedial program." But Section 28 also contains provisions for school officials to share sensitive legal status information with state, local, and federal officials. The data are aggregated only at the school level.

To understand the impact of such legislation, consider that on September 28, 2011, U.S. District Court Judge Sharon Lovelace Blackburn upheld the contested school-based provisions of Section 28 requiring schools to comply or risk legal action. Not surprisingly, the day after this ruling, the statewide public school student absentee rate in Alabama jumped from an average of 3%–4% to 6.86% (Alabama State Department of Education, 2011). In the immediate aftermath of Section 28's implementation and enforcement,

Latino student absentee rates tripled, while absentee rates for other groups of students remained virtually flat (Perez, 2012). Absentee rates eventually declined, but an even more alarming trend was uncovered. Through a Department of Justice (DOJ) Civil Rights Division inquiry into HB 56, Assistant Attorney General Thomas E. Perez (2012) found the following:

> the data [from the Alabama State Department of Education] show that compared with prior school years, the rate of total withdrawals of Hispanic children substantially increased. The data reflect that between the start of the school year and February 2012, 13.4 percent of Alabama's Hispanic schoolchildren withdrew from school. (p. 2)

The negative impact of HB 56 on Latino children in particular was clear and direct. The DOJ also argued that Section 28 disregarded the humane treatment of foreign nationals and discouraged parents from enrolling children in school by demanding proof of lawful presence (*United States of America v. State of Alabama & Governor Robert J. Bentley*, 2010). After a series of legal actions against HB 56, several controversial measures in the law have been blocked permanently, including Section 28 (*United States of America v. State of Alabama*, 2012).

The threat of deportation often leads undocumented parents and children to avoid public spaces and any interactions with police (Menjívar, 2011). Oklahoma enacted restrictive legislation through House Bill 1804 (State of Oklahoma, 2007), which promoted a pervasive "culture of fear" among immigrant families (Koralek, Pedroza, & Capps, 2009).[6] When immigration policy is directed at schools, the school setting itself is added to the list of uncomfortable, precarious public spaces for immigrant families to avoid. Restrictive immigration laws engender strong symbolism that affects behaviors and perceptions across individuals who live within and far from the jurisdiction of these laws (Santos, Menjivar, & Godfrey, 2013, p. 81).

What's troubling is that under the constant and real threat of deportation, undocumented immigrants generally go to great lengths to hide their legal status, and this often becomes a tremendous source of stress and insecurity (Abrego, 2008; Dreby, 2012). Schools that force the disclosure of legal status for all students and parents undoubtedly create an intimidating setting for immigrant families. Immigration legislation is real and palpable to school-age children whose educational experiences influence their self perceptions and where they see their place in society (Santos et al., 2013). We know, for example, that undocumented members of the young 1.5 generation often internalize legal status as a source of stigma (Abrego, 2011). Moreover, children of immigrants often feel a sense of stress and powerlessness, and they become fearful of authorities because of the looming threat of family separation (Dreby, 2012). In a survey of middle school students in Arizona after the passage of SB 1070, students who reported greater awareness of the law also reported a weaker sense of being American, particularly for first and second-generation youth across racial/ethnic groups (Santos et al., 2013). Researchers linked this dampened sense of Americanism and an increased sense of discrimination to diminished psychological health and lower levels of self-esteem (Santos et al., 2013).

Arizona HB 2281

Ethnic studies programs serve as restorative educational tools in the desegregation process. They are designed to academically engage students from diverse backgrounds and highlight the contributions of ethnic groups to U.S. literature, politics, science, history, and culture. Children of immigrants, as well as later-generation U.S. minority groups, stand to gain a more holistic understanding of their unique social and cultural space in the United States (Kunnie, 2010). In 1974, court cases filed by the National Association for the Advancement of Colored People and the Mexican American Legal Defense Fund accused the Tucson Unified School District (TUSD) of discrimination against Black and Latino students on the basis of race and national origin. Roy Fisher and Maria Mendoza became class representatives for the lawsuits in 1975 (*Fisher v. Tucson School District*, 1980; *Mendoza v. Tucson School District*, 1980). After the district court ruled against TUSD, the resulting settlement agreement established federal court oversight in the school district's desegregation process. To desegregate, TUSD agreed to remove discriminatory practices from faculty assignments, employee training, bilingual education policy, testing, and discipline. Ethnic studies at TUSD were part of the desegregation process ushered in by the Fisher-Mendoza court order (Kunnie, 2010). Almost 30 years later in 2008, TUSD was deemed "unitary" and the settlement agreement was lifted.

The progress made by TUSD faced a significant setback in 2010 with Arizona's HB 2281 that effectively dismantled the state's ethnic studies programs. HB 2281 prohibits public and charter school classes from offering courses that,

1. Promote the overthrow of the United States government, 2. Promote resentment toward a race or class of people, 3. Are designed primarily for pupils of a particular ethnic group, [and] 4. Advocate ethnic solidarity instead of the treatment of pupils as individuals. (State of Arizona, 2010)

Arguing that ethnic studies programs embody this, HB 2281 constituted grounds to defund a long-standing Mexican American studies (MAS) program for high school students in the TUSD. After facing a 10% budget penalty to maintain the MAS program, it was dismantled in January 2012.

Researchers who examined the impact of the Mexican American studies program in Tucson prior to its dismantling found that it successfully helped to keep minority youth from dropping out of school (Cammarota, 2007). Ginwright and Cammarota (2011) also found that students participating in MAS outperformed their peers on state tests in reading, writing, and math. Elsewhere, Cabrera, Milem, and Marx (2012) found MAS participation was a significant, positive predictor of graduation across four cohorts of recent high school students (graduating in years 2008–2011). Moreover, MAS students taking Arizona's Instrument to Measure Standards in reading, writing, and math all showed greater odds of passing than non-MAS students, though the relationship was not always statistically significant across cohorts.

HB 2281 differs from other restrictive policies because it does not request one's immigration status, and it does not threaten undocumented immigrants with deportation. Instead, it restricts minority students' access to community knowledge and educational resources. It is important to consider that Arizona's HB 2281 followed roughly one month after the implementation of SB 1070 (State of Arizona, 2010). Arguably, HB 2281 is one piece of a greater agenda at work in the state of Arizona that extends a comprehensive nativist legislative movement.[7]

Restrictive policies embedded in greater, comprehensive political agendas harm not only Latinos of all backgrounds and generations, but all U.S. ethnic minorities. SB 2281 delegitimizes ethnic scholarship and pedagogy (Cacho, 2010). Julian Kunnie, director of Africana studies at the University of Arizona wrote:

> The repressive character of the law violates the fundamental human, constitutional, and educational rights of freedom of expression and viewpoint.... The factuality of institutionalized racism that perpetuates racial and ethnic stereotypes will continue unabated and unaddressed because teachers will be hesitant and even fearful if they engage in class discussions centering on issues of race and ethnic identity. A general educational discomfort will obtain in classroom settings, leading to further social apathy and mistrust that will erode inter-ethnic engagement among students and teachers alike. (Kunnie, 2010, p. 21)

Students are sensitive to the dynamics of race and ethnicity both inside schools and in their communities. Yet, their educational settings face increased challenges in effectively engaging these important discussions and contextualizing them historically.

Lawsuits over HB 2281 have proceeded through the courts (*Acosta v. Huppenthal*, 2013; *Arce v. Douglas*, 2015). By 2015, the Ninth U.S. Circuit Court of Appeals issued a mixed judgement that upheld much of HB 2281's provisions, but acknowledged that the context of its legislative debates and administrative history, "raise at least a plausible inference that racial animus underlay passage of the legislation" (*Arce v. Douglas*, 2015, p. 18). The court ordered a trial to determine the law's discriminatory intent in violation of the Fourteenth Amendment.

Restrictive Immigration Policy Impacting the Greater Latino Community

Regardless of legal status, immigrants from Latin America and U.S.-born Latinos (Mexican-origin populations in particular) have largely been racialized as "illegal" immigrants in U.S. society (DeGenova, 2004; Dreby, 2012; Massey & Sanchez 2010). Within the school context, for example, undocumented students who arrived in the United States as young children are not necessarily discernible from documented students or their U.S.-born Latino peers because they are being schooled and socialized together (Abrego, 2006; Olivas, 1995). Latino students are therefore the most likely to encounter challenges related to immigration since their faces are most commonly associated with undocumented immigration (Darder, Torres, & Gutierrez, 1997; Gibson, 2002).

Given this context, how then does immigration policy impact the broader Latino experience in the United States? As immigration law becomes increasingly punitive and criminalized, it creates a context of social suffering for all immigrants that establishes long-term climates of normalized persecution, harm, and insecurity (Menjívar & Abrego, 2012). Moreover, the social stigma assigned to undocumented immigrants translates easily into broader, racialized stigmas against legal immigrants and U.S.-born Latinos as well. Latinos of all legal statuses, generations, and nationalities become susceptible to racial profiling under the pretext of immigration enforcement. A Pew Hispanic Center Study (Lopez, Morin, & Taylor, 2010) found that Latino respondents ranked immigration as the most important factor leading to discrimination, ahead of skin color, language skills, and income and education. Across immigrant youth and their U.S.-born peers, their American identity becomes undermined by punitive and discriminatory immigration legislation (Santos et al., 2013).

STATE AND FEDERAL HUMANITARIAN IMMIGRATION POLICY

A story of strife is never complete without a seed of hope. As immigration policies permeate the school experience of children of immigrants and others, the fundamental cause of universal public schooling remains intact because of *Plyler v. Doe* (1982), a case that firmly established a precedent granting equal K–12 public school access to noncitizen and citizen children alike (Olivas, 2010). *Plyler v. Doe* was filed in response to the Texas Legislature's 1975 education law revision that withheld state funds for educating undocumented children (and enabled districts to charge tuition fees to the parents of undocumented children). In 1982, the U.S. Supreme Court ruled against the state of Texas, explaining that the law did not serve a compelling government interest because it effectively imposed "a lifetime hardship on a discrete class of children" that would permanently render them to a social underclass (*Plyler v. Doe*, 1982). However, the movement to exclude undocumented students from public schools shifted focus to public institutions of higher education, specifically in passing legislation that either blocked undocumented students from attending public colleges, or prevented them from applying for financial aid and grants. Although the limitations are imposed in higher education, it undoubtedly shapes the K–12 educational experiences of children of immigrants, particularly those in high school who are transitioning into adulthood (Gonzales, 2011). However, humanitarian immigration policies have been shown to have a positive impact on students' identities and sense of self, their school experience, and their perspectives on the future.

California's AB 540

The federal government's Illegal Immigration Reform and Immigrant Responsibility Act of 1996 granted undocumented students the ability to apply to and attend public and private colleges, but it preempted any state's effort to qualify undocumented students for in-state tuition (Olivas, 2010). As a result, states were forced to pass special legislation to grant undocumented students access to in-state tuition. At the time of this writing, 16 states maintain active legislation extending in-state tuition rates to qualifying undocumented students, four states have passed legislation prohibiting undocumented students from receiving in-state tuition rates, and two states have prohibited undocumented students from enrolling at any public postsecondary institution.[8] Academically-oriented undocumented students find themselves in a peculiar space in which they are "criminalized for being undocumented, yet legitimated for their successful student status" (Abrego, 2008, p. 715). As undocumented children meet various transitions on their way to adulthood, knowledge of their tenuous legal status takes a damaging toll on the sense of self, leaving students in a "state of limbo" in which they feel separated from their peer support networks and harbor a sense of fear and shame due to their status (Gonzales, 2011, pp. 610–611). Students are often overcome with shock, confusion, anger, frustration, and despair (Gonzales, 2011, p. 615). Because of their legal status, undocumented students are forced to "transition to illegality" and retool their lives and aspirations (Gonzales, 2011). In many cases, students' grades fall, as does their self-image (Gonzales, 2011).

Enter AB 540, the 2001 law that revised the California Education Code to allow qualifying nonresident students to pay in-state college tuition, provided that they meet certain qualifications, including that they attended high school in California and earned a high school diploma or equivalent (State of California, 2011). Abrego (2008) conducted a longitudinal, qualitative study with undocumented youth to examine the legal and social ramifications of the law. Abrego interviewed 27 undocumented youth (17 to 24 years old) before the passage of AB 540, and followed up with them one year later, and again three to four years after the bill's passage. On the one hand, the study found that AB 540 achieved limited success helping undocumented students access a broader range of higher education options. However, the cost of college still proved too steep for many undocumented students and their families, and students were not allowed to compete for scholarships that required legal residence or citizenship (Abrego, 2008). This pushed some respondents toward the less expensive option of community college. While an important resource for students, community colleges sometimes divert students to vocational tracks rather than spur them toward a 4-year degree (Brint & Karabel, 1989).

Beyond this, undocumented students incorporated AB 540 into their everyday experiences, culture, and identity; these are "constitutive" effects of the law (Abrego, 2008, p. 721). Before AB 540, students reportedly internalized their immigration status, feeling stigmatized and embarrassed for being undocumented. In the years following AB 540, students were more willing to divulge their legal status. Respondents embraced the label of "AB 540 student" as a means of employing a "neutral, and more socially acceptable label" to communicate their legal status alongside their student status, which seemingly offered greater social legitimacy (Abrego, 2008, pp. 723 & 726). Stigma consciousness has been documented in psychological research to speak to individuals' self-consciousness about being a member of a stereotyped group (Brown & Pinel, 2003). In the wake of AB 540, undocumented students felt that some of the stigma was lifted.

DREAMs, Deferred Action, and Presidential Orders

Since 2001, each United States congressional session has been presented with variants of the Development, Relief, and Education for Alien Minors (DREAM) Act. Early incarnations of the DREAM Act offered the prospect of conditional lawful permanent resident status and an eventual path to citizenship for qualifying undocumented high school graduates and GED recipients, upon acceptance into college or registration for service in the military. Although the federal DREAM Act has yet to pass, in 2011, California's legislature passed a similarly-named policy that offers financial assistance for postsecondary education. The California Dream Act (based on Assembly Bills 130 and 131) was implemented in 2013 and allows undocumented youth who qualify for AB 540 to receive the same access to state-funded financial aid and scholarships that are available to in-state residents (State of California, 2011a, 2011b).

The federal DREAM Act is rooted in a mission to educate and invest in the future of undocumented youth as full-fledged members of American society. In this spirit, the Obama administration implemented the Deferred Action for Childhood Arrivals (DACA) Order of 2012, which directed the Department of Homeland Security to exercise prosecutorial discretion and halt the deportation of low priority cases, specifically, undocumented immigrants who came to the United States as young children (USCIS, 2016; USDHS, 2012). For individuals who submit applications and are granted deferred action, the order remains in place for 2 years (and is renewable). During that time the applicant may seek work authorization. To be considered for deferred action, applicants must be in school, high school graduates or GED recipients, or have served in the military. Among other requisites, applicants must have entered the United States before age 16, and cannot have records of felony conviction, or significant misdemeanor offenses. By November of 2014, President Obama announced the expansion of the population eligible for DACA program, and extended work authorization from 2 years to 3 years. Additionally, executive orders were issued for the Deferred Action for Parents of Americans and Lawful Permanent Residents (DAPA) program, which allows work authorization, and further provisions to legalize include spouses, sons, and daughters of lawful permanent residents and citizens (White House Office of Press Secretary, 2014). However, the 2014 expansion of DACA and the introduction of DAPA were enjoined by a federal judge in Texas in early 2015. After legal appeals, the issue is currently being considered before the Supreme Court (*United States v. Texas*, 2016).

Humanitarian policies such as this reflect the government's increasing awareness of undocumented youth, their plight, and the value of their future contributions to the United States. Instead of children of immigrants living in fear of family separation, these policies present a real opportunity to keep immigrants and their families together and emerge from the shadows of their legal status. As evidenced by AB 540 (State of California, 2001), undocumented students are keenly aware of the limitations of their legal status and they adjust their educational pursuits based on their perceived opportunity structure, a reality that is shaped in great part by legal status as well as socioeconomic status (Abrego, 2008; Guarneros, Bendezu, Perez Huber, Velez, & Solorzano, 2009). As children age, they become less engaged in school, particularly between middle and high school (Eccles & Roeser, 2005; Suárez-Orozco, Pimentel, & Martin, 2009). The loss of engagement is expedited among immigrant groups facing hardships (Eccles & Roeser, 2005; Portes & Rumbaut, 2001). Without humanitarian policies that grant qualifying students a fair opportunity to pursue education and upward mobility, it is likely that their school engagement will suffer.

CONCLUSION: IMPROVING EDUCATION
FOR CHILDREN OF IMMIGRANTS

Outside of the family, the individuals who have the greatest opportunity to encourage and connect with children of immigrants are educators. For both educators and school administrators who work with children of immigrants daily, there are at least three key, practical considerations to carry forward. Schools should: (a) continue outreach efforts to immigrant parents and families and link them with social and economic resources as needed; (b) employ instructional strategies to engage immigrant and later-generation youth, particularly as difficult social and policy-related dynamics emerge and likely impact their families; and (c) share realistic information on opportunities and support available to undocumented and U.S.-born students.

In order for outreach efforts to be successful, it is critical that school sites are perceived as receptive and welcoming. As we have demonstrated, immigration policy creates difficult and often hostile social contexts for immigrant families to navigate; in order to engage immigrant parents and their families, schools must become safe havens. Even without addressing restrictive immigration policies, research shows that immigrant parents (and undocumented parents in particular) find school settings intimidating (Crosnoe, 2010). Schools do best when they create a welcoming physical environment for families and treat all parents with dignity and respect. Principals and school administrators have a responsibility in setting the agenda for a welcoming school environment, and front desk staff and teachers who have frequent personal interactions with families are most critical in its implementation.

Beyond a welcoming school environment, what does successful outreach and parent engagement look like? Parent involvement has been linked to promoting children's learning and achievement (Cheadle, 2008; Pomerantz, Moorman, & Litwack, 2007). Crosnoe (2010) advocates a two-pronged, "direct" and "indirect" approach for involving immigrant parents with their children's education. The direct approach develops and reinforces education-oriented behavior among parents. Crosnoe (2010) cites several promising programs in line with the direct approach: Abriendo Puertas, Avance, Lee y Seras, Home Instruction for Parents of Preschool Youngsters, Parent Engagement Education Program, and Project Flame. These school- and community-based programs are driven by the following tenets: to help parents become teachers at home, make the home environment cognitively stimulating, bridge the gap between home and school, build connections between families and communities, and share useful information with parents about factors impacting their daily lives (tax assistance, financial literacy). For the most part, these programs offer low-cost or free opportunities for families to become full participants in the process of educating their children. Moreover, these services are especially needed in Latino immigrant communities, where parents are the least likely to read with their children, engage in home learning activities, and enroll their children in preschool, compared to U.S.-born Latinos, Whites, and immigrant and U.S.-born Asians (Crosnoe, 2010).

Crosnoe's "indirect" approach addresses outside factors known to limit parent involvement. For example, parents are less likely to engage with school personnel when they confront language barriers and a broad unfamiliarity with the American school system (Romo, 1986; Stanton-Salazar, 2001). In line with the "indirect" approach to immigrant parent engagement, Gerardo Lopez and his collaborators (Lopez, Scribner, & Mahitivanichcha, 2001) found that schools can successfully engage migrant families through nontraditional home involvement, which helps develop an understanding of families' socioeconomic context. With this understanding, schools are in a better position to connect immigrant families with targeted social and economic resources. This includes offering education awareness classes that help parents navigate the school site and broader educational system as well as parent "self-improvement" classes (GED, ESL, technical courses, citizenship classes), and coordinating within and outside of the school system to help families obtain the services they need. What's more is that these programs offer more extensive reach beyond immigrant families to all families facing socioeconomic difficulties. However, one caution is that programs often struggle to maintain parent participation (Crosnoe, 2010).

Ample opportunity exists to reach children of immigrants within the school setting itself. These students are regularly exposed to what Suárez-Orozco, Yoshikawa, and Tseng (2015) term a "cumulative intersectionality" of disadvantage experienced through living in poverty and language barriers (Hernandez, 2014 as cited in Suárez-Orozco et al., 2015), racialization (Telles & Ortiz, 2008), greater susceptibility to tracking (Valenzuela, 1999), and sometimes tenuous legal status (Abrego, 2008; Yoshikawa, Khloptseva, & Suárez-Orozco 2013). Smith-Maddox and Solórzano (2002) argue that to engage diverse student populations, Freire's problem-posing method is particularly effective because it breaches the typical dynamic of students listening only to teachers. The problem-posing method allows learning to grow through teachers and students actively engaging in dialogue, which allows students' insights and perceptions to become both recognized and valued in the learning process. Researchers have urged that teachers use writing prompts to encourage students to share some aspect of their experiences and engage in class discussion—this helps students understand commonalities among each other and furthermore allows teachers to become more versed in their students' lives (Suárez-Orozco & Suárez-Orozco, 2013; Suárez-Orozco et al., 2015). The delicate balance for instructors is to formulate topics that are engaging for children of immigrants, yet not so personal as to solicit information about students that would compromise their comfort in the classroom (such as questions about their legal status).

Also key in supporting children of immigrants is the communication of educational opportunities available to them. Department of Education-funded Trio programs (such as Upward Bound and Talent Search) focus on providing disadvantaged students with curricular and informational resources that will better prepare them to apply to and enroll in college. Latino youths' academic achievement is often hindered by inadequate information and low expectations about the opportunities available to them (Gasbarra & Johnson, 2008). Young Latinos and their parents are fully cognizant of the benefits of a college degree, even more than other ethnic and racial groups (Taylor, Kochhar, Wang, & Medina, 2009). The problem is likely that they don't know the optimal paths to obtain a college degree. The postsecondary reality is particularly daunting for undocumented students in states with the most restrictive tuition measures, though U.S.-born children of immigrants also often face socioeconomic constraints that make college seem unattainable. While college is a more immediate concern for upper classmen in high school, knowledge of legal or economic obstacles to higher education undoubtedly stream into the consciousness of younger students. It is critical that teachers and school personnel communicate the full array of educational options available to students, and explain resources that are available and where to find them. In other words, schools must be on top of immigration policy developments as they unfold, because they are in a prime position to advise students of their opportunities and to show them alternatives when laws place obstacles between students and higher education. When children's families are faced with adjusting to the sometimes-harsh social and economic realities of living in the United States, schools must become harbors of information, understanding, and support.

This chapter highlights the ways that immigration policy impacts the education of foreign-born and U.S.-born children of Latino immigrants. Students' identity and social-emotional well-being, school engagement, and outlook on future opportunities are all at risk within contexts of restrictive immigration policy. At this point, primarily qualitative data have linked immigration policy to students' educational experiences and outlooks; however, attendance trends in Alabama during the days following the implementation of Section 28 of HB 56 (State of Alabama, 2011) illustrate that there is also a quantifiable impact of these policies that needs further study (see Santos et al., 2013). Targeted quantitative studies would be well-served to look at established, measureable dimensions of school engagement to examine the relationship between immigration policy and children of immigrants, specifically in cognitive domains of school engagement that cover student beliefs and motivation to overcome difficult situations (Bandura, 1997; Fredricks, Blumenfeld, & Paris, 2004; Lee & Shute, 2010), self-efficacy

(Bandura, 1997), and goal orientation (Walls & Little, 2005). These areas conceptually align with qualitative findings on the student-level impact of immigration policy.

As immigration reform remains a divisive dialogue in the public realm and research on this important area continues, schools remain a constant, integral space in children's lives. To policymakers, we argue that an "inestimable toll" (*Plyler v. Doe*, 1982) is taken on children of immigrants when schools become purveyors of immigration law (State of Alabama, 2011, HB 56), and when students are intentionally barred from learning the valuable contributions of their community to the United States (State of Arizona, 2010, HB 2281). In the interest of investing in the future of children of immigrants and their communities, the policy takeaway is clear—support the DREAM Act and resurrect ethnic studies programs where they have been dismantled. Immigration reform must include provisions to keep families as in tact as possible, and we must work to keep schools in the business of educating and providing support to immigrant families and their communities.

NOTES

1. Generally, children who arrived in the United States after age 12 are considered first generation immigrants, and children who entered the United States before the age of 12 are part of the 1.5 generation (Rumbaut, 2004).
2. The Department of Homeland Security focuses on the immigration enforcement of high priority cases, which include "criminal aliens and national security threats, as well as repeat immigration law violators and recent border entrants" (United States Immigration and Customs Enforcement 2012).
3. The compilation of these policy categories is informed by Donnelly (2013), who uses the terms "pro-integration legislation" and "integrative/beneficial" to describe policies intended to help legal immigrants through social integration, citizenship, and education policy; and "pro-enforcement legislation" and "restrictive/punitive" describe policies that make life harder for unauthorized migrants through enhanced criminal sanctions and the denial of social services.
4. Proposition 187 won voter approval in 1994 to cut off nearly all social services and educational benefits for undocumented residents, but was ultimately deemed unconstitutional in U.S. District Court. The policy also required police, health care professionals and teachers to verify and report the immigration status of all individuals, including children.
5. The United States Supreme Court struck down SB 1070 provisions that created new misdemeanor offenses based on a failure to carry immigrant registration documents at all times (Section 3), undocumented immigrants seeking work (Section 5), and authorizing warrantless arrests when a person who has committed an offense is suspected of being undocumented and removable from the U.S. (Section 6). Section 2B was upheld, which required officers

conducting a stop, detention, or arrest to make efforts, in some circumstances, to verify the person's immigration status with the federal government. Since 2010, SB 1070-inspired legislation has passed in Alabama, Georgia, Indiana, South Carolina, and Utah (American Civil Liberties Union, 2016).

6. In particular, HB 1804 prohibited issuance of identification for unauthorized immigrants; made it a state crime to "transport, harbor, or shelter" undocumented immigrants (a particular difficulty in families of mixed legal status); and prevented undocumented students from receiving scholarships and financial assistance.

7. After Oklahoma's HB 1840 (a predecessor to SB 1070) was passed, researchers found that "...the legislation appears to have provided an opening for anti-immigrant sentiment in the state and to have furthered anti-immigration legislative proposals" (Koralek et al. 2009, p. iii).

8. States granting in-state tuition to undocumented students include California, Colorado, Connecticut, Florida, Illinois, Kansas, Maryland, Minnesota, Nebraska, New Mexico, New Jersey, New York, Oregon, Texas, Utah, and Washington. Oklahoma and Rhode Island offer in-state tuition to undocumented students through Board of Regents decisions. Arizona, Georgia, and Indiana have passed legislation that specifically prohibits undocumented students from receiving in-state tuition rates. Alabama and South Carolina prohibit undocumented students from enrolling at any public postsecondary institution.

REFERENCES

Abrego, L. J. (2006). "I can't go to college because I don't have papers": Incorporation patterns of Latino undocumented youth. *Latino Studies 4*(3), 212–231.

Abrego, L. J. (2008). Legitimacy, social identity, and the mobilization of law: The effects of Assembly Bill 540 on undocumented students in California. *Law & Social Inquiry 33*(3), 709–734.

Abrego, L. J. (2011). Legal consciousness of undocumented Latinos: Fear and stigma as barriers to claims-making for first- and 1.5-generation immigrants. *Law & Society Review 45*(2), 337–370.

Acosta v. Huppenthal, CV 10-623-TUC-AWT, 2013 WL 871948 (D. Arizona, 2013).

Alabama Department of Education. (2011). Alabama's immigration law-communicating section 28. *Public Relations in Our Schools*. Retrieved from https://www.alsde.edu/sec/comm/PROS/November2011.pdf

American Civil Liberties Union. 2016. "Arizona's SB 1070." Retrieved from https://www.aclu.org/feature/arizonas-sb-1070

Anti-Terrorism and Effective Death Penalty Act of 1996, Public Law No. 104-132, 110 Stat. 1214.

Arce v. Douglas, Nos. 13-15657 13-15760, D.C. No. 4:10-cv-00623-AWT (9th Cir. 2015).

Bandura, A. (1997). *Self-efficacy: The exercise of control*. New York, NY: Freeman.

Brint, S., & Karabel, J. (1989). *The diverted dream: Community colleges and the promise of educational opportunity in America, 1900–1985*. New York, NY: Oxford University Press.

Brown, R. P., & Pinel, E. C. (2003). Stigma on my mind: Individual differences in the experience of stereotype threat. *Journal of Experimental Social Psychology 39*, 626–633.

Cabrera, N. L., Milem, J. F., & Marx, R. W. (2012). *An empirical analysis of the effects of Mexican American studies participation on student achievement within Tucson Unified School District.* Report submitted June 20, 2012, to Willis D. Hawley, special master for the Tucson Unified School District desegregation case. Retrieved from http://posting.tucsonweekly.com/images/blogimages/2012/11/12/1352763151-112886925-emprical-analysis-mas-report-2012.pdf

Cacho, L. M. (2010). But some of us are wise: Academic illegitimacy and the affective value of ethnic studies. *The Black Scholar 40*(4), 28–36.

Cammarota, J. (2007). A social justice approach to achievement: Guiding Latina/o students toward educational attainment with a challenging, socially relevant curriculum. *Equity and Excellence in Education 40*, 87–96.

Chaudry, A., Capps, R., Pedroza, J. M., Castaneda, R. M., Santos, R., & Scott, M. M. (2010). Facing our future: Children in the aftermath of immigration enforcement. *The Urban Institute.* Retrieved from http://www.urban.org/UploadedPDF/412020_FacingOurFuture_final.pdf

Chavez, J. M., & Provine, D. M. (2009). Race and the response of state legislatures to unauthorized immigrants. *The Annals of the American Academy, 623*(1), 78–92.

Cheadle, J. E. (2008). Educational investment, family context, and children's math and reading growth from kindergarten through third grade. *Sociology of Education, 81*(1), 1–31.

Crosnoe, R. (2010). Two-generation strategies and involving immigrant parents in children's education. *Urban Institute.* Retrieved from http://www.urban.org/publications/412204.html

Darder, A., Torres, R. D., & Gutierrez, H. (1997). *Latinos and education: A critical reader.* New York, NY: Routledge.

DeGenova, N. (2004). The legal production of Mexican/migrant "illegality." *Latino Studies 2*(2), 160–185.

Diaz McConnell, E. (2013). Latinos in Arizona: Demographic context in the SB 1070 era. In L. Magaña & E. Lee (Eds.), *Latino politics and Arizona's immigration law SB 1070* (pp. 1–18). New York, NY: Springer.

Donnelly, R. (2013). State-level immigrant-related legislation: What it means for the immigration policy debate. In L. Magaña & E. Lee (Eds.), *Latino politics and Arizona's immigration law SB 1070* (pp. 1–18). New York, NY: Springer.

Dreby, J. (2012, August). How today's immigration enforcement policies impact children, families, and communities: A view from the ground. *Center for American Progress.* Retrieved from http://www.americanprogress.org/wp-content/uploads/2012/08/DrebyImmigrationFamiliesFINAL.pdf

Eccles, J., & Roeser, R. (2005). School and community influences on human development. In M. H. Bornstein & M. E. Lamb (Eds.), *Developmental science: An advanced textbook* (pp. 513–555). Mahwah, NJ: Erlbaum.

Espenshade, T., & Hempstead, K. (1996). Contemporary American attitudes toward U.S. immigration. *International Migration Review 30*, 535–570.

Fisher v. Tucson School District, No. 1, 625 F.2d 834 (1980).

Fredricks, J. A., Blumenfeld, P. C., & Paris, A. H. (2004). School engagement: Potential of the concept, state of the evidence. *Review of Educational Research* 74, 59–109.

Gasbarra, P., & Johnson, J. (2008). *A matter of trust.* New York, NY: Public Agenda.

Gibson, M. A. (2002). The new Latino diaspora and educational policy. In S. Wortham, E. G. Murillo, & E. T. Hamann (Eds.), *Education in the new Latino diaspora: Policy and the politics of identity* (pp. 241–252). Westport, CT: Ablex.

Ginwright, S., & Cammarota, J. (2011). Youth organizing in the Wild West: Mobilizing for educational justice in Arizona! *Voices in Urban Education 30,* 13–21. Retrieved from http://www.annenberginstitute.org/VUE/wp-content/pdf/VUE30_Ginwright.pdf

Glenn, E. N. (2011). Constructing citizenship: Exclusion, subordination, and resistance. *American Sociological Review, 76*(1), 1–24.

Gonzales, R. G. (2011). Learning to be illegal: Undocumented youth and shifting legal contexts in the transition to adulthood. *American Sociological Review, 76*(4), 602–619.

Guarneros, N., Bendezu, C., Perez Huber, L., Velez, V. N., & Solorzano, D. G. (2009). Still dreaming: Legislation and legal decisions affecting undocumented AB 540 students. *Latino Policy & Issues Brief, 23.* Retrieved from http://www.chicano.ucla.edu/files/pb23.pdf

Hernández, D. (2014). *Disparities in the well-being of diverse children with immigrant and U.S.-born parents.* Los Angeles, CA: UCLA Program on International Migration.

Illegal Immigration Reform and Immigrant Responsibility Act of 1996, Public Law 104-208, 110 Stat. 3009.

Jacobson, R. D. (2008). *The New Nativism: Proposition 187 and the Debate over Immigration.* Minneapolis: University of Minnesota Press.

Koralek, R., Pedroza, J., & Capps, R. (2009). Untangling the Oklahoma taxpayer and citizen protection act: Consequences for children and families. Washington, DC: *National Council of La Raza.* Retrieved from http://www.urban.org/UploadedPDF/1001356_oklahoma_taxpayer.pdf

Kunnie, J. (2010). Apartheid in Arizona? HB 2281 and Arizona's denial of human rights of peoples of color. *The Black Scholar, 40*(4), 16–26.

Lee, J., & Shute, V. J. (2010). Personal and social-contextual factors in K-12 academic performance: An integrative perspective on student learning. *Educational Psychologist, 45*(3), 185–202.

Lopez, G. R., Scribner, J. D., & Mahitivanichcha, K. (2001). Redefining parental involvement: Lessons from high-performing migrant-impacted schools. *American Educational Research Journal, 38*(2), 253–288.

Lopez, M. H. (2009). Latinos and education: Explaining the attainment gap. *Pew Hispanic Center.* Retrieved from http://www.pewhispanic.org/files/reports/115.pdf

Lopez, M. H., Morin, R., & Taylor, P. (2010). Illegal immigration backlash worries, divides Latinos. *Pew Hispanic Center.* Retrieved from: http://www.pewhispanic.org/files/reports/128.pdf

Magaña, L., & Lee, E. K. (Eds.). (2013). *Latino politics and Arizona's immigration law SB 1070.* New York, NY: Springer Press.

Massey, D. S., & Sánchez, M. R. (2010). *Brokered boundaries: Creating immigrant identity in anti-immigrant times*. New York, NY: Russell Sage Foundation.

McDowell, M., & Provine, D. M. (2013). SB 1070: Testing the 'frustration' hypothesis. In L. Magaña & E. Lee (Eds.), *Latino politics and Arizona's immigration law SB 1070* (pp. 55–78). New York, NY: Springer.

Mendoza v. Tucson School District, No. 1, 623 F.2d 1338, 1341 (9th Cir. 1980)

Menjívar, C. (2011). The power of the law: Central Americans' legality and everyday life in Phoenix, Arizona. *Latino Studies, 9*(4), 377–395.

Menjívar, C., & Abrego, L. J. (2012). Immigration law and the lives of Central American immigrants. *American Journal of Sociology, 117*(5), 1380–1421.

Miller, T. (2005). Blurring the boundaries between immigration and crime control after September 11th. *Boston College Third World Law Journal, 25*(1), 81–123.

National Center for Education Statistics. (2014). Racial/ethnic enrollment in public schools. *NCES.* Retrieved from http://nces.ed.gov/programs/coe/indicator_cge.asp

Olivas, M. (1995). Storytelling out of school: Undocumented college residency, race, and reaction. *Hastings Constitutional Law Quarterly, 22*, 1019–1086.

Olivas, M. (2010). The political economy of the DREAM Act and the legislative process: A case study of comprehensive immigration reform. *Wayne Law Review, 55*, 1757–1810.

Perez, T. E. (2012). *Letter to Dr. Thomas R. Bice, state superintendent of education of Alabama on behalf of Department of Justice Civil Rights Division.* Retrieved from http://media.al.com/bn/other/DOJ%20Letter%20May%202012.pdf

Plyler v. Doe, 457 U.S. 202 (1982)

Pomerantz, E., Moorman, E., & Litwack, S. (2007). The how, whom, and why of parents' involvement in children's academic lives: More is not always better. *Review of Educational Research, 77*, 373–410.

Portes, A., & Rumbaut, R. (2001). *Legacies: The story of the immigrant second generation.* Berkeley, CA: University of California Press.

Romo, H. (1986). Inequality in Bilingual Education: School Organizational Factors. *La Raza Law Journal, 1*(3), 227–294.

Rumbaut, R. (2004). Ages, life stages, and generational cohorts: Decomposing the immigrant first and second generations in the United States. *International Migration Review, 38*(3), 1160–1205.

Santos, C., Menjívar, C., & Godfrey, E. (2013). Effects of SB 1070 on children. In L. Magaña & E. Lee (Eds.), *Latino politics and Arizona's immigration law SB 1070* (pp. 79–92). New York, NY: Springer.

Smith-Maddox, R., & Solorzano, D. G. (2002). Using critical race theory, Paulo Freire's problem-posing method, and case study research to confront race and racism in education. *Qualitative Inquiry, 8*(1), 66–84.

Stanton-Salazar, R. D. (2001). Manufacturing hope and despair: The school and kin support networks of U.S.-Mexican youth. New York, NY: Teachers College Press.

State of Alabama. (2011). Beason-Hammon Alabama Taxpayer and Citizen Protection Act. House Bill 56. Retrieved from https://legiscan.com/AL/text/HB56/id/321074/Alabama-2011-HB56-Enrolled.pdf; http://www.ago.state.al.us/File-Immigration-Act-No-2011-535

State of Arizona House of Representatives. (2010). House Bill 2281. 49th Legislature, 2nd Regular Session, 2010. Retrieved from http://www.azleg.gov/legtext/49leg/2r/bills/hb2281s.pdf

State of Arizona Senate. (2010). Senate Bill 1070. 49th Legislature, 2nd Session, 2010. Retrieved from http://www.azleg.gov/legtext/49leg/2r/bills/sb1070s.pdf

State of California. (2011a). Assembly Bill 130. Retrieved from http://www.leginfo.ca.gov/pub/11-12/bill/asm/ab_0101-0150/ab_130_bill_20110725_chaptered.html

State of California. (2011b). Assembly Bill 131. Retrieved from http://www.leginfo.ca.gov/pub/11-12/bill/asm/ab_0101-0150/ab_131_bill_20111008_chaptered.html

State of California. (2001). Assembly Bill 540. 2001-2002 Leg., Reg. Sess. (Cal. 2001) (codified at Cal. Educ. Code § 68130.5). Retrieved from http://www.leginfo.ca.gov/pub/01-02/bill/asm/ab_0501-0550/ab_540_bill_20011013_chaptered.html

State of Oklahoma. (2007). Oklahoma Taxpayer and Citizen Protection Act of 2007. House Bill 1804, 51st Legislature. Retrieved from http://www.oklegislature.gov/BillInfo.aspx?Bill=HB1804&Session=0700

Suárez-Orozco, C., Pimentel, A., & Martin, M. (2009). The significance of relationships: Academic engagement and achievement among newcomer immigrant youth. *Teachers College Record, 111*(3), 712–749.

Suárez-Orozco, C., Yoshikawa, H., & Tseng, V. (2015). Intersecting inequalities: Research to reduce inequality for immigrant-origin children and youth. *William T. Grant Foundation.* Retrieved from http://blog.wtgrantfoundation.org/post/111903703827/intersecting-inequalities-research-to-reduce

Suárez-Orozco, M., & Suárez-Orozco, C. (2013). Taking perspective: Context, culture, and history. In M. G. Hernández, J. Nguyen, C. L. Saetermoe, & C. Suárez-Orozco (Eds.), *Frameworks and ethics for research with immigrants: New directions for child and adolescent development* (pp. 9–23). San Francisco, CA: Wiley.

Taylor, P., Kochhar, R., Wang, W., & Medina, J. (2009). *America's Changing Workforce: Recession Turns a Graying Office Grayer.* Washington, D.C.: Pew Research Center. Retrieved from http://www.pewsocialtrends.org/files/2010/10/americas-changing-workforce.pdf

Telles, E., & Ortiz, V. (2008). *Generations of exclusion: Mexican Americans, assimilation, and race.* New York, NY: Russell Sage Foundation.

United States Congress. (1996). Illegal Immigration Reform and Immigrant Responsibility Act of 1996. House of Representatives 3610, 104th Congress. Retrieved from https://www.congress.gov/bill/104th-congress/house-bill/3610

United States Department of Homeland Security. (2012). Press Release: Secretary Napolitano Announces Deferred Action Process for Young People who are Low Enforcement Priorities. Retrieved from https://www.nilc.org/wp-content/uploads/2015/11/PD-children-DHS-PR-2012-06-15.pdf

United States Immigration and Customs Enforcement. (2012). *Frequently asked questions on the administration's announcement regarding a new process to further focus immigration enforcement resources on high priority cases.* Retrieved from http://www.ice.gov/doclib/about/offices/ero/pdf/immigration-enforcement-facts.pdf

United States of America v. State of Alabama & Governor Robert J. Bentley, 11-J-2746-S (2011). Retrieved from http://www.justice.gov/opa/documents/motion-preliminary-injunction.pdf

United States of America v. State of Alabama. Nos. 11–14532, 11–14674. (11th Cir. 2012).

United States of America v. State of Texas, No. 15-674. (S Ct). Retrieved from: http://www.supremecourt.gov/oral_arguments/argument_transcripts/15-674_h3dj.pdf

United States Senate. (2011). S. 952, Development, Relief, and Education for Alien Minors Act of 2011, 112th Congress, 1st Session. Retrieved from https://www.congress.gov/bill/112th-congress/senate-bill/952

Valenzuela, A. (1999). *Subtractive Schooling: U.S.-Mexican Youth and the Politics of Caring.* Albany, NY: State University of New York Press.

Walls, T. A., & Little, T. D. (2005). Relations among personal agency, motivation, and school adjustment in early adolescence. *Journal of Educational Psychology, 97*(1), 23–31.

White House Office of the Press Secretary. (2014). Fact Sheet: Immigration Accountability Executive Action. Retrieved from https://www.whitehouse.gov/the-press-office/2014/11/20/fact-sheet-immigration-accountability-executive-action

Yoshikawa, H., Kholopstseva, J., & Suárez-Orozco, C. (2013). Developmental consequences of parent undocumented status: Implications for public policies and community-based organizations. *Social Policy Report, 27*(3), 3-17. Retrieved from: http://www.srcd.org/sites/default/files/documents/E-News/spr_273.pdf

CHAPTER 8

MISMATCHED ASSUMPTIONS

Motivation, Grit, and High-Stakes Testing

Julian Vasquez Heilig
California State University, Sacramento

Roxana Marachi
San José State University

Diana E. Cruz
Naperville School District 203

Since the onset of No Child Left Behind (NCLB) more than a decade ago, a lynchpin of accountability formulas for U.S. schools has included some form of a state-mandated exam. Accountability policies have utilized standardized tests as the basis of decisions that determine progression through grade levels, access to higher education, progress in achievement, and resource allocation to schools (Vasquez Heilig & Darling-Hammond, 2008). At the height of the NCLB era, about half of U.S. states required students to pass high school exit exams in order to graduate from high school (Vasquez Heilig & Home, 2013). In elementary and middle schools, these exams are

Educational Policies and Youth in the 21st Century, pages 145–157

considered "high-stakes" because they are often used to determine grade retention.

The prevailing theory of action behind the exam requirements and accountability movement is that schools and students held accountable to these measures will automatically increase educational output due to the accountability pressure. The assumption inherent in these policies is that when students and educators are faced with the pressure of examinations, they will simply try harder. Pressure to improve test scores is assumed to produce gains in student achievement as schools work to improve their instruction for low-achieving students (Vasquez Heilig & Darling-Hammond, 2008).

Despite two decades of high-stakes testing linked to accountability formulas, the United States has not closed achievement gaps. At the miniscule rate that the gaps are closing under NCLB, it would take 80 more years for the achievement gaps to close (Reardon, Greenberg, Kalogrides, Shores, & Valentino, 2012). A possible explanation for the stagnant gaps may be that assumptions about human behavior based on test-based accountability systems fundamentally ignore decades of research on human development and motivation.

HIGH-STAKES TESTING AND ADVERSITY

Current research investigations have considered student achievement in the midst of testing (Vasquez Heilig, Young, & Williams, 2012), but it is also necessary to understand how high-stakes testing may impact students' psychosocial well-being. Understanding whether and how high-stakes examinations diminish achievement motivation is a hypothesis that runs contrary to the prevailing theory of motivation underlying No Child Left Behind and subsequent high-stakes testing policies. However, the lack of improvement of student success in the midst of accountability warrants this careful examination as several prominent policy reports have documented the detrimental impacts of high-stakes testing pressures on youth. For example, Holbein and Ladd (2015) explored how high-stakes accountability pressures influenced "non-achievement student behaviors" and conclude the following:

> Accountability pressure has the unintended effect . . . of increasing the number of student misbehaviors such as suspensions, fights, and offenses reportable to law enforcement. Further, this negative response is most pronounced among minorities and low-performing students, who are most likely to be left behind. (Holbein & Ladd, 2015, p. iii)

Earlier research also documented the harms of overreliance on account-ability-based systems. In *Raising Standards or Raising Barriers?* McNeil and Valenzuela wrote,

> Those who promote state systems of standardized testing claim that these systems raise the quality of education and do so in ways that are measurable and generalizable. They attribute low test scores to management's failure to direct its "lowest level" employees (i.e., the teachers) to induce achievement in students. In Texas, the remedy to this situation has been to create a management system that will change behavior, particularly the behavior of teachers, through increased accountability. The means of holding teachers and administrators accountable is the average scores of each school's children on the state's standardized test, the Texas Assessment of Academic Skills, or TAAS... this over-reliance on test scores has caused a decline in educational quality for those students who have the greatest educational need. (McNeil and Valenzuela, 2001, p. 2)

In a 2010 report, Advancement Project outlined data from the intersections of high-stakes testing and "zero-tolerance" policies highlighting the double hit of harmful policies that funnel youth into the school-to-prison pipeline.

> Perhaps more important is the damage done by high-stakes testing to the student experience in school. Not only do formulaic, test-driven reforms neglect the important role schools have to play in helping students become well-rounded citizens, they also turn school into a much less engaging, even hostile, place for youth by eliminating the components of education they find most interesting. Additionally, the emphasis placed on test results above all other priorities has an alienating and dehumanizing effect on young people, who resent being viewed and treated as little more than test scores.... The effects can accumulate even more when additional consequences are attached to the tests. For example, there is a long record of research demonstrating the consistent association of high-stakes exit exams with decreased graduation rates and increased dropout rates. Additionally, the results from standardized tests are often used to retain students in grade. Yet, grade retention has been shown to be the greatest predictor of student dropout. (Advancement Project, 2010, p. 5)

Researchers have argued that resilience is the process (Olsson, 2003) of overcoming the negative effect of risk exposure, coping successfully with traumatic experiences, and avoiding the negative trajectories associate with those risks (Masten & Powell, 2003). Considering the predominance of high-stakes exams in the current educational policy environment, a promising avenue of discussion lies in marshaling psychological research to conceptualize how grit or resiliency may or may not interact with high-stakes exams. In this chapter we discuss the (in)adequacy of the current testing and accountability environment for stimulating student success, and marshal established psychological research to consider the paradigm of assessment beyond the uneasy dichotomy that currently pits assessment as a technical exercise incentivizing the enhancement of cognitive abilities versus assessment as a potential disincentive to learners' academic persistence and success.

RESILIENCY AND ENVIRONMENT

In recent years there has been growing public interest in understanding why some children grow up to be healthy and well-functioning adults despite having to overcome various forms of adversity in their lives. The phenomenon of successful development under high-risk conditions is known as "resilience" in the research literature and much research has been devoted to identifying the protective factors and processes that might account for children's successful outcomes (Masten, 2001). In short, resilience theory seeks to address the strengths that people and systems demonstrate that enable them to rise above adversity.

Emmy Werner, a University of California child psychologist, conducted a groundbreaking resiliency study in the early 1990s. Werner followed a group of Hawaiian students into adulthood (1955–1986) while monitoring the impact of a variety of biological and psychosocial risk factors, stressful life events, and protective factors on their development (Werner & Smith, 1992). She found that about one third of the students who were affected by conditions of "risk" escaped to adulthood without much permanent damage. Werner noted that children who emerged from the risk conditions had at least one person who accepted them as they were, such as teachers, counselors, and other adults who served as role models.

Frequently, resilience studies focus on specific subgroups that represent marginalized communities and their achievements. From an educational perspective, these are usually students from low-socioeconomic status (SES) and students from communities that are statistically less likely to achieve academically (Moote & Wodarski, 1997). Examples of specific groups who have been studied related to resilience include high-achieving African American middle school children participating in athletics (Hawkins & Mulkey, 2005), Mexican American students from low-socioeconomic backgrounds who excelled in high school (Gonzalez & Padilla, 1997), and bilingual Latinos who excelled in academic situations (Hassinger & Plourde, Lee, 2005).

Academic resilience can be defined as "the process and results that are part of the life story of an individual who has been academically successful, despite obstacles that prevent the majority of others with the same background from succeeding" (Morales, 2008, p. 198). Henderson and Milstein (2003) emphasized the importance of the educational environment in the development of resilience when they said, more than any institution (except the family) schools can provide the environment and conditions that foster resiliency in today's youth and tomorrow's adults. Achieving the stated goals of academic and life success for all students and an enthusiastic, motivated, change-oriented staff involves increasing student and staff resiliency.

More recently, an emerging area of research that intersects many related research fields overlapping with resilience is in social, affective, and educational neuroscience. Immordino-Yang and Damasio (2007) posited in the inaugural article of *Mind, Brain & Education* that,

> The neurobiological evidence suggests that the aspects of cognition that we recruit most heavily in schools, namely learning, attention, memory, decision-making, and social functioning, are both profoundly affected by and subsumed within the processes of emotion; we call these aspects emotional thought. Moreover, the evidence from brain-damaged patients suggests the hypothesis that emotion-related processes are required for skills and knowledge to be transferred from the structured school environment to real-world decision making because they provide an emotional rudder to guide judgment and action. Taken together, the evidence we present sketches an account of the neurobiological underpinnings of morality, creativity, and culture, all topics of critical importance to education. (Immordino-Yang & Damasio, 2007, p. 3)

While there is no single encompassing definition of resilience, numerous authors, both inside and outside the field of education, have developed their own perspectives over the past several decades. In summary, resiliency is characterized as the heightened likelihood of success in school and other life accomplishments despite environmental adversities brought about by early traits, conditions, and experiences (Wang, Haertel, & Walberg, 1994).

YOU ALREADY KNEW "GRIT"?

The conceptualization of grit is not new. Stemming from a long history of theorizing about the nature of resilience, it has been addressed by researchers, social workers, psychologists, sociologists, educators, and many others over the past few decades. More recently, however, the concept of grit has been discussed as a "hidden power" in student educational success (Tough, 2013) with many using the idea to imply that if American students had more grit would they find more success in a testing and accountability environment. This attribution of responsibility provides an ideal scapegoat for the chronic failures of test-based accountability, because if students fail they might have greater chances to develop grit. And, with all the empowering notions associated with grit (resiliency, efficacy, mastery, growth mindsets), it offers a seemingly positive spin on situations where students actually experience chronic failure. Although an enticing framework, we need to be aware of the potential drawback of taking such a narrow approach. As grit has become popularized in the public narrative, so too have critiques of how it may be (mis)applied.

Discussions of student grit that focus on protective, positive factors of success such as wellness, adaptation, protective factors, capacity building, and improvement to emphasize the possible and the belief that things will work, seem to offer an alternative to deficit-oriented models of development (Duckworth, Peterson, Matthews, & Kelly, 2007). However, many would assert that the grit narrative actually perpetuates a deficit approach since it assumes the responsibility for learning as a character trait located within the child. The ensuing message is that as long as the child works hard and puts forth persistent effort (despite any other hardships they may be enduring), they should/will be able to succeed academically (Gow, 2014). Although the notion of grit seems proactive, it actually serves as just another way to blame children for their failures rather than their social circumstances or opportunities.

Schwartz (2015) discussed controversies in grit and refers to teachers who have expressed concerns that the grit narrative ignores many of the structural barriers that make it difficult for some children from low-income homes—or those who have learning differences—to succeed in school. She noted that many educators have questioned whether the current definition of grit is more about compliance with predetermined norms in schools settings than about possessing personal determination, particularly amid pressures on academic achievement.

DO HIGH-STAKES TESTS
AND ACCOUNTABILITY LEAD TO MORE GRIT?

Despite soaring rhetoric in support of high-stakes tests by policymakers and others, to date there is a dearth of empirical research detailing the relationships between high-stakes testing and student emotional responses. The initial theory of action underlying testing and accountability was that students would be motivated to try harder when faced with feedback that they have not performed to some standards (Vasquez Heilig & Darling-Hammond, 2008). However, 10 years after the nationwide implementation of Texas-style accountability, all students did not reach proficiency and proponents are looking for an explanation for why the regime has not performed better.

How a student responds to the experience of challenge or failure will depend on a host of contextual, cognitive, and emotional variables. If school leaders do not create healthy learning conditions that foster success and allow for "safe" experiences of failure, we may well be undermining students' motivation and exacerbating disparities that already exist in the midst of testing. Furthermore, if students are given constant feedback of failure from testing and accountability monikers of failure assigned their school, with a default assumption that it means something about their intelligence (rather than effort), then lessons in grit, effort, or other attempts to put forth effort may be dismissed as pointless.

Why high-stakes testing and accountability have failed to deliver on their promise is an open question with many possible explanations. Basch (2010) documented extensive evidence from the fields of neuroscience, child development, epidemiology, and public health that highlight health disparities that disproportionately affect educational opportunities and outcomes of youth in urban settings and that significantly contribute to the existence and exacerbation of achievement gaps. Basch provides compelling evidence that unless we address the deep and systemic health gaps that drive the roots of student functioning and learning, we will likely not see improvements despite the best of intentions to close the "achievement" gaps.

Yes, resiliency and grit matter. However, so too do other critical factors including resources, opportunities for enrichment, social supports, health, and guidance that would strengthen opportunities for youth to succeed despite the odds. The key rests with unlocking how these features come together. We know poverty is a sizable barrier for many (see Chapter 5). However we also know that a sizable percentage of economically disadvantage children and adolescents overcome this adversity, exhibit competence in the face of economic hardship in their lives, and go on to lead highly successful, well-adjusted and productive lives (Werner & Smith, 1982, 1992, 2001). The challenge becomes how best to coordinate economic, social, and psychological opportunities along with resilience-building messages that build on student strengths in guiding them to optimal, positive, student developmental outcomes.

Waxman, Padrón, and Gray's (2004) review of recent studies provided persuasive evidence of a growing body of research that points to the conclusion that students exhibiting academic success have family and peer support, have supportive feedback, and are involved in school life. Conversely, students who exhibit low self-esteem have little parental support and involvement, are not engaged positively with their schools, are not usually motivated to succeed, and do not achieve good academic results. Much discussion among educators has centered on the search for strategies that reduce adversity and advance opportunities for learning. Two major guidelines have received increasing recognition for potentially reducing the risk factors associated with urban life and the achievement gap in urban schools (Williams, 1996). First, schools need to forge better connections with families and the community to support resilience development and student learning. Second, reducing educational segregation within schools and implementing responsive and powerful instructional practices also result in improved student retention, a more positive school climate, and improved academic outcomes (Milstein & Henry, 2008).

Absent addressing the aforementioned issues, grit has the potential to be a vehicle for education leaders and policymakers continuing to drive blind focus on tests scores while ignoring health and opportunity gaps. There is no research to support the assumption that high-stakes tests and accountability ratings lead to higher levels of grit, perseverance, and/or motivation. Similarly, we have no way of knowing the role grit may play in persevering through ongoing test-based experiences. On the contrary, decades of research in the field of educational psychology documents the harm of shame-based, competitive, punitive, and/or fear-based learning environments that often coincide with high-stakes testing experiences. Interpretation, context, support, and resources matter in determining how scores will be perceived, what beliefs will result, and what resulting behaviors will be most likely. Thus, future research in the fields of human development and motivation should consider whether widening student success gaps in the future—especially as standards are artificially raised without any corresponding supports to authentically improve student learning or engagement—are due to mismatched assumptions about motivation, grit, and high-stakes testing.

IMPLICATIONS FOR EDUCATIONAL POLICY

Accountability was born in Texas based on a "gut feeling" about how tests and a rating system would impact the motivation of students (Vasquez Heilig, Young, & Williams, 2012). Considering decades of research, testing and accountability may not foment grit, academic resiliency, or increase achievement motivation. For the many students who put forth maximum effort, who face ongoing difficulties and limited resources at home, and who may be repeatedly receiving failing scores on these high-stakes assessment, we need to acknowledge the possibility that the conditions being created would be ripe for the development of "learned helplessness" that can explain a great deal of academic disengagement among youth. The experience of learned helplessness has been found to strongly relate to depression, poor health, and motivational problems. Individuals who have failed at tasks in the past have a tendency to conclude erroneously that they are incapable of improving their performance in the future (Stipek, 1988).

Children experiencing learned helplessness are more likely to fail academic subjects and are less intrinsically motivated than others, and students experiencing repeated failures will often in turn give up trying to gain respect or promotion through academic performance (Ramírez, Maldonado, & Martos, 1992). The symptoms of helplessness and uncontrollability, most commonly felt by people who are depressed, are also correlated with the experience of learned helplessness (Maier & Watkins, 2005).

Many questions abound for those on the ground interacting with youth who are required to take the current high stakes tests. What kinds of student responses should individual teachers keep in mind as they administer the tests? In what ways can educators best support student motivation given the projected high rates of failure built into the system of cut scores? And given the complexity of the grit narrative, is it a good idea to suggest that students need to have more grit in the face of failing an unfair test or might that approach backfire and be better replaced with full disclosure about the lack of validity of the tests? What if educational leaders and policymakers were to engage in perspective taking of the students' experiences as they encounter learning climates where these high-stakes tests define all activity? Will they see experiences created by these exams as encouraging students at an appropriate level of challenge (and with an array of accompanying supports) to succeed with effort? Or will the repeated, failure-based experiences lead students to make conclusions that it's simply not worth it to try any more?

When defining and striving for excellence, it is best to focus on all students. However, our current public educational system fails to meet the needs of many students of underserved communities. This is apparent when we discuss the achievement gap or disparities seen in academic performance between various groups of students. Unfortunately, for many students of marginalized communities, the achievement gap increases until they drop out of school. With the passage of the No Child Left Behind Act (NCLB), closing the achievement gap demands that all students learn, stay in school, and meet state standards. In addition, NCLB's framework of accountability, assessment, and evaluation has become a driving force in education as educators attempt to close the achievement gap that exists between Anglo students and students representing the minority (Fuller, Wright, Gesicki, & Kang, 2007).

According to Horsford (2011), the politicization of education has resulted in a high-stakes accountability culture, and in some cases privatization of public schools that distract efforts from meaningful systemic education reform. Our children have become commodities and a means to an end, rather than an opportunity to improve an educational end. Furthermore, when addressing the achievement gap and the needs of students from marginalized communities, educational leaders should seek to address structural and institutional manifestations of exclusion and segregation that permeate administrative structures, policies, processes, and practices (Horsford, 2011). If we focus solely on grit, perseverance, and/or motivation and ignore structural realities in policy, by default we maintain racialized hierarchies and inequities in schools and school systems. Educational policy must address school structures and foster school climates and cultures that support school, family, and community relations built on the mutual respect, caring, and trust of communities of color (Horsford, 2011).

Another educational policy solution often discussed is the integration of technology in schools. However, the current policy environment pressed by foundations and the numerous educational technology startups also portends a variety of computer-based assessments aimed at measuring learning and enhancing "college and career." While user-interface design issues on computerized tests may not currently be at the forefront of concern for policymakers and test developers, future research is warranted to examine user experiences with the interface of the tests (i.e., serious flaws documented by Rasmussen, 2015, for tests administered to more than 10 million children in 19 states). Factors to consider include students' (and teachers') facility with using the technology as well as potential negative cognitive and affective impacts on their testing experience. If technology is to be integrated into assessment, it must be efficacious and valid. Additionally, educational decisions should not be based on one form of test scores, such as a single score on a high-stakes test. Educational progress for all students regardless of their background, will involve the use of multiple forms of assessment data (Valencia, 2011), developing resiliency (Milstein & Henry, 2008; Williams, 1996), and evaluating structural and institutional barriers (Horsford, 2011).

This chapter also suggests important implications for practice. Teachers should communicate to their teacher organizations and other allies the real life lived experiences of students of color with exams. Currently, teacher organizations, foundations and policymakers and other influential organizations have pledged support to Common Core and the high-stakes exams that are married to the standards. However, the lived experience of students of color in relation to the new gauntlet of Common Core exams it still unknown in the literature, but the potentially deleterious impact of the new regime of exams on students of color is predictable considering the history of standards and testing in the United States (Vasquez Heilig & Darling-Hammond, 2008). As a result, teachers should be mindful and communicate to their teacher organizations, local communities, policymakers, researchers, and other stakeholders the challenges of handling student motivation in the new Common Core high-stakes test based environment.

In conclusion, it is profoundly problematic to link underperformance on tests to "grit, growth mindset" or effort-based remedies when the core assessments being administered fail to meet basic standards for testing and accountability. Many of the new, experimental, computerized assessments administered to millions of children in 2015 "field" tests have been fraught with technological user-access barriers (Marachi, 2015; Rasmussen, 2015). As discussed in this chapter, grit and high-stakes tests should be understood within the current context of poverty and other structural factors, the fact that failure rates have arbitrarily been set to fail a majority of students, and the resulting potential disengagement, frustration, anger, stress, and feelings of despair from "learned helplessness." In conclusion, is it fair or just for millions of students of color to fail an unfair state-mandated test, despite working hard in the classroom, and this failure be blamed on a lack of grit rather than the real issue—the structure and scoring of unreliable and unvalidated tests?

REFERENCES

Advancement Project. (2010). *Test, punish, and push out: How "zero-tolerance" and high stakes testing funnel youth into the school-to-prison pipeline.* Retrieved from http://b.3cdn.net/advancement/50071a439cfacbbc8e_suxm6caqe.pdf

Basch, C. E. (2010, March). Healthier students are better learners: A missing link in school reforms to close the achievement gap. *Equity Matters, Research Review 6.* Campaign for Educational Equity, Teachers College, Columbia University. Retrieved from ERIC database. (ED523998)

Duckworth, A. L., Peterson, C., Matthews, M. D., & Kelly, D. R. (2007). Grit: Perseverance and passion for long-term goals. *Journal of Personality and Social Psychology, 92*(6), 1087–1101.

Fuller, B., Wright, J., Gesicki, K., & Kang, E. (2007) Gauging growth: How to judge No Child Left Behind? *Educational Research, 36*(5), 268–278.

Gonzalez, R., & Padilla, A. M. (1997). The academic resilience of Mexican American high school students. *Hispanic Journal of Behavioral Sciences, 19*(3), 301–317.

Gow, P. (2014). What's dangerous about the grit narrative and how to fix it. *Education Week,* Retrieved from http://blogs.edweek.org/edweek/independent_schools/2014/03/ whats_dangerous_about_the_grit_narrative_and_how_to_fix_it.html

Hassinger, M., & Plourde, L. A. (2005). Beating the odds: How bilingual Hispanic youth work through adversity to become high achieving students. *Education, 126*(2), 316–327.

Hawkins, R., & Mulkey, L. (2005). Athletic investment and academic resilience in a national sample of African American females and males in the middle grades. *Education and Urban Society, 38*(1), 62–88.

Henderson, N., & Milstein, M. M. (2003). *Resiliency in schools: Making it happen for students and educations.* Thousand Oaks, CA: Corwin Press.

Holbein, J. B., & Ladd, H. (2015, February). Accountability pressure and non-achievement student behaviors: Working paper 122. *Center for analysis of longitudinal data in education research.* Retrieved from http://www.caldercenter.org/sites/default/files/WP%20122.pdf

Horsford, S. (2011). *Learning in a burning house: Educational inequality, ideology, and (dis)integration.* New York, NY: Teachers College Press.

Immordino-Yang, H., & Damasio, A. (2007). We feel, therefore we learn: The relevance of affective and social neuroscience to education. *Mind, Brain, and Education, 1*(1), 3–10.

Maier S. F., & Watkins, L. R. (2005). Stressor controllability and learned helplessness: The roles of the dorsal raphe nucleus, serotonin, and corticotropin-releasing factor. *Neuroscience and Biobehavioral Reviews, 29,* 829–841. Retrieved from http://www.uvm.edu/~shammack/Maier%20and%20Watkins%202005%20review.pdf

Marachi, R., (2015). *Critical questions about computerized assessments and smarter balanced test scores.* Retrieved May 23, 2016 from https://eduresearcher.com/2015/07/06/critical-questions-computerized-testing-sbac/.

Masten, A. (2001). Ordinary magic: Resilience processes in development. *American Psychologist, 56,* 227–238.

Masten, A., & Powell, J. (2003). A resilience framework for research, policy, and practice. In S. S. Luthar (Ed.), *Resilience and vulnerability: Adaptation in the context of childhood adversities* (pp. 1–28). New York, NY: Cambridge University Press.

McNeil, L., & Valenzuela, A. (2001). The harmful impact of the TAAS system of testing in Texas: Beneath the accountability rhetoric. In M. Kornhaber and G. Orfield (Eds.), *Raising standards or raising barriers? Inequality and high stakes testing in public education* (pp. 127–150). New York, NY: Century Foundation. Retrieved from http://www.edb.utexas.edu/latino/McNeil%20&%20Valenzuela.pdf

Milstein, M., & Henry, D. (2008). *Leadership for resilient schools and communities.* Thousand Oaks, CA: Corwin Press.

Moote, G. T., & Wodarski, J. S. (1997). The acquisition of life skills through adventure-based activities and programs: A review of the literature. *Adolescence, 32*(125), 143–167.

Morales, E. E. (2008). Exceptional female students of color: Academic resilience and gender in higher education. *Innovative Higher Education, 33*(3), 197–213.

Olsson, C. A. (2003). Adolescent resilience: A concept analysis. *Journal of Adolescence, 26,* 1–11.

Ramírez, E., Maldonado, A., & Martos, R. (1992). Attributions modulate immunization against learned helplessness in humans. *Journal of Personality and Social Psychology, 62*(1), 139–146.

Rasmussen, S. (2015). Smarter balanced tests are fatally flawed and should not be used. *S. R. Education.* Retrieved May 23, 2016 from http://mathedconsulting.com/wp-content/uploads/2015/04/Common-Core-Tests-Fatally-Flawed.pdf

Reardon, S., Greenberg, E., Kalogrides, D., Shores, K., & Valentino, R. (2012). *Left behind? The effect of No Child Left Behind on academic achievement gaps* (Working paper). Stanford, CA: Stanford University Press.

Schwartz, K. (2015). Does the grit narrative blame students for school's shortcomings? *KQED Mindshift,* Retrieved from http://ww2.kqed.org/mindshift/2015/05/05/does-the-grit-narrative-blame-students-for-schools-shortcomings/

Stipek, D. (1988). *Motivation to learn: From theory to practice.* Englewood Cliffs, NJ: Prentice Hall.

Tough, P. (2013). *How children succeed: Grit, curiosity, and the hidden power of character.* Boston, MA: Mariner Books.

Valencia, R. (2011) *Chicago school failure and success: Past, present and future.* New York, NY: Routledge.

Vasquez Heilig, J., & Darling-Hammond, L. (2008). Accountability Texas-style: The progress and learning of urban minority students in a high-stakes testing context. *Educational Evaluation and Policy Analysis, 30*(2), 75–110.

Vasquez Heilig J., & Holme, J. (2013). Nearly 50 years post-Jim Crow: Persisting and expansive school segregation for African American, Latina/o and ELL students in Texas. *Education and Urban Society.* doi: 10.1177/0013124513486289

Vasquez Heilig, J., Young, M., & Williams, A. (2012). At-risk student averse: Risk management and accountability. *Journal of Educational Administration, 50*(5), 562–585.

Wang, M. C., Haertel, G. D., & Wahlberg, H. J. (1994). What helps students learn? *Educational Leadership, 51*(4), 74–79.

Waxman, H. C., Padrón, Y. N., & Gray, J. P. (Eds.). (2004). *Educational resiliency: Student, teacher, and school perspectives.* Charlotte, NC: Information Age.

Werner, E., & Smith, R. (1982). *Vulnerable but invincible: A longitudinal study of resilient children and youth.* New York, NY: Adams, Bannister, and Cox.

Werner, E., & Smith, R. (1992). *Overcoming the odds: High-risk children from birth to adulthood.* New York, NY: Cornell University Press.

Werner, E. E., & Smith, R. S. (2001). *Journeys from childhood to midlife: Risk, resilience and recovery.* Ithaca, NY: Cornell University Press.

Williams, B. (1996). *Closing the achievement gap: A vision for changing beliefs and practices.* Alexandria, VA: Association for Supervision and Curriculum Development.

PART III

IMPLICATIONS FOR BETTER POLICY DEVELOPMENT FOR 21ST CENTURY YOUTH

CHAPTER 9

SEARCHING BEYOND SUCCESS AND STANDARDS FOR WHAT WILL MATTER IN THE 21ST CENTURY

Luke Reynolds
Harvard Public Middle School

*The central problem is this: How can the oppressed, as divided, unauthentic
beings, participate in developing the pedagogy of their liberation? Only as they discover themselves to be "hosts" of the oppressor can they contribute to the
midwifery of their liberating pedagogy. As long as they live in duality in which
to be is to be like and to be like is to be like the oppressor, this contribution is impossible. The pedagogy of the oppressed is an instrument for their critical discovery that
both they and their oppressors are manifestations of dehumanization.*

—Paulo Freire, *Pedagogy of the Oppressed*, 1970, p. 30

My 11th-grade honor student looks up at me and calls my bluff. "I got everything on the rubric," he says and smirks.

The classroom is quiet, and Timothy has come to this after-school writing conference at my request after he questioned the grade I gave his essay
on the novel, *The Great Gatsby*. The assignment included a "personal connection" section whereby students were challenged to look at the inner

Educational Policies and Youth in the 21st Century, pages 161–175
Copyright © 2016 by Information Age Publishing
All rights of reproduction in any form reserved.

turmoil of a character and connect it to some kind of inner turmoil in their own lives.

Timothy's essay contained no such personal connection. In terms of the critical/analytical essay goals, Timothy's work was spot-on, and should that have been the only focus for this essay, he would have received an A for his analysis. Instead, I gave Timothy a C+ because he left out a large requirement of the essay. However, in conjunction with the assignment, I also gave students our English department's official rubric, which adheres to the Connecticut Frameworks and the standardized test preparation program standards. This rubric contains no mention of the words inner turmoil and personal connection in regards to the critical/analytical essay.

So, we have a problem.

"I know the personal connection requirement is not included on the rubric, Timothy, but it's on the assignment, and it's a hugely important part of my goal for this piece of writing." I give him my best face of encouragement—eyes wide open, bright smile—and I even pat him on the shoulders. It's my attempt to say: Hey, come on. What we're doing here is about more than rubrics, right? It's about life and growth and learning!

Timothy gives me a blank look. "But it's not on the rubric, Mr. Reynolds. I did everything on the rubric, and the rubric should decide my grade, not some stuff about inner turmoil."

I decide to level with him. "Look, Timothy. The rubric takes the cake when it comes to grading, sure, and when you take the state test in the spring, they won't ask about your inner turmoil. But *I am asking*, because I care about it, and because if you don't start noticing and caring then you're not going to learn anything this year except how to pass a test." I take a breath, try to keep a lightness in the air with a smile.

But Timothy's next words destroy that levity completely. "Isn't learning how to pass the test all that matters?" Timothy leans back in his chair like he knows he's got a full house: The deck is stacked and I've got nothing but a hand of mismatched cards.

Is he right?

THE BOTTOM LINE IN OUR
CURRENT EDUCATIONAL CLIMATE

With the onslaught of a nationally standardized curriculum, as well the meteoric rise in high-stakes, standardized testing over the last 20 years, we must ask ourselves as practitioners and policymakers: What is getting lost? If rubrics, standards, and high-stakes testing were truly the trinity of positive education reform, then we have to wonder: What about students like Timothy, what about students who can ace the standards and yet lose something of themselves—perhaps the willingness to connect to literature (or any other subject) in a way that enhances the values, self-awareness, and civic agency they possess? Or, take the other extreme: What happens to students who cannot ace the standards by gaming the system? Students in schools that underperform on standardized testing often revert to "soulless" pedagogy that would seek to save district takeovers of their schools. Michael Apple (2008) characterizes the result this way:

> We should be clear that the curriculum has always been the result of tensions, struggles, and compromises. . . . What counts as core knowledge has all too often been someone's core, not everyone's core. Most often, the rhetoric of common intellectual heritage is simply that—rhetorical. (Apple, 2008, p. 35)

And so our schools are left with "someone's core" that may disregard empowerment, agency, and authentic 21st century skills. Students in underperforming districts are left with the mantra to memorize and master "core knowledge" that manages to assert one skill only: test taking.

Beverly Williams, a public middle school teacher in Roxbury, Massachusetts, bemoans the current climate of competition over cooperation and civic responsibility. A Teacher of the Year in Boston in 2007, Williams has taught at the inner-city Timilty Middle School (recently euphemized with the label Renaissance School due to low test scores) for more than 20 years. She claims, "If we do not teach our children about civic responsibility, we will continue to suffer the injuries from insensitive and disingenuous behaviors" (Williams, 2012). But how can the current educational climate—enmeshed within a program like Race to the Top and allegiance to No Child Left Behind—allow for civic responsibility, character values, and cooperation to be taught? We've become so focused on success and achievement (measured only on the barometer of test scores) that we're often forced to disregard other essential methods and modes of education. Indeed, we are persuaded by politics and policies that what matters most are not values, character, cooperation, or personal connection, but scores. Numbers trump everything.

This terrifying trend is bolstered earlier and earlier in American educational culture. Education writer and researcher Paul Tough writes poignantly about the way in which the current numbers-drenched climate steers his fear and hope for his own newborn son, Ellington.

> Two years before Ellington's birth, the Kumon chain of tutoring centers opened New York City's first Junior Kumon Franchise, where children as young as two spent their mornings filling out worksheets and completing drills on letter and number recognition. . . . Ellington would be growing up in a culture saturated with an idea you might call the cognitive hypothesis: the

belief... that success today depends primarily on... the kind of intelligence that gets measured on IQ tests. (Tough, 2012, p. xiii)

With a cultural philosophy of education firmly rooted in test-taking skills, strictly-cognitive abilities, and intense competition, the current divergent trend in public and private schools is likely to continue, and increase. Policy and political pressure placed on district and school-based administrators will continue to ensure that, in "racing to the top," we leave so many students bereft on the bottom of the mountain while simultaneously we shutter to think that those on top will be our leaders. Those students forgotten at the bottom lack the intensive, relationship-rich, content-delving education they need, and those who succeed on our numerical measures and make it to the top lack the kind of character and values so crucial to the 21st century.

A BROKEN EVALUATION TOOL
THAT HIDES THOSE IN POWER

In his bestselling book, *What the Dog Saw*, social commentator and *New Yorker* staff writer Malcolm Gladwell makes a fascinating, lucid, and deeply discouraging case for what kind of educational reform is needed in schools. Interestingly, while his reflections prove to offer some new thoughts, they take the hard line of crunching numerical data to find out what's working or not within a classroom. For example, Gladwell cites numerous economists and eventually makes his case that hiring teachers should match a process that financial firms utilize. He casts his lot with many of the economic-centered education reformers and claims that what needs to happen is "for the teaching profession to copy what firms like North Star have been doing for years" (Gladwell, 1999, p. 333). And what North Star does, as Gladwell depicts it, is to hire financial advisers based not on their experience or training but by trying them out, then looking at the numerical value of success they have, and then retaining their services or firing them based on these financial results. In other words, instead of focusing on learning the skills required to become effective and inspiring teachers, our culture should look for latent talent by trying out many teachers, than firing those who don't produce strong numerical figures in terms of student test score growth. Such an idea trends with the stringent focus on numerical success we're seeing within our schools: if something doesn't produce fast growth (measured solely by high-stakes test score increases) then it isn't worth our time, energy, or money.

Thus, we find ourselves enmeshed in a contemporary culture obsessed with test data. If we can't measure an increase in skill ability, then nothing else matters. Documentaries like *Waiting for Superman* (Guggenheim,

2010) advance this sentiment, and ultimately the impossibly high pressure on teachers and administrators—and via them, on to students—to succeed at all costs on high-stakes testing trumps everything else. Whole education programs and reforms are designed based on this mentality of competition and numerical success. Most fascinating of all in this steep cultural trend is what has gone almost completely unexamined in the literature on education reform and research—both in the mainstream media and within academic journals.

When Paulo Freire questioned how the oppressed can participate in the creation of their own pedagogy, our current educational climate affords no space for a morally acceptable answer. How are inner-city teachers like Beverly Williams supposed to find time, energy, and inspiration to teach civic responsibility, cooperation, values, and character amidst policies threatening her school and her job should she not produce certain numerical test gains? How should I have responded to my suburban student, Timothy, who blatantly argued (with the support of our entire culture at his back) that the checklist is what matters—not the personal connections and the inner growth? The truth is, we don't have a good response. There's no way to fight such sentiments because they are everywhere in the language and lingo of how we talk about education and learning: race to the top, test-gains, IQ, percentages. The financial bottom line becomes synonymous with the goals and philosophy of our educational policies, so much so that respected, insightful social commentator like Gladwell can come to the conclusion that the way to solve problems in our schools is to run them the way a financial investment firm like North Star is run: net worth, high yield, and good returns. What is lost is any discussion of authentic learning, overcoming modes of oppression, and education that equalizes opportunities for children of all demographics to live value-rich, character-driven, community-oriented lives.

But there is a way to change, to turn the status-quo on its head and educate for true 21st century skills like cooperation, community orientation, character growth, and collective problem solving—skills that will avert the steep problems and crises we face. In his powerful documentary film *Tough Guise*, the sociologist Jackson Katz (1999) claims that one of the ways that dominant groups retain dominance is through their non examination. He claims that when passive language is applied to any population, it has the effect of hiding the aggressor and showcasing the wounded, as if the wounding happens without a perpetrator. Katz's articulation can be of some aid here, as we deal with a numbers-based terminology that casts students and teachers as passive recipients of a status quo system where dominant groups can form educational policies without consent or involvement. Another way to form this notion might be that if so many students are struggling and being wounded by public school systems, might there be another oppressor at large other than teachers? Might it be possible to explore a whole new set of numbers and crunch data that seeks to put into place a new set of standards? Thus far in our modern educational reform movements—and especially those within public schools—efforts have amounted to more standards and pressure being placed on local teachers and administrators. In this realm, reform efforts like the ones Gladwell documents and bolsters have as their aim to find the good teachers, fire the rest, and produce test-score gains for students. Economics-minded education researchers like Eric Hanushek and Steven Rivkin (2007) additionally advance the notion that what improves learning quality is placing more stringent links between student test scores and teacher pay. In other words: create highly pressurized, competitive environments within schools so that students, teachers, and schools are all competing against one another. What goes completely unexamined in ideas like these is what Freire might term the *oppressors*—those with large amounts of power higher up in the system whose policies and approaches are assumed to be untouchable. And why? Because they are the power-holders. The system is assumed to be unchangeable—and small changes in the lower levels are what reformers and researchers must focus on.

The predominant energy and outrage in our system now trends toward the standards that apply to students and teachers—in other words, we ask: What should our students and teachers be able to achieve, and how can we measure the results to be sure they have achieved it? The impetus is squarely placed on what those in the lower reaches of autonomy and empowerment do and produce—they are the ones we test, examine, and evaluate. Such a system allows those in power to evade any responsibility and ensures that the status-quo system continues, while hiding any real possibility for change.

STANDARDIZING THE MEANS

Perhaps no more scathing indictment of systematized inequality has been crafted than Jonathan Kozol's (1991) *Savage Inequalities*. Taking as its baseline the notion that all students—in all geographic areas of the country—are entitled to the same education with the same class sizes and expenditures per pupil, the book offers a treacherous overview of how that seemingly basic principal of educational equality is seemingly impossible. What is fascinating to me is the reception of Kozol's book. Critics everywhere praised the lucid writing, the way in which Kozol showed a light on the despicable inequalities within the funding system, and the need for immediate reform. When the book was released in 1991, reviewers rallied to its reasoning, claiming the systematically unequal system of education was an "outrage," "shocking," and "heartbreaking." And yet, following the release of the book, education trends continued to evolve into increased standards for students and teachers rather than any top-down reforms. In other words, we have an account that produced a collective indignation nationally as a bestselling book, and yet the policies that continued to gather steam in the years afterwards pressured students to do better on high-stakes testing and pressured teachers to pressure students to do better on high-stakes testing. In the 20+ years since *Savage Inequalities* was published, the result is a sad, continuing lack of funding for the inner-city schools he researched, as well as growing class sizes for said schools, and increased pressure on administrators, teachers, and students therein.

What would happen, however, if stringent measures of standardization were placed on policymakers before being placed on teachers and students? As a hypothetical case in point, let's focus on some perennially discouraging figures. As a teacher in two public school systems (first in Connecticut, and then in Massachusetts), I taught five classes, like many other teachers across the country. And like my colleagues, I continually felt like the class sizes I had to work with and the sheer pace of the day afforded little time to collaborate with colleagues, give each student the kind of individualized attention they needed, and create authentic assessments that would advance learning and values. Tony Danza's intriguing recent project corroborates this kind of pressure and frenzied pace at which many teachers work. In his memoir-cum-commentary book *I'd Like to Apologize to Every Teacher I Ever Had: My Year as a Rookie Teacher at Northeast High,* Danza recounts his year as a public school teacher in an inner-city school in Philadelphia. The book is surprisingly poignant, deeply empathetic, and engrossing. What I find most fascinating about Danza's reflections on his time as a public school teacher is his enormous shock at the difficulty of the job—at wanting badly to meet the needs of his students, and yet feeling totally burned out, bereft of energy and time enough to do the kind of teaching he wanted to do. And the toll this takes on all new teachers is painfully clear. Danza writes, "More than one hundred of the new teachers who went through orientation with me in August quit before we even got to Christmas. There has to be a better solution," (Danza, 2012, p. 192). Researcher Richard Ingersoll's overwhelming results of a 2004 study showed just how daunting the task that's set before new teachers is (Ingersoll & Smith, 2004). He found that within their first three years of teaching, 50% of all new public school teachers will quit their jobs. That's a retention rate of half—and this finding denotes an active choice to leave the profession, not a pink slip or a forced departure. Danza offers his own humble solution: "Three classes per teacher, instead of five. Teachers would have more time to prepare for their classes and follow through with each student," (Danza, 2012, p. 192). In other words, someone who has made a life of rigorous acting schedules, performances, constant travel, and the need to always be "on" ventures into the world of teaching and corroborates what 50% of new teachers already know: the way the system is designed sets up teachers as well as students for failure. And why? Because the value system that guides marketplace policies in our country is the same system that guides ideas regarding student success: the bottom line of high-yield numbers. Instead of asking, what would allow each student to receive the best, most individualized, value-rich, learning environment possible, we ask how can we educate as many children as possible in the cheapest possible manner, while also demanding ever higher test scores on standardized tests. And furthermore, when test scores don't rise the way we demand they should, policymakers, media culture (evident in documentaries such as *Waiting for Superman*) and many social critics are quick to point at public school systems and say it's their fault. Indeed, the powerful policymakers evade any kind of examination, and the status-quo system remains, with the most intense stakeholders of teachers and students consistently shouldering blame.

A massive change we can make is to remove the focus on standardizing the results and start standardizing the means. Instead of standardizing the test scores that students must obtain—and which teachers must help their students obtain—we could start standardizing the means that policymakers in power must fulfill. The changes could be stunning. Some possible standardized means might be that every public school teacher in America would teach three classes per day instead of five; class sizes of all public school classes in America would not exceed 15 students per class; guidance counselors within public schools would carry loads of no more than 100 students, and have built-in time to meet regularly with students in their load in a one-on-one manner; and teachers' aides and tutoring help would be available in a one-on-one or small-group basis to every student seeking such aid in a public school system.

Many of us reading through these kinds of standardized means might be tempted to scoff at them. As if! Ridiculous! How can class sizes go from 40 plus students in some inner-city schools to 15? How could we ever afford to hire enough new teachers to allow for every public school teacher to teach only three classes? Impossible. We might be tempted to view an opportunity like this one and deem it simply unachievable. And yet, we read essays like the one by Gladwell suggesting we hire teachers and fire them as soon as they don't work out, even though the cost would be high and the retention rate disastrous. We often encounter pieces that claim we need to run schools more like businesses, but CEOs at the top are rarely held to account, and those at the bottom end up working enormously hard to achieve the sales data required by those in power, yet often without the strategies, systems, and means in place to achieve them. But the current climate is quite willing to look only to the students who fail and the teachers who fail and deride both. We are also quick to place on pedestals those few teachers who produce uncanny results: teachers like Rafe Esquith, Ron Clark, or Erin Gruwell. But what such pedestal popping hides is the notion that certain individuals can do extraordinary things even in the face of steep difficulties, but not everyone can function at that level. It's the lie of a capitalistic society that everyone can be a millionaire: It's not possible. Some people will always do extraordinary things, but by framing those rare exceptions as the rule, we cheat our children out of a holistic system that is equitable, justice-minded, and truly learning-rich. In fact, we need only look at what happens to some of those teachers whom we place on pedestals: They leave. After three years, Erin Gruwell left her inner-city public school to take a university position. Ron Clarke left his public school to become an administrator in his own, upstart school. And Rafe Esquith remains in his public school, with the commitment that he will never have children of his own, as his life as a teacher will continue to be all-consuming if he wants to maintain the pace and standards he has set for himself. These teachers have all done—and continue to do—remarkable work, but to use them as models of what every public school teacher should be able to do is both disingenuous and also hides those in power who refuse to change an unequal, broken system. Instead of raising the standardized requirements on students and teachers, we need to raise the high-stakes testing on policymakers and those in power. As Freire suggests, it's only by realizing that the education system as it currently exists is a dehumanizing mechanism, whereby we assent to notions of status-quo inequality and the fact that not every child deserves a liberating, creative, and learning-rich education.

But where can we find funds to make these kinds of changes—to standardize the means rather than the results? This kind of question begins to open up doorways of creativity, compassion, and collective problem solving. As we start to ask questions like these, we also become models for our students of the kind of education that matters in a 21st century society. The problems we face currently are not those that competition and self-seeking can solve. Indeed, on every indicator available we have seen that the divide between rich and poor has grown more extreme than it has ever been; global warming is increasing; and other issues like job loss, human trafficking, poverty, poor health, decreasing food standards, and increasing mass production are all facing this generation. It's a daunting task to solve even one of these crises. And competition and self-seeking only encourage the rise of certain individuals, not the collective benefit and humanizing growth of a population.

Thus, as our school system reforms to value standards set on those in power, demanding that conditions be provided in which rich learning and character growth are possible, these values become both cultural and emulative for students. In other words, as we provide more stringent standards for the means by which we educate our children, we massively increase the chances for our students to then carry those kinds of character-driven, collaborative, community-oriented values into their own future jobs and contributions to culture and crisis solving.

One small, practical way we could begin to approach this shift in values would be with the following hypothetical possibility. In January of 2007, each of the 261 elected members of the House of Representatives made approximately $165,200 per year. Each of the 100 senators made approximately the same salary (Dwyer, 2006). Meanwhile, in 2008 the national average salary for a public school teacher in America was $53,910 (Snyder & Dillow, 2010). What if we cut the salaries of Congress down a significant amount, but still allowed them to bring home more than the average public school teacher—say around $65,200 per year? That would free up additional revenue (361 x $100,000), which would total approximately $36 million. This money could be translated into implementing some of the aforementioned proposed standardized means. We could begin to reduce the class load for teachers and reduce the number of students per class. Such changes could have a dramatic effect on the quality of education a child receives, and also on the retention rate of those who choose to become teachers. This would create additional revenue in all kinds of ways: lower costs to interview, hire, and train new teachers since the retention rate may decrease; lower costs on criminal actions taken by schools and law enforcement as students receive more focused and individualized attention and care within schools; and a host of other possibilities could result. In this manner, we could continue to reduce spending on salaries of those in power, and transition that funding into areas where students could reap massive benefits. Instead of paying expensive business consultants so that test scores will rise, or forming new charter schools or pouring money into school voucher programs, we can begin putting money toward creative avenues to increase the quality, values, and individualized education every student in a public school system receives. But even beyond the effect this would have on the education students in America actually receive, perhaps the biggest benefit would be the modeling of truly essential 21st century skills and abilities.

CREATIVITY, COMPASSION, AND COLLABORATION

An unprecedented increase in competition as a motivating tool within schools and between schools has come completely into vogue in the last decade. We regularly assume that the language of business is also the language of schools—we talk about score results, adequate yearly progress, and comparison data between districts and even between individual students. In other words, the current values of a highly-pressurized American public school system are competition, results-driven data, and traditional notions of success (tied to economic explanations of school achievement, as we've seen in Gladwell's analysis). However, these kinds of standards implemented since the formation of NCLB in 2001 haven't yielded solutions. Indeed, as Marilyn Cochran-Smith and Susan Lytle claim, "By requiring that teachers concentrate so heavily on raising scores in a limited set of school subjects, the law [NCLB] virtually assures a narrowing of the curriculum with conspicuous inattention to the broader social and democratic goals of education," (Cochran-Smith & Lytle, 2006, pp. 682–683). In essence, stringent standardization of both teachers and students effectively creates a marketplace educational system, complete with the values of the marketplace: capitalism, competition, self-seeking financial (or score) gains, and intense comparison. Alternately, we can model different values and actively work to confront 21st century problems by prioritizing creativity, compassion, and collaboration.

The logic of the marketplace can create pressurized classrooms, and as a public school teacher, I felt the pressures to ensure my students made test-score gains and achieved proficient results. However, one classroom project yielded an unexpectedly powerful result. With my 11th-grade students, I designed a classroom anthology unit that would consist of my students working collaboratively to create a publishable book devised of their own essays on the theme of love, loss, and learning. These personal narratives allowed students some freedom from the consistent focus on critical/analytically writing projects, yet afforded them no lapse in steep writing requirements and rounds of revision. However, there would be no grades given for these writing assignments, nor would the work affect their overall grade for the term. In other words, both the competition and the traditional success notions were removed from the writing experience and its result. Instead, students worked collaboratively to revise one another's essays and begin to combine their essays in a logical fashion in order to construct the best possible book as a whole. Additionally, funds raised from the sales of the eventual anthology, *Inside Out and Outside In* (Reynolds, 2007) would be donated to charity. Students researched various charities and learned about where the funds would go and how they would be utilized before they made their vote for the recipient. Most fascinating to me was the level of student interest and motivation during a month-long project that yielded no ability to enhance their grades or help prepare them with any specific set of high-stakes test-preparation skills. And yet, after the completion of the volume, anecdotal evidence of my class showed me massively increased enthusiasm, homework completion rates, class attendance rates, and deeper more energetic discussions about the literature we would read during the rest of the term.

By focusing on values like creativity through an authentic project, compassion by using both research skills and eventual funds to go to charity, and collaboration by the necessity of working together to create one product rather than working individually to create 25 products that would then compete and compare with one another, students were drawn into their own education and took more active roles in their learning. Researcher Gloria Ladson-Billings powerfully claims that "meaning is made as the product of dialogue between and among individuals" (Ladson-Billings, 1995, p. 473). If we desire for education to have meaning for students—and for teachers—then it must involve more than narrow goals of competition and high-stakes testing. Heavily standardizing the work of teachers and students does the exact opposite of creating a space for dialogue; indeed, it often works, instead, to suppress creativity, collaboration, and compassion. Via the avenues of focusing on the self and comparison between the self and others, marketplace educational practices do little to solve problems within or among people. And this kind of education is poor preparation for the tasks facing our contemporary society.

A similar trend of collaboration and creativity yielding more learning-rich, enthusiastic educational environments can be seen, too, among teachers themselves: When teachers are able to work with one another, in relationship and collaboration rather than competition, the retention rates and passion for classroom work increases dramatically. Among those studies that assert positive relationships between teacher collaboration (via programs like mentoring and aid-oriented groups) and retention, the goal and role of skirting teacher burnout is often mentioned. Schlichte, Yssel, & Merbler (2005) claim that among five novice, special education teachers, the most important defense against burnout and the desire to quit was relationships among colleagues, and specifically mentoring. They claim that "mentoring has been identified as a critical factor in eliminating feelings of isolation as experienced by first year special education teachers" (Schlichte et al., 2005, p. 36). In other words, school environments where meaningful, compassionate relationships are stressed over competition for testing results, teachers are more excited to remain in the profession and retain their enthusiasm for classroom work.

CONCLUSIONS

If we seek an educational system that prioritizes competition and privatization, we are well on track. However, if we seek to model creativity, compassion, and collaboration for our students, then we must begin by using these skills as our measures of success. How compassionate are we as teachers, administrators, parents, and policymakers; how creative are we; and how collaborative? Instead of measuring student achievement by the disingenuous numerical value on a for-profit designed, high-stakes test, we can instead begin to measure the quality of our education system by the means we equip it with. Small class sizes, collaborative learning opportunities, authentic projects that require both rigor and creativity, relationship-rich environments, and teacher-student encouragement rather than fear-based discouragement are all essential in our schools.

I began this chapter by sharing the story of my student, Timothy, and his attitude toward an essay in which I asked my students to include authentic and creative personal connections to the literary text that weren't required by the department rubric. Perhaps it was Timothy's response to this assignment—that smirk in which he claimed he could game the system because that's the kind of value the system itself rewarded: numerical success at all costs. Or, perhaps it was because I saw other of my students, from less advantaged homes than Timothy, who looked at long lists of requirements and rubrics, and the overwhelmed fear in their eyes made me want to weep. Or perhaps it was because the reason I'd become a teacher in the first place was being stolen from me by standardization, and by high-stakes test preparation that did nothing for my own teacher's soul. Maybe it was a combination of all three reasons that I created the novella project. In essence, my students would craft 50–70 page novellas: entirely creative work, entirely of their own choosing, and entirely as fiction writers rather than symbols of test-score growth. In the course of the two months during which we workshopped these novellas, discussed them in class, laughed about the odd settings and characters, and wept along with the deeply tragic accounts, I watched, mesmerized by the way creativity took hold of each student. I watched as the value of collaboration trumped competition, and zest for creative flair trumped a grade point average. Indeed, when each student handed in their final draft of the novella, Timothy stayed after class. Lingering by the doorway as I shuffled the massive pile as best I could, Timothy watched me. I stopped shuffling, looked up at him, and found not a smirk but a smile. He nodded his head and said only a handful of words. "That was real cool, Mr. Reynolds."

In the weeks afterwards, reading these hefty efforts of my students, I saw something I hadn't seen in my eleventh graders yet: their deeply impassioned love of learning. The kind of love we speak of when we ask a group of 5-year-olds if they want to hear a story; the kind of love that can never be influenced by the bottom line of scores, money, or marketplace terminology. But here's the real kicker: years later, students in this novella-writing experiment were still writing. The value of creativity had awoke in them again. We never need to pressure 5-year-olds to draw a picture with crayons, or listen to a fabulous tale, or craft their own magical, strange story. It's an innate desire in kids to be creative. It's considered a joy. Teaching and learning can embody this same kind of joy even in secondary schools—even in difficult places. But this kind of value system can only occur in a wide-scale way if the system that supports it has its standards in the right places. Instead of standardized test-score results of students and their teachers, it's high time we put pressure on those further back up the river. As the situation stands, we're grabbing bucketfuls of nutrient-drained water and then complaining that those who live by its immediate shores need to fix it. In reality, those living upstream need to receive the stricture of standards that no longer allows them to pollute the water and then claim it's not their responsibility.

Bill Ayers argues poignantly that

> When the aim of education and the sole measure of success is competitive, learning becomes exclusively selfish, and there is no obvious social motive to pursue it. People are turned against one another as every difference becomes a potential deficit. Getting ahead is the primary goal in such places, and mutual assistance, which can be so natural in other human affairs, is severely restricted or banned. It's no wonder that cheating scandals are rampant in our country and fraudulent claims are commonplace. (Ayers, 2012)

If we want to help create a 21st century that doesn't increase the gap between rich and poor, that doesn't encourage success at all costs, and that doesn't worship money while ignoring need, then we must demand a reprioritization of values. As teachers, we can join the effort by working the craft learning experiences for our students that foster their creativity, value their compassion, and demand their collaboration. We can join with our colleagues to claim these skills as more important than test results, and we can, as needed, work under the radar to design lessons that skirt the rhetoric and deliver the authentic. As administrators, we must believe that creativity, compassion, and collaboration will always lead us to better places than competition and the bottom line. Positions of leadership allow for a modeling of these priorities that can set the tone for schools in deeply profound ways. As policymakers and citizens who elect policymakers, we must resist the easy lie that a failing school or education system is the result of its teachers and students alone. The destruction begins further upriver, and we must refuse to allow those in power to set an agenda that keeps us on track for comparisons and belittling.

Our students sit in front of us, charged with the task of meeting a 21st century society embroiled in its own tragedy, which is simply this: believing there is no other way. We must stand at the front of our classrooms, town halls, and government chambers and declare that there is another way, which we've simply resisted trying because it seeks to change the power dynamics. But the new way is essential if we actually care about all children. From here, the only way to truly move forward is to stop competing and start collaborating; to stop self-seeking and start embodying compassion; and to stop assessing schools as though they are business and students as though they are products, and to start prioritizing creativity over test scores.

The measure of whether or not we rise to the challenge will not be the numerical value stamped on a numerically coded student's standardized test, but the look of that students face as she solves a science problem, engages in a heated classroom history debate, and learns in an environment rich with passion, joy, and growth. In the two decades that have passed since Kozol's *Savage Inequalities*, we have miserably failed that test. This time around, let's try something different.

REFERENCES

Apple, M. (2008). Curriculum planning: Content, form, and the politics of accountability. *The Sage Handbook of Curriculum and Instruction*. Los Angeles, CA: Sage.

Ayers, B. (2012). *An open letter to President Obama from Bill Ayers*. Retrieved from: http://www.good.is/posts/an-open-letter-to-president-obama-from-bill-ayers

Cochran-Smith, M., & Lytle, S. L. (2006). Troubling images of teaching in No Child Left Behind. *Harvard Educational Review, 73*(4), 668–697.

Danza, T. (2012). *I'd like to apologize to every teacher I ever had: My year as a rookie teacher at Northwest High School*. New York, NY: Crown.

Dwyer, P. (2006). *Salaries of members of Congress: A list of payable rates and effective dates, 1789-2006* (97-1011 GOV). Washington, DC: Congressional Research Service.

Freire, P. (1970). *Pedagogy of the oppressed*. New York, NY: Continuum.

Gladwell, M. (1999). *What the dog saw: And other adventures*. New York, NY: Penguin.

Guggenheim, D. (Director), & Chilcott, L. (Producer). (2010). *Waiting for Superman* [Motion picture]. United States: Walden Media & Participant Media.

Hanushek, E., & Rivkin, S. (2007). Pay, working conditions, and teacher quality. *The Future of Children, 17*(1), 69–86.

Ingersoll, R., & Smith, T. (2004, March). Do teacher induction and mentoring matter? *NASSP Bulletin, 88*(638), 28–40.

Katz, J. (1999). *Tough guise*. [Video]. Amherst, MA: Media Education Foundation.

Kozol, J. (1991). *Savage inequalities: Children in America's schools*. New York, NY: HarperCollins.

Ladson-Billings, G. (1995, Fall). Toward a theory of culturally relevant pedagogy. *American Educational Research Journal, 32*(3), 465–491.

Reynolds, L. (Ed.). (2007). *Inside out and outside in: Essays on the nature and experience of love*. Moraga, CA: Stonegarden.net.

Schlichte, J., Yssel, N., & Merbler, J. (2005, Fall). Pathways to burnout: Case studies in teacher isolation and alienation. *Preventing School Failure, 50*(1), 35–40.

Snyder, T. D., & Dillow, S. A. (2010). *Digest of education statistics 2009*. Washington, DC: National Center for Education Statistics.

Tough, P. (2012). *How children succeed: Grit, curiosity, and the hidden power of character*. New York, NY: Houghton-Mifflin Harcourt.

Williams, B. (2012). Everybody is somebody. *Intersections*. Retrieved from: http://reynoldsluke.blogspot.co.uk/2012/10/one-true-thing-from-beverly williams.html

CHAPTER 10

NEW POLICIES
FOR THE 21ST CENTURY

Sharon L. Nichols
University of Texas at San Antonio

Nicole Svenkerud-Hale
Texas A&M University

Language is a good place to start reform.
—Susan Ohanian, 2009

In the 2008 movie *Slumdog Millionaire* (Colson, Boyle, & Tandan, 2008), the opening scene shows a police officer brutally interrogating a young teenage boy. From the very beginning, viewers are thrust into an emotionally charged violent scene that raises many initial questions. Who is this boy? Why is he in trouble? How did he get here? This short opening scene is a jarring introduction that gives the viewer only vague impressions about characters and possible plots. The rest of the movie proceeds through a sequence of scenes that toggle back and forth in time slowly filling in answers to the questions raised by the first scene of the movie. The movie then provides audience members a sort of catharsis effect by revisiting the interrogation scene at the end, only now of course, audience members understand the who, what, when, and why of what is happening.

Educational Policies and Youth in the 21st Century, pages 177–192
Copyright © 2016 by Information Age Publishing
All rights of reproduction in any form reserved.

This approach to storytelling is often referred to as "framing," since the whole idea is to begin and end (or frame) the story with the same scene. In framing movies and books in this way, authors strategically influence the way viewers and readers will experience the story. In *Slumdog*, moviegoers were specifically primed to look again for this interrogation scene and therefore, their experience of learning about the characters and other plot points are viewed through this expectation. The frame influences how they experienced the rest of the movie. Consider if the movie began in another place, such as when the boys were young and foraging through the trash on the streets of Mumbai. Audience members would experience the subsequent story much differently, noticing different features, characters, and plot elements as the movie unfolded. Thus, frames in the world of narratives serve to direct and influence readers' and viewers' interpretations of events as stories unfold.

Frames exist in other disciplines where individuals are asked to understand or interpret some type of problem, scenario, or dilemma. For example, cognitive psychologists study framing effects when it comes to risky decision making. Political scientists examine how politicians frame their political platforms in the run up to Election Day. And, sociologists and media analysts look at how journalistic framing impacts how readers interpret societal problems. In all cases, data suggest that the way in which problems are framed, or described, impacts the way in which consumers interpret them.

Framing effects are widespread when it comes to educational policy. For at least 50 years, politicians and journalists alike have used frames to sell their views of what is wrong with America's schools and why. A widely referenced example of this comes from the 1950s when Russia beat us into space. At the time, an infamous cover story in *Life* magazine blamed America's schools and students for this failure by comparing characteristics of one "typical" American student and one "typical" Russian student (Sochurek & Wayman, 1958; Wilson, 1958). Of course, the American student was cast as lazy and defiant, whereas the Russian student was cast as studious and obedient. This story was exceedingly popular and fed the emerging narrative that America's schools and their students are to blame for our economic and societal ills.

But this "story" is absurd. Most of America's students are not lazy (Nichols & Good, 2004) and there is no data to connect education with economic productivity. And yet, headline after headline since that time seem to contend that America's students and their teachers are to blame. If anything, this has only worsened over time. The ways in which our educational problems have been framed by politicians and media outlets have defined our view of America's public education system.

Unfortunately, we are moving further away from understanding the relevance of these frames. In a 2009 speech to educational writers, Obama's

Secretary of Education Arne Duncan called for citizens to contribute to the debate of school reform. He called for a solution-driven debate: "It's not enough to define the problem. We've had that for 50 years. We need to find solutions—based on the very best evidence and the very best ideas." We do need solutions; however, we contend that better solutions come from a careful examination of our fundamental problems. Mr. Duncan's assumption that we somehow know (and agree upon) the problems we face in improving America's schools implies there are single, easily identifiable solutions.

If we are going to enact educational policies in the 21st century that will have a meaningful impact on the lives of our increasingly diverse student body, then it is absolutely crucial that we take a step back and examine how problems are defined in the first place. Throughout this book, authors have persuasively pointed out how various policies can be deleterious to our youth. Many have offered promising policy solutions that could counteract these problems currently set in motion. The goal of this chapter is to take a step back from specific policy discussions and offer critical insight into the nature of problem definitions and how they constrict how we help our youth.

FRAMES

One way to understand the nature of problems, is to think through how that problem is defined in the first place—or how it is framed. Just as the example from *Slumdog Millionaire* illustrates, narratives that are framed a particular way cause us to think about it in just that way. The first author has written a lot about the problems with high-stakes testing. When teaching, she was often asked, "If you don't like tests, what else should we be doing then?" This very common question is partly what prompted the ideas explored in this chapter, because instead of thinking of an alternate solution, all I can think of is what is the problem? This lack of problem "critique" compels us to understand why. The answers rest with a rich literature that has explored how frames dictate how we see problems.

Decision Making

The effect of frames have been most commonly studied when it comes to risky decision making. According to Tversky and Kahneman (1981), a decision frame is defined as a "decision maker's conception of the acts, outcomes, and contingencies associated with a particular choice" (p. 453). As a consequence, the frame a decision maker adopts, "is controlled partly by the formulation of the problem and partly by the norms, habits, and personal characteristics of the decision-maker" (p. 453). Thus, decisions are highly contingent upon the information given as well as the attributes of the decision maker. Data on decision making illustrates how the way in which problems are framed influences a decision maker's choices.

In a typical study of its kind, participants are faced with a hypothetical problem in which 600 individuals are likely to die as a result of some infectious disease. In light of this problem, decision makers are given one of two possible options for saving lives. If program A is adopted, 200 people will be definitely saved (72%). If program B is adopted, there is one-third probability that 600 will be saved, and two-thirds probability that no one will be saved. The question is, which one is favored? Most opt for the sure thing; the scenario in which 200 will be saved even though in the other scenario there is a good chance all people could be saved. Researchers then ask the question what if this exact same set of circumstances were framed differently. To address this question, participants are presented with the same hypothetical scenario, however their options are framed in the negative. If program A is adopted, 400 people will die. If program B is adopted, there is a one-third probability that nobody will die and a two-thirds probability that 600 people will die (78%). Data show people change their minds. Individuals would prefer to take a chance rather than opt for the sure thing. The point is that in both cases, the outcome is the same, 400 individuals in program A are sure to die and yet it is more acceptable when it is framed positively (200 people will live) rather than when it was framed negatively (400 people will die).

In this "standard view" of framing (Levin, Schneider, & Gaeth, 1998), participants' choices of risk versus nonrisk depended on whether options were described in positive or negative terms. Participants demonstrated "choice reversal" selecting certainty when options are framed positively and risk when framed negatively. These data provide support for what Tversky and Kahneman (1981, 1992; Kahneman & Tversky, 1979) refer to as prospect theory: the idea that framing manipulation determines whether outcomes are evaluated in terms of gains or losses. Research since this time more or less consistently supports the tendency "for people to be more likely to take risks when options focus attention on the chance to avoid losses than when options focus on the chance to realize gains" (Levin, Schneider, & Gaeth, 1998, p. 153).

In the decision-making literature, other types of framing effects include attribute and goal framing. In attribute framing, only one feature is manipulated at a time. For example, Levin and Gaeth (1988) demonstrated that perceptions of good and bad influenced the choice between meat that was described as either 75% lean or 25% fat. Although these representations are exactly the same, most preferred meat labeled in positive terms (leanness) instead of negative (fat). Numerous studies have confirmed this trend. Studies of decision-making in terms of all types of scenarios including resource allocation (invest in company with 40% failure rate or 60% success rate) (Dunegan, 1993, 1995), gambling (Levin, Chapman, & Johnson, 1988), medical treatment (Levin, Schnittjer, & Thee, 1988) have yielded similar results. People are much more likely to subscribe to scenarios that are framed more positively than ones framed in terms of a deficit even if the outcome is exactly the same.

Goal framing, by contrast, includes studies that look at the effects of persuasive communication on tendencies to act. For example, women are more inclined to engage in breast self-examination when presented with information that stressed the negative consequences of not engaging in such behavior than when information stressed the positive consequence of engaging in it (Meyerowitz & Chaiken, 1987). When presented with an opportunity to make some decision, the way in which options are framed influences the choices we make and the way we behave.

Problem Solving

Similar to decision making, when it comes to solving complex problems, the way in which the problem is framed, or represented, impact the kinds of solutions that appear. In their seminal book on problem solving, Newell and Simon (1972) describe ways in which the structure or presentation of problems dictate the type of solutions paths that emerge. When problems are well-defined, there is a clearly articulated solution path, such as when students are asked to find the area of a parallelogram or to define the word "batiks." Here, there is very little ambiguity as to what is being asked or how it should be solved. By contrast, when problems are ill defined, the goal state is much less clear and potential solution paths more numerous, as when we are asked how to increase business sales, how to save money for college tuition, or how to engage in (or end) war. In these instances, problem solutions are dependent upon the information given and the problem solver's internal representation of what is being asked of them (Dunbar, 1998; Halpern, 2003).

A known problem of problem solving is the notion of "functional fixity" (Duncker, 1945). That is, not only are we confined by the problem space that is defined for us, but this confinement acts as a barrier for seeing new or spontaneous ways of solving the problem. The nine-dot problem is a perfect example of this. After drawing three rows of three dots that are lined up horizontally and vertically, problem solvers are asked to draw four straight lines without lifting the pencil but at the same time going through each of the dots. The answer lies in drawing lines that literally go "outside the box." Problem representations often constrain our perceptual field such that alternative solutions that ask us to go beyond the perceptual (or conceptual) boundaries of the problem are restricted from view. As Newell and Simon (1972, p. 819) state when faced with a problem with multiple solution paths, "The subject immerses himself in an informational environment that evokes *only* elements belonging to the environment" (emphasis added).

Of course, most of our societal problems would be categorized under the "ill-defined" category described previously, and therefore, susceptible to problem representation and functional fixity effects. Thus, the way in which we as a culture face some of our most difficult and intractable societal ills is partly contingent on the way in which these problems are described and understood. Politicians, who are at the forefront of proposing some of the alleged solutions, then, have much to gain in convincing the populace that certain problems require the solutions they wish to endorse. This is where problem representation comes in handy. For example, the problem of gun violence gets framed according to interests of gun proponents such as the NRA. Their slogan "guns don't kill people, people kill people" leads very naturally to problem solutions that focus efforts on reactive type approaches (policing, convicting, and locking up those who use guns) instead of proactive ones (investing in early childhood programs, focusing on gun control).

Poverty is another complex social problem that is susceptible to problem representation constraints. The willingness of a society to help its poor population is related to how the problem of poverty is framed. As Weiner (1980, 2005) has examined, the attributions we ascribe to persons and situations are linked to our affective reactions and tendencies to help. In terms of conditions of poverty, he suggests that when the causes of poverty are attributed to individuals instead of societies, we are less likely to provide support or help. By contrast, if poverty is framed in terms of social disadvantages and lost economic opportunities, then solutions emerge that focus more on the environmental conditions instead of the individual. When the media pointed to Katrina victims and asked why didn't they just leave, then one can see how the lack of assistance to those left behind is rationalized by a problem representation that situates poverty as a problem of lazy (or dumb) individuals instead of inept policies, lack of community resources, and social good will.

The role of problem representation plays out when it comes to our willingness (or lack therefore) to invest in our youth. It is common for adults to believe that adolescence is a time of "storm and stress" or inevitable rebellion, social unrest, and hostility (Arnett, 1999; Bandura, 1964; Holmbeck & Hill, 1988; Offer & Schonert-Reichl, 1992). When adolescents are viewed this way, then their acting out is expected and unavoidable. Not surprising, we see policies enacted that are influenced by this belief across many areas of youth's lives (Nichols & Good, 2004). When it comes to youth violence, the expectation that some youth will be violent prompts policies aimed at controlling youth (e.g., three strikes you're out, or zero tolerance programs). And, when it comes to education, the current emphasis conse-quence-based testing suggests that youth require the pressure of external enticements or threats to have a reason to do well in school (the underlying assumption being they won't do it on their own). This monolithic framing of youth's behavior communicates to them (and the broader society) the expectation that they will fail, act out, do wrong, and the promise that bad things will happen if (and when) they do.

The Role of the Media

Problem representation and functional fixity are useful devices for ex-amining how policies aimed at correcting complex social problems are framed and therefore, the nature of the solutions they imply. Although politicians are at the forefront of policy development, journalists perpetu-ate politicians' agenda in the way they frame events, stories, and problems. For example, in framing newsworthy events, specific aspects are made stra-tegically more salient to consumers than others, and in doing so, become more "noticeable, meaningful, or memorable to audiences" (Entman, 1993, p. 51). Of course, saliency does not necessarily predict how readers/ consumers interpret events, but at a minimum it is more likely to be re-membered (e.g., Fiske & Taylor, 1991; Halpern, 2003). The strategic use of saliency as in the "if it bleeds, it leads" philosophy of reporting, is meant to grab (and hopefully sustain) readers' attention.

But, media analysts find that framing does so much more than just grab our attention. The way a story is framed offers a specific version of events that is characterized by the language used as well as the perspective taken (e.g., Kahneman, & Tversky, 1984). Entman defines it this way,

> To frame is to *select some aspects of a perceived reality and make them more salient in a communicating text, in such a way as to promote a particular problem definition, causal interpretation, moral evaluation, and/or treatment recommendation* for the item described. Typically frames diagnose, evaluate, and prescribe. ... Frames, then, *define problems*—determine what a causal agent is doing with what costs and benefits, usually measured in terms of common cultural values; *diagnose causes*—identify the forces creating the problem; *make moral judgments*—evalu-ate causal agents and their effects; and *suggest remedies*—offer and justify treat-ments for the problems and predict their likely effects. (Entman, 1993, p. 52)

Thus, mass media define social problems for audiences—presenting the who, what, where, why, and when. The strategic choices of how to discuss story knowns and unknowns not only influences the beliefs and attitudes of consumers (e.g., Iyengar & Kinder, 1987), but in turn, also help to shape how social problems get addressed through policies and legislation (Gamson, 1992).

Media expert David Altheide (1997) makes this point when it comes to how violence against children, in these case child kidnappings, gets framed. He argues the following,

> Focusing on "stranger kidnappings" of which there were very few each year (e.g., 67 in 1983), sparked an unprecedented multimedia barrage of "missing child" photos and pleas on milk cartons, billboards, network news, millions of pieces of mail, and of course numerous movies and documentaries. The children of America were reportedly under siege. Such action fueled legislation, policy changes, increased criminal sanctions and budget allocations in the millions of dollars. Ignoring the far more numerous "runaway" and "throwaway" children left most cities with paltry resources to help and protect several hundred thousand children "on the road." (Altheide, 1997, p. 655)

In this case, the slanted emphasis on stranger abductions in an environment where the problems of youth runaways are significantly more prevalent, played a significant role in subsequent resource allocations and policy implementation.

FRAMING AND PROBLEM REPRESENTATION IN EDUCATIONAL POLICY

No Child Left Behind and Race to the Top both leave little doubt as to what the problems are with American education and who is to blame. Both laws emphasize tests as the only evaluator of school success and very clearly defines the problem with our schools as a problem of academically failing students (as measured by standardized achievement tests across math, reading, writing, social studies, and science). The law also clarifies for us who is to blame: lazy, unfocused, and ineffective teachers and our lazy, uninspired, and unmotivated students. By holding teachers and students directly accountable for their performance on a test, the policy specifically positions the problem of education as a problem of academically challenged students and their lazy and ineffective teachers and school leaders. Although this "blame it on public schools" orientation is not new, as McCaslin (1996) and others argued in 1996 (e.g., Amrein & Berliner, 1996; Berliner, 1996; Good, 1996) and as many have vigorously and articulately debunked before and since that time (e.g., Berliner & Biddle, 1995; Bracey, 1997), NCLB's version seems to be one of the most aggressive indictments against our nation's schools and its teachers and students to date.

Redefining Our Problems: Toward a Newer Narrative

Educators, politicians, and citizens must become savvy about framing devices in order to see through the underlying agendas politicians use them to promote. For example, Edelman (1988) argues that pervasive references to educational "crises" throughout the years (see also Glass, 2008) are constructed, packaged, and sold (and easily bought) in order to justify political action. The Phi Delta Kappan polls are evidence of this. Consistently and for at least 30 years, the public rates their local schools much higher than national schools. Negativity of other schools invade citizens' consciousness even when personal experiences are so much more positive. Our educational problems must be better defined and more inclusive of what we know about the in and out of school factors that influence students (Berliner, 2006).

One approach for moving forward is to offer more strategic frames surrounding the variables that are targeted by our politicians. One starting point may be to broaden our representations of schools, teachers, and students. Under the current climate, educational quality is defined by adequate test scores that necessarily mean students are defined as test scores, schools viewed as test-score factories, and teachers as test training technicians. In order to redefine solutions, it is useful to redefine the problem variables—students, teachers, and schools.

Students

In McCaslin's (1996) original essay on how politicians frame educational reform, she argues policies that emphasize academic achievement as the sole purpose of schooling narrowly define the experience of being a student. She argues for a view of students as "social beings" who, in school settings, must bring to school a range of experiences, needs, and dispositions. She notes,

> Students are social beings; student is but one feature of their lives. Students live in social worlds of home, peers, neighborhoods, and schools that do not always provide support and safety. Life for children, students, in the 1990s is challenging for most, horrific for some.
>
> The representation of students as social beings who are more than their achievement and who learn more than the intended formal curriculum has implications for how to consider the experience of being a student and how to influence that experience so that, among other things, we might achieve our goals for student achievement. (McCaslin, 1996, p. 14)

By expanding our conception of student from "academic test score" to "social being" it naturally broadens ideas for how we might enhance a students' level of success.

We think, as McCaslin argues, students should be viewed as social beings who are also viewed as collaborators in their own learning process. By expanding the role of students from that of subject matter learner to collaborator in the learning process, then the focus shifts again from the idea that students are blank slates in need of heavy doses of subject matter, to the idea that they are active agents in their own learning.

Scholars who have strategically viewed students as collaborators have studied how giving students a voice in their education impacts their motivation and achievement (Cook-Sather, 2006). In this line of research, the idea of actively listening to our students extends beyond the superficial layer of asking what they like or dislike about school. It involves deeper, more meaningful, and collaborative conversations, between teachers and students. In one study, Rudduck and colleagues (Rudduck, Chaplain, & Wallace, 1996) report that when students were asked their opinion on what conditions support a suitable learning environment, most report respect and fairness for pupils as individuals, active engagement in the learning environment, and autonomy in the school environment. That is, when students are invited to actively participate in an on-going dialogue with teachers regarding their own learning process, they develop a greater sense of responsibility toward their education and academic success.

Mitra (2009) discusses the many potential benefits for incorporating student voice into the decision-making process for educational change. Mitra states,

> Student voice initiatives have served as catalysts for educational change, including improvements in classroom practice made directly by teachers working with students to co-create curriculum and to engage in dialogues about ways to shape the learning process in the classroom. (p. 1837)

Most importantly, current research supports that when teachers and schools take the time to incorporate student voice into educational change, this has long-term positive benefits for student development outcomes, as students are able to learn how they can make a difference in their own life and in the lives of others (Mitra, 2009). Even more compelling is the positive changes associated when students are asked to participate in faculty meetings. Research shows that when students are present at these meetings, the intent of conversation dramatically changes; professional behaviors demonstrated by teacher's increase (i.e., not completing crossword puzzles during staff meetings), there is less hostility exhibited between teachers, and there is an increase in the number of positive interactions between colleagues (Flutter & Rudduck, 2004; Rudduck & Demetriou, 2003). Furthermore, when students are able to provide immediate feedback regarding their curriculum, not only does this facilitate curriculum development, but it also strengthens and improves student-teacher relationships (Mitra, 2009) and positively influences professional training and development for teachers (Donohue, Bower, & Rosenberg, 2003).

Teachers

We must view teachers as professionals and not as test technicians. This positioning of our educators could have enormously positive impact on the quality of teachers recruited into the profession as well as the quality of their development throughout their career. One of the main reasons the nation of Finland does so well on international tests and is regarded by many as one of the strongest educational systems in the world is because of their view of teachers as esteemed professionals. Because of this view, they are treated with a great deal of respect from members of the culture, provided intensive professional development opportunities, and are paid well.

Perhaps if we also adopted this view, our teachers would be provided the support, respect, and reverence their craft deserves. Teachers, like doctors, require extensive training and practice to improve. and even then they can only exert so much control over their students. This is understood when it comes to our medical professionals, and yet teachers continue to fall prey to what social psychologists refer to as a fundamental attribution error. As described by Kennedy (2010), this is a problem whereby we tend to "overestimate the influence of personal characteristics on behavior and underestimate the influence of the situation itself" (p. 591). As a culture, we confuse the quality of the teacher (how nice they are) with the quality of their teaching. This conceptual mistake leads us to believe that if only teachers were caring enough, perseverant enough, excited enough, these qualities would overcome whatever types of students they face. This perspective fundamentally overlooks the many aspects of a teacher's work that are outside of their control, such as resources, planning time, and student characteristics (e.g., student poverty, see Biddle, Chapter 5).

Schools

Currently, conceptions of schools are guided by a business model view of education where schools are seen as black boxes where only inputs and outputs matter. We propose that we view our schools as communities. From this new perspective, then, what naturally emerges is a concern not just for inputs and outputs, but also for the processes that occur within. Research suggests that when schools are able to create a strong sense of community, a wide variety of immediate and long-term benefits are associated with this process. For example, Osterman (2000) discusses that when students experience a strong sense of belonging to their schools, they demonstrate an increase in academic motivation, develop a higher level of social competence and altruistic behaviors, students' prosocial behaviors increase, and relationships with teachers are built upon trust and respect. A school that embodies a strong sense of community is linked to students' academic motivation, social and emotional competencies, as well as the prevention of alcohol use, drug use, violent behavior, dropouts, and other risky behaviors (Battistich, Schaps, Watson, Solomon, & Lewis, 2000; Solomon, Battistich, Watson, Schaps, & Lewis, 2000) as well as academic achievement. Teachers also benefit from this perspective, as they experience higher morale and job satisfaction when working in schools that support learning communities (Battistich, Solomon, Kim, Watson, & Schaps, 1995).

Elbers and Streefland (2000) generated a community of mathematicians that included teachers and students (ages 11 and 13 years old). The teachers were viewed as "senior researchers" and the students were viewed as "junior researchers." In this study, the senior researchers collaborated with the junior researchers to solve everyday problems. As a result, all the participants developed new mathematical intuitions and more advanced patterns of thoughts as they shared, suggested, analyzed, evaluated, rejected, or constructed upon the ideas of each researcher (teachers and students) in the study. As a result of this style of learning community, each participant was able to move past his or her own individual limitations and exponentially expand their learning possibilities. More importantly, they were able to build their own understandings and concepts rather than passively receive the knowledge.

Another study compared the interaction patterns of students who attended a traditional school to students enrolled in a community of learners' school (Matusov, Bell, & Rogoff, 2002). Results indicated that students in the community of learners' school more frequently promoted knowledge within each other's ideas and initiated leadership; compared to the students in the traditional school, who asked questions for answers they already knew and they withheld knowledge from their peers to test and judge one another. This study demonstrates a deeper understanding that students learn more in school than what is simply taught. They learn how to interact with each other, regardless if it is positive or negative.

CONCLUSION

Policymakers must be more cognizant of the assumptions embedded in policies they endorse. High-stakes testing accountability communicates that the only purpose of America's schools is to help students to perform better on tests. This positioning is a very restricted view of who are students are, what the profession of teaching entails, and how schools function. By expanding our conceptions of schools as communities, teachers as professionals, and students as collaborators and social beings, we find new ways of thinking about the problems and solutions for schooling emerging. The literature reviewed here is just a starting point for how these representations play out for students. High-stakes testing reform is failing miserably and harming so many of our youth. It is critical we adopt broader frames of references for thinking about the problems of education and therefore pursuant solutions.

At the height of high-stakes testing accountability implementation in 2008, the first author participated in a community forum event on education in a border town in the South. Panel members included a cross section of community members with different perspectives on the local education and accountability system. Among the participants were an elementary teacher, a special education teacher, an 8th-grade student, a parent, and myself. We were all aligned in sharing stories of the destructive nature of high-stakes testing. The student was perhaps the most convincing panelist sharing with us how he didn't go a day in school without his social studies teacher referring to the state test and how the principal basically "begged" his mom to bring him to school on test day because he would score high (and subsequently help the school look better on accountability).

Toward the end, a local businesswoman, who came in late, raised her hand wanting to participate in a discussion she had largely missed. She shared with the room her discontentment with students from one local school sharing that oftentimes her applicants can't spell *there* versus *their*. Troubled by this state of affairs, she seems to have already concluded that the answer is to test students more. Her obvious frustration with one student compelled her to look for someone to blame. Not only did she fail to see these moments as opportunities to mentor new employees, but her frustration was so big that she concluded the best way to fix this state of affairs was to test them more! This punishing attitude is what fuels the policy.

Business-minded citizens would be better advocates for schools if their views of students, teachers, and schools broadened. If they viewed students as collaborators, teachers as professionals, and schools as communities perhaps more citizens would be willing to invest in their proper development and education. All of the policies discussed throughout this book require critical examination of the problems for which policy prescriptions are being offered. Only then can we advocate for policies that will support, not undermine, our vast, diverse student population.

REFERENCES

Altheide, D. L. (1997). The news media, the problem frame, and the production of fear. *The Sociological Quarterly, 38*(4), 647–668.

Amrein, A., & Berliner, D. (2006). High-stakes testing, uncertainty, and student learning. *Education Policy Analysis Archives, 10*(18). Retrieved January 31, 2007, from http://epaa.asu.edu/epaa/v10n18/.

Arnett, J. J. (1999, May). Adolescent storm and stress, reconsidered. *American Psychologist, 54*(5), 317–326.

Bandura, A. (1964). The stormy decade: Fact or fiction? *Psychology in the Schools, 1*, 224–231.

Battistich, V., Schaps, E., Watson, M., Solomon, D., & Lewis, C. (2000). Effects of the child development project on students' drug use and other problem behaviors. *Journal of Primary Prevention, 21*, 75–99.

Battistich, V., Solomon, D., Kim, D., Watson, M., & Schaps, E. (1995). Schools as communities, poverty levels of student populations and students' attitudes, motives, and performance: A multilevel analysis. *American Educational Research Journal, 32*, 627–658.

Berliner, D. C. (1996). Uninvited comments from an uninvited guest. *Educational Researcher, 25*(8), 47–50.

Berliner, D. C. (2006). Our impoverished view of educational reform. *Teachers College Record, 108*(6), 949–995.

Berliner, D. C., & Biddle, B. J. (1995). *The manufactured crisis: Myths, fraud, and the attack on America's public schools.* New York, NY: Addison-Wesley.

Bracey, G. W. (1997). *The truth about America's schools: The Bracey Reports 1991–1997.* Bloomington, IN: Phi Delta Kappa Educational Foundation.

Colson, C. (Producer), Boyle, D., & Tandan, L. (Directors). (2008). *Slumdog Millionaire.* USA: Warner Bros.

Cook-Sather, A. (2006). Sound, presence, and power: "Student voice" in educational research and reform. *Curriculum Inquiry, 36*(4), 359–390.

Donohue, D. M., Bower, J., & Rosenberg, D. (2003). Learning with and learning from: Reciprocity in service learning in teacher education. *Equity and Excellence in Teacher Education, 36*, 15–27.

Dunbar, K. (1998). Problem solving. In W. Bechtel (Ed.), *A companion to cognitive science* (pp. 289–298). London, England: Blackwell.

Duncker, K. (1945). *On problem solving: Psychological monographs, 58*(5), No. 270. Washington, DC: American Psychological Association.

Dunegan, K. J. (1993). Framing, cognitive modes, and image theory. Towards an understanding of a glass half full. *Journal of Applied Psychology, 78*, 491–503.

Dunegan, K. J. (1995). Fines, frames and images: Examining formulation effects on punishment decisions. *Organizational Behavior and Human Decision Processes, 68*, 58–67.

Edelman, M. (1988). *Constructing the public spectacle.* University of Chicago Press: Chicago, IL.

Elbers, E., & Streefland, L. (2000). Collaborative learning and the construction of common knowledge. *European Journal of Psychology of Education, 15*(4), 479–490.

Entman, R. (1993). Framing: Toward clarification of a fractured paradigm. *Journal of Communication, 43*(4), 51–58.

Fiske, S. T., & Taylor, S. E. (1991). *Social cognition* (2nd ed.). New York, NY: McGraw-Hill.

Flutter, J., & Rudduck, J. (2004). *Consulting pupils: What's in it for schools.* London, England: Routledge/Falmer.

Gamson, W. A. (1992). *Talking politics.* New York, NY: Cambridge University Press.

Glass, G. V. (2008). *Fertilizers, pills, and magnetic strips: The fate of public education in America.* Charlotte, NC: Information Age Publishers.

Good, T. L. (1996). Educational researchers comment on the education summit and other policy proclamations from 1983–1996. *Educational Researcher, 25*(8), 4–6.

Halpern, D. (2003). *Thought and knowledge: An introduction to critical thinking.* Mahwah, NJ: Erlbaum.

Holmbeck, G. N., & Hill, J. P. (1988). Storm and stress beliefs about adolescence: Prevalence, self-reported antecedents, and effects of an undergraduate course. *Journal of Youth and Adolescence, 17*(4), 285–306.

Iyengar, S., & Kinder, D. R. (1987). *News that matters: Television and American opinion.* Chicago, IL: University of Chicago Press.

Kahneman, D., & Tversky, A. (1979). Prospect theory: An analysis of decision under risk. *Econometrica, 47,* 263–291.

Kahneman, D., & Tversky, A. (1984). Choice, values, and frames. *American Psychologist, 28,* 107–128.

Kennedy, M. M. (2010). Attribution error and the quest for teacher quality. *Educational Researcher, 39*(8), 591–598.

Levin, I. P., Chapman, D. P., & Johnson, R. D. (1988). Confidence in judgments based on incomplete information: An investigation using both hypothetical and real gambles. *Journal of Behavioral Decision Makings, 1,* 29–41.

Levin, I. P., & Gaeth, G. J. (1988). Framing of attribute information before and after consuming the product. *Journal of Consumer Research, 15,* 374–378.

Levin, I. P., Schneider, S. L., & Gaeth, G. J. (1998). All frames are not created equal: A typology and critical analysis of framing effects. *Organizational Behavior and Human Decision Processes, 76*(2), 149–188.

Levin, I. P., Schnittjer, S. K., & Thee, S. L. (1988). Information framing effects in social and personal decisions. *Journal of Experimental Social Psychology, 24,* 520–529.

Matusov, E., Bell, N., & Rogoff, B. (2002). Schooling as a cultural process. Shared thinking and guidance by children from schools differing in collaborative practices. In R. Kail & H. W. Reese (Eds.), *Advances in child development and behavior* (Vol. 29, pp. 129–160). New York, NY: Academic Press.

McCaslin, M. (1996). The problem of problem representation: The summit's conception of student. *Educational Researcher, 25*(8), 13–15.

Meyerowitz, B. E., & Chaiken, S. (1987). The effect of message framing on breast self-examination attitudes, intentions, and behavior. *Journal of Personality and Social Psychology, 52,* 517–522.

Mitra, D. (2009). The role of intermediary organizations in sustaining student voice initiatives. *Teachers College Record 111*(7), 1834–1868.

Newell, A., & Simon, H. A. (1972). *Human problem solving.* Englewood Cliffs, NJ: Prentice-Hall.

Nichols, S. L., & Good, T. (2004). *America's teenagers—myths and realities: Media images, schooling, and the social costs of careless indifference.* Mahwah, NJ: Erlbaum.

Offer, D., & Schonert-Reichl, K. (1992). Debunking the myths of adolescence: Findings from recent research. *American Academy of Child and Adolescent Psychiatry, 31*(6), 1003–1014.

Ohanian, S. (2009, June 5). Accountability and the slippery language of public relations: An essay review. *Education Review, 12*(7). Retrieved June 10, 2009 from http://edrev.asu.edu/essays/v12n7index.html

Osterman, K. (2000). Students' need for belonging in school. *Review of Educational Research, 70*(3), 323–367.

Rudduck, J., Chaplain, R., & Wallace, G. (1996). *School improvement: What can pupils tell us?* London, England: David Fulton.

Rudduck, J., & Demetriou, H. (2003). Student perspectives and teacher practices: The transformative potential. *McGill Journal of Education, 38*(2), 274–288.

Sochurek, H. & Wayman, S. (1958, March 24–April 21). Crisis in education. *Life, 44*(12–16).

Solomon, D., Battistich, V., Watson, M., Schaps, E., & Lewis, C. (2000). A six-district study of educational change: Direct and mediated effects of the Child Development Project. *Social Psychology of Education, 4*, 3–51.

Tversky, A., & Kahneman, D. (1981). The framing of decisions and the psychology of choice. *Science, 211*, 453–458.

Tversky, A., & Kahneman, D. (1992). Advances in prospect theory: Cumulative representation of uncertainty. *Journal of Risk and Uncertainty, 5*, 297–323.

Weiner, B. (1980). A cognitive (attribution)-emotion-action model of motivated behavior: An analysis of judgments of help-giving. *Journal of Personality and Social Psychology, 39*(2), 186–200.

Weiner, B. (2005). *Social motivation, justice, and the moral emotions: An attributional approach.* Mahwah, NJ: Erlbaum.

Wilson, S. (1958, March 24). It's time to close the carnival. *Life, 44*(12), 37–38.

CHAPTER 11

SOCIAL POLICIES AND THE MOTIVATIONAL STRUGGLES OF YOUTH

Some Closing Comments

Mary McCaslin
University of Arizona

I have been asked to comment on the issues raised within this book and to somehow add to the authors' considerations of youth, the social and educational policies that affect them, and what might be done to improve the situation. This is a daunting task, but I will try my best. I begin with a brief representation of the co-regulation theoretical perspective I bring to this task so readers can more clearly judge the potential relevance of my comments. See McCaslin (2009; 2016), and McCaslin, Vriesema, and Burggraf (2016) for a more extended discussion.

CO-REGULATION FRAMEWORK

The construct of co-regulation (McCaslin, 2009) is rooted in a sociocultural perspective influenced by Vygotskian (1962, 1978) and neo-Vygotskian activity perspectives. Here I stress two basic assertions within this approach.

Educational Policies and Youth in the 21st Century, pages 193–203
Copyright © 2016 by Information Age Publishing
All rights of reproduction in any form reserved.

First, co-regulation takes as a given the social origins of "higher psychologi-cal processes." There are two implications of this assertion. First, cultural expectations and regulations, which capture cultural "probable" beliefs about groups of individuals, matter. Second, social opportunities and rela-tionships, what I call "practicable" experiences that can and do matter, do in fact matter. Together, cultural norms and challenges, and social oppor-tunities and relationships matter greatly. Thus, the arguments within this book are important not only in terms of capturing the behavior of a more powerful other—the "they" and "their policies" that appear in each chap-ter—but authors remind us as well of the power of that dynamic to restrict, if not undermine, youth potential. These arguments are important for what that means for youth now and for the citizens youth might become.

Second, co-regulation views personal identity as a continuous process that emerges through individual "personal potential" immersed in partici-pation and validation in social and cultural relationships. Thus, identity is socially situated and historical. Differences among individuals matter to themselves and to others. Individual differences include the usual array of potential constructs (e.g., readiness to learn) as well as personal disposi-tions and "adaptive learning" within contexts. Adaptive learning involves the internalization of goals; the motivation to commit, challenge, or re-form them; and the competence to enact and evaluate those commitments (Rohrkemper, 1989). Adaptive learning is part of emergent identity; thus, it may be expressed in the present, but it is linked to the past and informs the future. More recently, I have used the term "emotional adaptation" to capture adaptive learning in classrooms (McCaslin, Vriesema, & Burg-graf, 2016). Emotional adaptation foregrounds emotion and coping strate-gies that seem central to, yet are not considered determinants of, academic achievement. Emotional adaptation informs a sense of personal compe-tence, control, and power. It relates to many of the concerns expressed by Part I authors.

These positions inform a model of co-regulation that captures the dy-namic relationships and tensions among cultural, social, and personal sources of influence. Together they challenge, shape, and guide (co-regu-late) possibility. The co-regulation perspective foregrounds the tensions—the mutual press—among them. This perspective stresses as well that no source of influence—personal, social, or cultural—is equally distributed. One result, then, is differential opportunity for culturally valued, socially validated, personally desirable adaptive learning (McCaslin, 2009).

Finally, because the co-regulation perspective asserts that individuals are social by nature and by nurture, it is more focused on opportunity and re-lationship (and the challenge, intrigue, negotiation, and compromise they afford) than it is focused on individual choice and decision making that un-dergirds much motivation and self-regulation theory. As stated elsewhere,

"The model allows us to consider, for example, the co-regulation and motivational struggles of those who have, have not, and have more cultural capital, social support, and personal resources" (McCaslin, 2009, p. 140). It is the lens I bring to this commentary.

THE PROBLEM OF PROBLEM REPRESENTATION

As Nichols and Svenkerud-Hale discuss in Chapter 10, there is a close relationship between how a problem is represented and what is perceived as reasonable ways to go about solving it. I find it a useful framework for authors to consider in that it provides one strategy that might influence reform processes. It begins with a better understanding of current problem representations. In the Preface of this book, Nichols writes:

> This edited book including leading authors from across the country highlights how educational policies impact youth's development and socialization in school contexts. In most cases, policies are constructed by adults, implemented by adults, but are rarely informed by the needs and opinions of youth. Not only are youth not consulted but policymakers often neglect what we know about the psychological, emotional, and educational health of youth. Therefore, both the short and long term impact of these policies have but limited effects on improving students' school performance or personal health issues such as depression and suicide. (p. xiii)

This is a poignant statement. It helped me think about "how did we get here" and for that I am both grateful and dismayed. Grateful because it helped me think; dismayed because of what I remembered.

Societal Worries and School Reform

First, it is useful to think about the temporal context of current school reforms. Modern federal involvement in school reform began in earnest with the appearance of A Nation at Risk in 1983. It is important to know that school reform was just one of several major societal concerns in the 1980s. Societal worries also included the increasing cost of health care, with judgments about who was responsible for health problems and solutions. For example, smoking was now seen as the major cause of (costly) lung cancer, obesity and (costly) diabetes had been linked, and at the end of the day alcohol was more than a personal lifestyle. It was a (costly) social problem. By 1984 acquired immune deficiency syndrome (AIDS) was an "acquired" (costly) epidemic. Victims were vilified; it was "their" own fault.

Costly illnesses were now open to perceptions of individual lifestyle choices, choices that unfairly taxed the social network.

Adding to healthcare and cost worries, the baby boomers were getting older, their parents living longer, and women were not as willing to stay home to care for them. Seniors looked outside the family for financial support and security. They (the Grey Panthers) fought for and won the establishment of the AARP (American Association of Retired Persons), whose sole purpose was their welfare. Concerns about health care and aging played out in the context of continued high levels (10%) of adult unemployment. Who was going to pay for all of this? When? Importantly, there was a sense of immediacy and urgency in the popular culture. These were big problems and they had to be fixed now; two aspects of problem representation known to undermine quality of thinking and problem solving (Weick, 1984).

These social concerns had one thing in common: they were mostly grown-ups' problems. Adults were concerned about their own welfare, arguably more than they were concerned about the welfare of youth. Youth were termed "the forgotten constituency" (Takanishi, DeLeon, & Pallak, 1983). Throughout the decade, policies aimed at youth, including reducing federal expenditures in most social programs, were described as assaultive, mean-spirited, and ultimately culturally self-defeating. This is the context within which A Nation at Risk was released. It called for students to do more: spend more time in school through more and longer school days, and spend more time on school at home. The era of never-ending homework had begun. There is more. A Nation at Risk fundamentally linked youths' achievement failures to declining U.S. global competitiveness (rather than, e.g., the increasing number and size of the holes in the social safety net, corporate decision making, union overreach, a crumbling rust belt, or adult unemployment). Youth were blamed for the situation adults feared they were in: youth were choosing to not achieve.

The Role of Psychology in Popular Culture

Societal concerns and solutions emerged as psychology was shifting its focus away from environmental and biological controls over human behavior to more "uniquely human" cognitive issues of self-control and personal responsibility. Self-help initiatives that purported to guarantee success emerged as a cottage industry. It is a quick step between self-help supports and "help yourself" demands. Two trends in motivational scholarship reinforced this dynamic. The first addressed the role of the individual and self-reliance in attainments. Albert Bandura (e.g., 1978, 1982, 1989) was a major influence throughout this decade. His concept of "self-efficacy," by which personal beliefs can drive attainment above and beyond known aptitude, captured the "can-do" American spirit. His assertion of "triadic reciprocal determinism" thankfully muddied the causal chain, taking some of the pressure off the environment and focused attention on the potential of the individual to rise above it all. By the end of the decade, Bandura had persuasively argued that freedom was "self-control," a perspective that resonated with social policies of benign neglect and enlightened self-interest.

Second, attribution theory emerged in this decade as a major representation of naïve psychology, the study of how popular culture understands the human condition (e.g., Weiner, 1991). Bernard Weiner brought attribution theory to classroom learning in particular. The study of why things happen "to me" was extended to the study of why things happen "to you." Each was rooted within a simplified causal system of dichotomous appraisals (e.g., internal or external) that inform emotion, which fuels behavior. The initial study of self-understanding made room for the study of interpersonal judgments that informed whether a person deserved assistance or sanctions for her actions. Attribution theory codified cultural rules and roles, and helped clarify when and why society supports, invests in, neglects, or punishes its citizens. These two research streams—self-reliance and causal judgments of responsibility—are still dominant perspectives in educational psychology. Their fusion is most easily detected in the subfield of "self-regulated learning."

Defending the Public School

Similar to now, as this book so clearly establishes, not everyone was on the same page then. Real debates and changing conceptions were under way in the academy and education. Concerns with education encompassed both the work of the school, known by student achievement, and how that achievement would be measured. The Nairn and Nader Report in 1980 was a scathing attack on the role of testing in intelligence and achievement in general, and on the Educational Testing Service in particular. The report well-represented societal distrust of the very notion of intelligence, the tests that would define it, and their potential for test bias. Similar concerns could be found within the academy. Then as now, test use was especially suspect among social groups who were not advantaged by them.

Eleanor DiMarino-Linnen and I wanted to mark the turn of the century by learning what we could about the role of research and theory in shaping and being shaped by the context of social and educational policies. We completed a 50-year review of articles published in the *American Psychologist* (McCaslin & DiMarino-Linnen, 2000). Our analysis seems especially useful in light of this current book. DiMarino-Linnen and I summarized tensions in the 1980s:

Societal challenges to psychological conceptions of student learning, intelligence, and achievement were played out in the popular press. As educational psychologists turned to more-process-than-product orientations of learning, thinking, and intelligence and the learning and motivational implications of the multicultural realities of American schools were explored, society was demanding concrete outcomes to facilitate student and teacher accountability. To many citizens (and educators) psychology was taking the "learning" out of learning in classrooms; for some, psychology also was replacing "American" with "multicultural," but it would be educators and students in American schools who would be held accountable even so. (pp. 125–126)

This statement captures current tensions surprisingly (or not) well.

THE PROBLEM OF PROBLEM REPRESENTATION REDUX

Nearly 20 years ago I wrote about "the problem of problem representation" in the then current reform movement called the National Education Summit Policy Statement (1996), or the Summit. The conception of "students" in Summit documents was unidimensional; essentially, "those who achieve." The primary goal of the Summit reform was to raise the bar on what counted as achievement. I argued then that the Summit's extremely limited conception of students doomed any possibility of attaining reform goals; indeed upping the ante for "what counts" would likely undermine both students and reform initiatives (McCaslin, 1996). Ironically, the 1996 Summit was a product of the National Governors' Association (NGA) and has much in common with the current Common Core reforms, which are also a product of NGA involvement. We are back to higher standards and college readiness as the educational gold standard for the academically talented with a trustworthy work ethic and basic skills for those destined for work in service and trades. Since NCLB, however, this time around school reforms have more teeth. Thus, the latest reform increases standards whose attainment is to be known by performance on high-stakes tests: high difficulty standards x fixed-schedule power assessments x high accountability consequences. Sounds more like a formula for creating debilitating anxiety than the promotion of meaningful learning.

How Did We Come To This?

It seems reasonable to ask, why were the education reforms of Nation at Risk followed by the Summit, then NCLB, then Race to the Top (RttT—it even looks in a hurry) and now possibly Common Core? I would argue first, that a flawed representation of "student" underlies and undermines each.

The authors of this book have much to say about that. They have done a very good service by bringing to the "problem representation" an essential prestep; namely, problem recognition. There is a serious lack of recognition—either due to naiveté or willful ignorance—of the lived experiences of today's youth. Intentional or not, this false innocence is dangerous (May, 1972). It fuels economic (Biddle, see Chapter 5), immigration (Gutierrez & Cerecer, Chapter 3; Alvear & Turley, Chapter 7) language (Morales, Trujillo, & Kissell, Chapter 1; Lopez, Chapter 6), social (Penn, Kinloch, & Burkhard, Chapter 2; Patterson, Blanchfield, & Riskind, Chapter 4), and educational (Heilig, Marchi, & Cruz, Chapter 8; Reynolds, Chapter 9; Nichols & Svenkerud-Hale, Chapter 10) policies that are anything but benign in their effects, as is amply documented by the authors in this book.

Second, the conception of motivated learning that is implicit in each reform bears examination. The acquiring worker of A Nation at Risk and the challenged active learner of the Summit became the anxious test taker of NCLB. McCaslin and Lavigne (2010) argued that the motivational fuel of A Nation at Risk was validated success; in the Summit it was engaged interest. In *NCLB* it was failure avoidance. Who might be the learner and what would be the fuel of Common Core? Some students are likely to immerse themselves in conceptual understanding and exploration more than in acquisition of a series of discrete basic facts and skills. Other students are more likely to struggle with uncertainty. The "flow" of understanding and exploration is motivating (Csikszentmihalyi, 1990); the stress of experienced ambiguity is much more open to individual differences in emotion and coping. What about the continued use of high-stakes tests? The Obama administration recently (October 24, 2015) announced a plan to decrease the amount of testing in the new reform. Time on testing is to be restricted to 2% of academic learning time. Given newer theories of learning, however, it is easy to imagine that test practice will be recast as "instruction through retrieval." It seems important to ask if testing continues to be high-stakes, are fewer tests more or less stressful than more tests? Are tests perceived as chances to succeed or to fail? Perhaps the stress debates—is acute or chronic stress more destructive—will help inform the outcome.

Third, it appears that greater attention is still needed to representations of students, motivated learning, and what that means for the role of the teacher. For example, as Vasquez Heilig, Marachi, and Cruz discuss in Chapter 8, currently school reforms are tinged with the notion of "grit," a modern variation of self-efficacy. Only now it is more about a sheer determination character trait—pick yourself up—than optimistic belief about meeting a discrete challenge. What does it mean for the student who arrives at school depleted from already negotiating a challenging start to the day? What does it mean for the role of others—teachers, for example—in helping students learn, in curricula that are accessible, in assignments that are reasonable? In my work, the students who "take care of myself" do not flourish. Perhaps help is not available; or they are overconfident, distrustful of others, feel a need to hide their inability, simply mistaken, or do not care. For whatever reason, however, these take-care-of-myself students do need the assistance of others to achieve, not more evidence that they are having difficulty or that others will not help them. Grit advocates need to dig deeper.

I have similar concerns with the "successful mindset" of incremental intelligence, a modern variation of attribution theory, in which increased effort is the solution to learning difficulty. That is too simple. Failure attributed to lack of effort is meant to fuel guilt or regret, so that the learner attempts to fix or repair the situation by trying harder. Repeated exposure to failure in the context of effort, however, informs an attributional appraisal (internal to the person, uncontrollable, stable over time and therefore expected to happen in the future) that leads to feelings of shame—certainly not the fuel of achievement (McCaslin, Vriesema, & Burggraf, 2016).

Fourth, the chain links of school reforms suggests two things. One, a change in reform is not a new start. Students live in families; generations within families have experienced different links in the school reform chain. Successful studenting within one reform is not necessarily successful—or useful—in another. Homework "help" at home scenarios ("But that's not how teacher does it!") come to mind. But it is about more than homework, it is about the very definitions of what valuable knowledge and abilities are. The chain of school reforms suggest that there is confusion, or at least disagreement, over just what is the work or purpose of schools. I assert that schools are not businesses, achievement is not an outcome, and education is an investment not a cost of doing business. Knowing ideally what schools are not about is useful. However, we need a better representation of what schools are for and what that means for being a student so that being a valued student can transfer to what it means to be a valued adult. "Achievement" seems rather limited in this respect. Some time ago, Alyson Lavigne and I offered the following for consideration as the Obama administration was garnering support for RttT, involving seemingly every segment of society in the process, except students.

> Motivation researchers need to help the administration define their model of the learner and what that means for the four broad reform goals and the realization of successful school reform. We have suggested a co-regulation model that defines students as social beings. It links motivation and identity—participation and validation—through student negotiation of the press among their own wants and needs, the opportunities and relationships available to them, and the cultural norms and challenges about who they are and the adults they may become. Our model of the learner has a lot in common with adults who struggle and juggle to coordinate multiple demands, tasks, and

goals. Like adults, our learners negotiate conflicts that remind them that they can't have it all, that what they want often comes with a cost, and that sometimes their needs and desires simply do not matter. Our learners learn that some times and some situations do not allow choice; rather, they must adapt, compromise, substitute, or settle to make progress. We believe our model of the learner is a powerful one because it captures what it is like to be a student and an adult; thus, it can and does transfer beyond the public school, linking student motivational dynamics with emergent adult identity. We hope our co-regulation and other models of the learner can generate competing hypotheses that can be subjected to deliberate study to better understand and improve motivated learning in the varied conditions of the public school. It may be the most important work we do. (McCaslin & Lavigne, 2010, pp. 241–242)

What if representations of youth aligned better with representations of what it means to be an adult? Would youth be welcomed to a seat at the adults' social policy table—and know what to do with it when they got there?

Summary

Major societal concerns of the 1980s resonate today. Adults are still worried about the social costs of personal lifestyle "choices" such as obesity and exposure to secondhand smoke. Concerns about health care top the list, amplified by the rising costs—some say the greed—of the pharmaceutical industry. Concerns about unemployment have recently abated; however, concerns about wages and the quality of employment have taken their place. Women able to stay home to assist family members is now as much, if not more, the concern than women willing to assist them. The 1980s problem representation of inadequate student achievement as a threat to adults' and national security arguably remains. We are still trying to solve the problem of students who will not achieve. The major solution strategy, school reform now with sanctions to make students achieve, continues (as compared, for example, with tackling poverty and inequality to improve the conditions of schooling). Surface features of reforms have changed over the years, but the underlying solution belief remains constant: (a) improved schools are known by improved student achievement on standardized or standards-based tests; (b) improved student achievement will restore, or retain (depending on political persuasion), U.S. excellence; and (c) U.S. excellence will secure the future of the country and our old age.

We can do better than this. Our youth deserve better than this. Let's start with a different representation of the work of the public school. Schools as places that support home and community to enhance student well-being, relationships, and personal attainment seem good places for children and their families to thrive. It broadens the purpose of schools to participation and validation in community, to contribution and citizenship. Schools can be about so much more than individual achievement or the lack thereof. If adults want students to achieve in the belief that it will ensure our future, then we need to make that future desirable for and to our children. A shared problem representation of shared investment—adults in youth and youth in adults—seems more fruitful than the current zero-sum perspective that dominates the school reform era.

CLOSING COMMENT

Finally, I want to acknowledge the authors of this book for tackling such important and difficult scholarship. The United States tolerates considerable variation in the treatment of youth. It isn't fair, it isn't right, and it isn't easy to put to words. It isn't easy to read, either. Readers are to be commended for seeking out the lived experiences of those who do not, and without meaningful change likely will not, negotiate their lives on a level playing field. I hope in their next book, authors can speak to how changes in conceptions of youth have informed and been informed by social and educational policies. Together, social policies and conceptions of youth coregulate—challenge, shape, and guide—the developmental tasks, opportunities, and validated milestones of youth. It is time to prioritize and optimize that dynamic.

REFERENCES

Bandura, A. (1978). The self-system in reciprocal determinism. *The American Psychologist, 33*(4), 344–358.

Bandura, A. (1982). Self-efficacy mechanism in human agency. *The American Psychologist, 37* (2), 747–755.

Bandura, A. (1989). Human agency in social cognitive theory. *The American Psychologist, 44* (9), 1175–1184.

Csikszentmihalyi, M. (1990). *Flow: The psychology of optimal experience.* New York, NY: Harper & Row.

May, R. (1972). *Power and innocence: A search for the sources of violence.* New York, NY: W.W. Norton.

McCaslin, M. (1996). The problem of problem representation: The Summit's conception of student. *Educational Researcher, 25,* 13–15.

McCaslin, M. (2009). Co-regulation of student motivation and emergent identity. *Educational Psychologist, 44*(2), 137–146.

McCaslin, M. (2016). Commentary: The co-regulation of cultural, social, and personal sources of influence on student emotional adaptation and achievement. In K. R. Wentzel & G. B. Ramani (Eds.), *The handbook of social influences in school contexts: Social-emotional, motivation, and cognitive outcomes* (pp. 329–346). New York, NY: Routledge.

McCaslin, M., & DiMarino-Linnen, E. (2000). Motivation and learning in school: Societal contexts, psychological constructs, and educational practices. In T. Good (Ed.), *Schooling in America: Yesterday, today, and tomorrow, 100th yearbook of the National Society for the Study of Education* (pp. 84–151). Chicago, IL: University of Chicago Press.

McCaslin, M., & Lavigne, A. L. (2010). Social policy, educational opportunity, and classroom practice: A co-regulation approach to research on student motivation and achievement. In T. Urdan & S. Karabenick (Eds.), *The next decade of research in motivation and achievement. Advances in motivation and achievement* (Vol. 16, pp. 211–249). London, England: Emerald Group.

McCaslin, M., Vriesema, C. C., & Burggraf, S. (2016). Making mistakes: Emotional adaptation and classroom learning. *Teachers College Record, 118*(2).

Nairn, A., & Nader, R. (1980). *The reign of ETS: The corporation that makes up minds: The Ralph Nader report on the Educational Testing Service.* Washington, DC: Learning Research Project.

Rohrkemper, M. M. (1989). Self-regulated learning and academic achievement: A Vygotskian view. In B. Zimmerman & D. Schunk (Eds.), *Self-regulated learning and academic achievement: Theory, research, and practice* (pp. 143–168). New York, NY: Springer-Verlag.

Takanishi, R., DeLeon, P., & Pallak, M. (1983). Psychology and public policy affecting children, youth, and families. *The American Psychologist, 38*(1), 67–76.

Vygotsky, L. S. (1962). *Thought and language.* Cambridge, MA: MIT Press.

Vygotsky, L. S. (1978). *Mind in society: The development of higher psychological processes.* Cambridge, MA: MIT Press.

Weick, K. (1984). Small wins: Redefining the scale of social problems. *The American Psychologist, 39*(1), 40–49.

Weiner, B. (1991). Metaphors in motivation and attribution. *The American Psychologist, 46*(9), 921–930.

ABOUT THE EDITOR

Sharon L. Nichols is an associate professor of educational psychology at the University of Texas at San Antonio. Dr. Nichols has authored or co-authored two books and more than two dozen journal articles and book chapters related to youth development and motivation, and educational policy. She is coauthor of *Collateral Damage: How High-Stakes Testing Corrupts America's Schools* (with D. C. Berliner) and *America's Teenagers—Myths and Realities: Media Images, Schooling, and the Social Costs of Careless Indifference* (with T. L. Good).

Dr. Nichols is the past chair of the Adolescent Development Special Interest Group of the American Educational Research Association and past treasurer of Division 15 (Educational Psychology) of the American Psychological Association. She is on the editorial boards of *Educational Policy Analysis Archives* and *Teachers College Record*.

Her current work focuses on the impact of test-based accountability on instructional practice and adolescent motivation and development.

Educational Policies and Youth in the 21st Century, page 205
Copyright © 2016 by Information Age Publishing
All rights of reproduction in any form reserved.

Made in the USA
San Bernardino, CA
27 January 2018